Twenty-Firs

Weapons Proliferation

Twenty-First Century Weapons Proliferation

Are We Ready?

Edited by

HENRY SOKOLSKI

and

JAMES M. LUDES

With a Foreword by John J. Fialka

FRANK CASS
LONDON • PORTLAND, OR

First published in 2001 in Great Britain by
FRANK CASS PUBLISHERS
Crown House, Chase Side, Southgate
London N14 5BP

and in the United States of America by
FRANK CASS PUBLISHERS
c/o ISBS, 5824 N. E. Hassalo Street
Portland, Oregon 97213-3644

Website http://www.frankcass.com

British Library Cataloguing in Publication Data

Twenty-first century weapons proliferation: are we ready?
1. Arms race
I. Sokolski, Henry II. Ludes, James
355.8'2

ISBN 0-7146-5095-1 (cloth)
ISBN 0-7146- 8137-7 (paper)

Library of Congress Cataloging-in-Publication Data

Twenty-first century weapons proliferation: are we ready? / edited by Henry Sokolski
and James M. Ludes; with a foreword by John J. Fialka.
    p. cm.
Includes bibliographical references and index.
ISBN 0-7146-5095-1 (cloth) – ISBN 0-7146- 8137-7 (pbk.)
1. United States–Military policy. 2. World politics–21st century. 3. Weapons of mass
destruction. 4. Nuclear nonproliferation. 5. Arms control. 6. Security, International. I.
Sokolski, Henry. II. Ludes, James M.

UA23.T877 2001
355'.033573–dc21
                                                                        00-065675

Typeset in 10.5/12 Baskerville by Vitaset, Paddock Wood, Kent
Printed in Great Britain by
MPG Books Ltd, Bodmin, Cornwall

Contents

PART III. IS THERE CAUSE FOR OPTIMISM?

Foreword

Perhaps the most spectacular, yet least remembered physical event of the twentieth century was called 'TEAK'. It was a thermonuclear warhead detonated nearly 50 miles high over the Pacific by US nuclear weapons scientists on 1 August 1958. The explosion, at least 20 times more powerful than the atomic bomb that incinerated Nagasaki, produced an amazing show of light, heat, radiation and electronic effects. Some of them raged over the entire Pacific. Nothing like it had ever been seen before on Earth, and we should pray, think deeply and work hard so that nothing like it will be seen again.

The point of this book is that, as we open the glittery doorway into a new century, we should not forget the lessons of the recent past. It was visions of endless prosperity and hope for a rapidly civilizing world based on the electronic transfer of information that led us into the twentieth century. The visions were soon dashed by two ugly wars that unleashed the most powerful weapons that humanity has ever devised. Like it or not, these weapons are part of the burden we carry into the twenty-first.

Take TEAK, for example. To the scientists that sent it aloft, it had a terrible beauty. It started with an acetylene-like flash of bright light surrounded by an astonishing fireball that shot upward and outward. Within six minutes it was 600 miles in diameter, a death star burning in the ionosphere. It could be seen in Hawaii, over 700 miles away. As the nation's first unclassified primer of the nuclear age, a 700-page US Army manual called *The Effects of Nuclear Weapons*, noted in 1962, TEAK rose to a height of 90 miles and it was surrounded by a 'luminous' red ring. It was apparently caused by shock waves ripping through the thin air at the edge of the Earth's atmosphere. 'A brilliant aurora appeared from the bottom of the fireball, and purple streamers were seen to spread toward the north.' They could be seen from the Samoan Islands, more than 2,000 miles away. While TEAK produced the most stunning fireworks display ever seen, the scientists were interested in effects that could not be seen. One of them was a force called 'electromagnetic pulse', a raging storm of electrons spreading at 2,000 miles per hour. It knocked out radio communications over much of the Pacific. In some areas, the blackout lasted as long as ten hours.

As you will learn from reading this collection of essays, the number of nations pondering the effects, both physical and political, of nuclear weapons is spreading. One of the ways these weapons might be used against a prosperous nation that is heavily dependent on electronic gear and space-based communications (such as the USA) would be to launch another shot like TEAK. It could be a twenty-first century Pearl Harbor – a bold stroke that leaves a prospective enemy blind and dumb at the moment of attack. Unthinkable, you might be tempted to say. But US and Russian scientists spent decades weighing the pros and cons of attacks like this. Now others, from Baghdad to Pyongyang to Beijing, are avidly studying the arts of this kind of war. One of the most poorly understood lessons of our recent past is that putting hard problems into the memory hole marked 'unthinkable', or papering them over with diplomatic controls that do not work, may be politically expedient, but in the final summation are downright dangerous. Such exercises in wishful or non-thinking led directly to the buildup of German and Japanese forces that introduced us to the prolonged campaign of terror, pain, expense and death that was the Second World War.

The few books we have about nuclear proliferation are often hand-wringing, jargon-laden affairs, written for a small group of technical and military cognoscenti – people who often seem incapable of getting the attention of a larger audience. This book tries to broaden the message. One writer even puts his finger on the communications problem. The gurus of anti-terrorism, says David C. Rapoport, feel tempted to exaggerate potential threats to enhance their careers. That way, whatever happens, they will not have understated the problem. In the meantime, however, they have frightened the politicians and the defense planners – the very people they need to reach. Exaggerating the risks and costs that must be met, as Rapoport notes, is like urging the purchase of a huge insurance policy 'with someone else's money'. Instinctively, all but the most courageous policy makers flee such scenarios, preferring to spend their time and money working on easier problems that give more obvious and immediate benefits to constituents.

This book tells us that the problems of proliferating nuclear states and terrorist groups that possess weapons of mass destruction are threats that loom in the near future. They are threats that are certainly thinkable and probably solvable if we have the time and the patience and if we apply the resources necessary to do the work. We know that stuffing things like TEAK down the memory hole will not make them go away. Simply setting our collective hair on fire with worst-case visions is not the answer, either.

Thomas G. Mahnken notes that the scenarios of the gurus are so powerful that the US military has fought mightily not to engage its thinkers in this area. How do they do that? Well, he says, they avoid dealing with potentially embarrassing tactics such as a surprise nuclear attack using the effects of electromagnetic pulse or the use of chemical weapons on forward military bases by simply not putting them in war games. That makes it easier for players to look good – a major objective of the modern military. While their generals and admirals may indulge in such ostrich-like strategies, industrial nations have nonetheless developed powerful weapons that can be used to lure emerging powers away from the ugly arsenals that some of them are contemplating. These are democracy, booming economies and border-penetrating communications that show, as West Germany showed East Germany, that a nation that has only a grim war footing to hold it together will have a decidedly grim future.

Henry S. Rowen sees us careening into a rapidly changing world where governments will slim down, markets will take over and the economic distance between the USA and rising, young economic powers in Asia will shrink. This could be either good or bad, he says. In diplomacy, as in basketball, we will make our own luck. The growth of grass-roots politics and the rule of law could make China not only a powerful economy, but a powerful civilizing influence.

On the other hand, China and other modernizing countries, such as Iran, could opt to resist these globalizing forces and assemble world-threatening military machines by buying off-the-shelf hardware and dabbling in nuclear, chemical and biological warfare technology. In this century, they are much more cheaply acquired than they used to be. Moreover, the disarming lure of democracy does not seem to take on Muslim nations where gifted young men and women continue to join angry fundamentalist groups.

Michael Barletta shows us how courageous leaders in Argentina and Brazil managed to break the strong political and military forces that were leading them toward a nuclear confrontation. The results were good neighbors, economic prosperity and an end to secret establishments turning wealth into instruments of mass destruction.

Making our own luck in the twenty-first century will require taking on realities that an earlier generation of thinkers chose to ignore, or assumed that somebody else (like us) would handle. Frank von Hippel notes that part of this ugly inheritance is an arsenal of nuclear weapons that is far, far beyond what we need together with mountains of spent nuclear power-plant fuel that could become nuclear weapons tomorrow unless we think more clearly about effective ways to dispose of it today.

One of the more laid-back theories making the rounds is that proliferation of nuclear weapons may be good: a 'stabilizing' presence that will keep nations like India and Pakistan deterred from making war on each other in much the same way that it kept the Cold War between the USA and the Soviet Union from becoming hot. One of the selling points of this school of thought is that it requires us to do nothing, a feature which more than a few policy makers will find appealing.

But the military conservatism, the rich infrastructure of scientists and the multiple layers of internal checks and fail-safe controls that kept the USA and Russia safe from nuclear misadventures may not be there to restrain the leaders of smaller nations. In our military literature, we have talked glibly about the possibility of 'guillotine strikes' and other nuclear strategies that might annihilate enemies. The new students of this literature might be tempted to try it. Or they may find themselves the hapless victims of accidents. What would happen if a weapon with the power of TEAK were stolen or detonated while in transit? Surely terrorist groups who dabble with weapons of mass destruction will have such accidents. As David C. Rapoport points out, *Aum Shinrikyo* – the Japanese cult that had the equivalent of $1 billion and a cadre of PhDs to develop chemical and biological weapons – blundered down this path, killing its own people. It launched 12 attacks, which all fizzled. It had the scenario figured out: a subway train acts like a giant piston and could move enough nerve gas to kill 10,000 people. But the Japanese were lucky.

I first stumbled across *The Effects of Nuclear Weapons* as a reporter covering the Pentagon for the *Washington Star* in the late 1970s. In the later stages of the Cold War, experts had begun to worry about the damage that a terrorist group armed with a nuclear weapon might create. The book talks about 'flash burns' that left people as mere white images on a charred wall, and 'profile burns' that penetrated a woman's clothing, leaving the pattern of her dress branded on her back. There are also 'beta burns', disfigurement caused by radioactive fallout – a seemingly harmless rain of fluffy ashes – hours after the attack. Then there is radiation sickness: 'the usual vomiting and nausea followed, in more or less rapid succession, by prostration, diarrhea, anorexia and fever' ... and death. While we have developed movies and novels that deal with terrorist threats, most of them do not seem to get to this point. After a great deal of shooting (always in the conventional sense) some devilishly handsome mid-level officer, often accompanied by a nuclear physicist who looks more like a super model, manages to thwart the bad guys and save us from (nuclear, biochemical, whatever) destruction. Whew! They also save a lot of us from having to think about our changed circumstances. A nuclear weapon, however small, would be a gruesome tragedy if it exploded in any of our cities. The burn victims alone would quickly overwhelm the available medical care. Are we ready? We will probably never be totally ready, but that does not excuse creative people for not thinking about it.

Andrew Carroll, an historian, recently published in the *New Yorker* a collection of moving letters from US soldiers writing home from our wars. In one, Richard King, an infantryman who won the Silver Star fighting in the Pacific, tells his family about a gruesome firefight in which one soldier had his jaw, tongue and nose shot off. 'This is a horrible thing to write about, but people should understand what war means: maybe then they won't start another so soon.'

Proliferation is a horrible thing to write about, but more people should understand what it means. I had a rude introduction to one aspect of it during the Gulf War as a reporter for the *Wall Street Journal*. I was with the Third Armored Division in its successful dash across the Kuwaiti desert to outflank Iraq's Republican Guard. One thing that was on every infantryman's mind was that Iraq's army was equipped with artillery that could fire nerve gas shells. We wore charcoal-impregnated suits and were shown how to use a kit that contained five hypodermic needles filled with a chemical to block the effects of nerve gas. (If it didn't work, a sixth needle contained a sedative.) The training regime was that, upon a given signal, you put the mask on and make it seal tightly against your face. If you did not manage to do that within nine seconds, the gas would begin to attack the involuntary nervous system, leading quickly to death. One obvious problem here, I thought as we bumped along, was that we had no handy detection device that could quickly distinguish nerve gas. If the threat were biological weapons, there was no detection gear at all. Fortunately, the wind was blowing at our backs until the war ended. As we later learned, Iraq's generals had chemical-tipped shells deployed, ready to fire. But they did not. Perhaps they did not want the wind blowing it back into their troops' faces. Perhaps they took our threat seriously. The message we had delivered to Saddam was that our response to a chemical attack might be tactical nuclear weapons. Whatever happened (and it would be good, someday, to find out), I was disturbed to read the essay by Ashton B. Carter and L. Celeste Johnson that says that almost ten years later we still lack essential defenses against such weapons. Running on luck may still work in the movies, but the real world is more like Las Vegas where luck does not last.

As this book points out, part of the legacy from the last two generations is that there are lots of hard puzzles that need solving. We need 'nuclear archeology' that gives us a better sense of how many nuclear warheads were made and tougher accounting to tell us where they are. We need to use the lessons that police and fire squads have learned in anti-terrorist drills, assuming use of nerve gas in an American city. While it may seem counter-intuitive, what they have learned is that the first things that must be shut and guarded are the doors to hospitals, before they become hopelessly contaminated with mobs of victims and thus rendered unusable. The use of biological weapons poses problems that are more formidable. Release of a contagious disease, like anthrax, presents rescue crews with an inverted pyramid. It can take hours or days before the release becomes deadly, forcing investigators to backtrack the victims to the place and time where the attack happened.

Would you like to read a real thriller? Would you like to grapple with real scenarios that could happen to you, your family, your children, your work force, your friends, your city, your country? Find a soft chair and curl up with this book.

John J. Fialka
McLean, Va.
January 2001

Acknowledgments

Any edited volume has at least as many parents as it has chapters. This book is no exception. Besides being the result of the book's authors, though, this volume benefited from several generous grants and critical editorial advice. Without such help, the book's publication would not have been possible.

Although the original essays were commissioned by the Nonproliferation Policy Education Center, Stewart Cass and David C. Rapoport grandfathered the project and assured publication with Frank Cass Publishers. Co-editor Jim Ludes, meanwhile, prepared many of the essays for publication in the summer 1999 edition of his Georgetown University journal, *National Security Studies Quarterly*. Marianne Oliva, research coordinator at the Nonproliferation Policy Education Center, and Sally Green of Frank Cass Publishers tackled many of the final volume's remaining production details.

Financial support was also critical. All of the book's chapters were funded by the William H. Donner Foundation and the Smith Richardson Foundation. In addition, the University of California's Institute for Global Conflict and Cooperation lent support to two of the book's chapters. Finally, earlier research support was afforded by the United States Institute of Peace.

Introduction: What World Awaits Us?

HENRY SOKOLSKI

Ten years after Desert Storm's targeting of Saddam's missile, nuclear, chemical and biological weapons capabilities, public concern about strategic weapons proliferation has only grown. Smaller nations' interest in acquiring nuclear weapons, which had waned in the late 1980s and early 1990s, is again on the rise. Also, with the end of the Cold War, vast surpluses of nuclear weapons-usable materials in the USA and Russia as well as in Japan and Europe have increased concerns over nuclear leakage and theft. Then, there is the prospect of terrorist use of nuclear, chemical or biological munitions that was so dramatically highlighted by the Japanese subway sarin attacks of 1995. Finally, the last five years have seen the increasing pace of space technology proliferation underscored by ever more advanced Chinese, North Korean, Iranian, Indian and Pakistani missile and satellite launches.

How should we think about these threats? Are the planned responses of the USA and its allies sufficient? Is there cause for optimism in the growing number of peaceful democracies world-wide or in the long run will proliferation be our doom? These questions are the focus of *Twenty-first Century Weapons Proliferation: Are We Ready?*

The first of these issues – what the strategic weapons proliferation challenges are that the USA and its allies will face – is covered in the book's first section. Is nuclear proliferation a more serious worry after the Indian and Pakistani nuclear tests? Just prior to these tests, the conventional wisdom was that acquiring nuclear weapons was a mistake. Nuclear weapons, it was argued, lacked any true military utility. As for deterrence, a mere option to acquire them was considered superior to announcing possession of such weapons.

India and Pakistan's tests challenged this thinking. They also destroyed the myth that there are only five nuclear nations (the USA, Russia, Britain, France and China). How important are these changes? Former US Nuclear Regulatory Commissioner Victor Gilinsky examines them in his chapter, 'Nuclear Proliferation After the Indian and

Pakistani Tests'. In it, he argues that the tests destroyed the major pretenses of US and international nonproliferation and that, unless a stricter international system of controls is instituted, more nuclear proliferation is likely. One thing, he contends, is certain: the broad-based support necessary for such controls can only come 'on the basis of a uniform standard, applicable to all states, including the current official nuclear states'.

International controls, even strict ones, however, are unlikely to prevent the threat of terrorism. How likely is the use of nuclear, chemical and biological weapons by terrorist groups? David C. Rapoport, editor of the *Journal of Terrorism and Political Violence,* answers this question in his chapter, 'Terrorism and Weapons of the Apocalypse'. In it, he examines the evidence for why such terrorism and even states' use of such agents, although technically possible, is not likely. The military utility of the current generation of chemical and biological agents, he points out, is limited. As for their terrorist use, this is rarer still: since 1970 there have been 12 chemical or biological attacks in the USA and only one fatality. This does not mean such attacks will not happen, only that we need to understand the various reasons why they have not. Indeed, as more and more public officials voice their concerns without reflection, the likelihood of terrorists actually acting on their worries increases.

Nuclear war and terrorism, of course, have long been at the center of public attention. Only since Desert Storm has much attention been paid to missile proliferation and the spread of advanced conventional weapons. Tim D. Hoyt, a young adjunct professor of national security studies at Georgetown University, focuses on this set of emerging threats in his chapter, 'The Next Strategic Threat'. In it he analyzes three conventional weapons developments that have strategic impli-cations: India's development of precise ballistic missiles, Iran's development of sea denial capabilities in the Persian Gulf, and China's development of advanced space technology. Countering these emerg-ing threats, Hoyt argues, will require more than export controls; it will require the USA to develop a new set of long-term, highly leveraged military, economic and diplomatic strategies.

This, then, leads to the volume's second section, which is devoted to gauging the adequacy of planned US and allied responses. This section's opening chapter, 'What Strategic Weapons Proliferation Will Demand of Us' by Henry Sokolski, critiques the current crop of Cold War arms control and military prescriptions offered by both hawks and doves. In their stead, Sokolski suggests a broad menu of measures aimed at achieving the type of single-standard weapons restraint called for by Victor Gilinsky.

Former Assistant Secretary of Defense for Counterproliferation

Ashton B. Carter and L. Celeste Johnson are also frustrated with existing US counterproliferation efforts. In their chapter, 'Beyond the Counterproliferation Initiative', Carter and Johnson argue that far more resources and attention need to be focused on the original Counterproliferation Initiative announced by the US Defense Department in 1993. They call for a 'Revolution in Counterproliferation Affairs'.

Tom Mahnken, Associate Professor of Strategy at the US Naval War College, however, is doubtful. In his chapter, 'Counterproliferation: A Critical Appraisal', Mahnken points out that, while Carter and Johnson call for a revolution in counterproliferation affairs, their proposed revolution is little more than the original initiative 'clothed in new rhetoric'. More important, Mahnken argues, is that the deficiencies of the original initiative are basic. If the USA and its allies are to command the proliferation threats that face them, Mahnken argues that they will have to do far more than Carter and Johnson call for. In addition to protecting their forces against weapons of mass destruction, they will have to 'take into account the strategic character of different potential opponents' and these opponents' ability to use advanced conventional weapons systems. This, in turn, requires nothing less than the development of a comprehensive set of long-term, country-specific strategies targeted against key proliferators.

This, then, brings us to this section's last chapter, which considers what substantive steps the USA and its friends would have to take if they were serious about nuclear proliferation. In 'Getting Back to Basics: Controlling Fissile Materials', Frank von Hippel of Princeton University's Center for Energy and Environmental Studies details the technical challenges the world's nuclear nations would face in any effort to reduce existing civil and military stockpiles of nuclear weapons-usable materials. These challenges are technically surmountable assuming there is sufficient political will to tackle them. 'What is needed', von Hippel notes, 'is an administration with both the understanding and the commitment at the presidential level to a comprehensive strategy to contain and shrink the world's huge stockpiles of fissile materials'.

All of this, of course will require time. The question that the book's last section focuses on is do we have it? Henry S. Rowen, former Assistant Secretary of Defense in the Bush Pentagon and Professor of Business at Stanford University, answers with a provisional yes. In his chapter, 'Why a Rich, Democratic and (Perhaps) Peaceful Era Is Ahead', Rowen quantifies and explains the strong relationship between persistently rising earned incomes, higher levels of education, growing demand for liberal self-government, and increasingly pacific relations between nations. Although this democratic wave will eventually expand the world's zones of peace beyond the Western Hemisphere and Europe, Rowen warns that the growing availability of strategic weapons technology may make the transition to this more peaceful world less than smooth. Indeed, persistent exceptions to the democratic wave theory are the many highly Islamicized nations in north Africa, the Middle East, central Asia and the Persian Gulf. For many states in these regions, growth in personal wealth and demand for liberal democratic rule seem to be inversely related.

This negative exception and its implications are explained by Daniel Pipes, editor of *Middle East Quarterly,* in the book's next chapter entitled 'Muslim Exceptionalism: Why the End of History (and of Proliferation) Will Not Be Easy'. In it, Pipes details the historical causes of antipathy between intensely Islamicized and Western and Christian cultures. Far from being ameliorated by increased wealth, these sources of friction, Pipes argues, are only heightened by it. The best the West can do to reduce these frictions is to work actively to dispel the distortions about the West propagated by Islamic radicals.

This last point – that nations' attraction to democracy and peace is not simply driven by economics – is taken one step further in the next chapter, 'Argentine and Brazilian Nonproliferation: A Democratic Peace?'. Written by Michael Barletta, Senior Research Associate at the Monterey Institute of International Studies, it argues that more than the nominal emergence of democracy is required to encourage peaceful relations between nations. Barletta details how the leaders of Argentina and Brazil increased nuclear relations between 1985 and 1988 to facilitate the strengthening of democratic institutions, economic interdependence, civilian rule and peaceful relations before any of these institutions or practices had taken root. The leaders in both nations, in short, used politics to catalyze Argentine–Brazilian trade, and executive secrecy to promote more peaceful relations.

This, then, brings us to the book's concluding chapter, which argues for the primacy of sound theory in divining and shaping our proliferation fate. In 'Proliferation Theory and Nonproliferation Practice', Peter D. Feaver, Professor of Political Science at Duke University, insists that the supposed gap between various theorizing about proliferation and promoting sound nonproliferation policy is neither necessary, nor conducive to good policy. After evaluating the practical value of the most popular academic debates concerning proliferation, Feaver is led to a fundamental conclusion. The only alternative to bringing sound theory to practice is a profoundly undesirable future. It is a world where policy makers make policy though ignorant of the problems and opportunities that good theory would expose, while 'theorists spin arcana without a view to producing something that matters'. It is a world the gist of which *Twenty-First Century Weapons Proliferation* was specifically geared to avoid.

Part I

The Strategic Weapons Proliferation Challenges Ahead

Nuclear Proliferation After the Indian and Pakistani Tests

VICTOR GILINSKY[1]

INTRODUCTION

The May 1998 nuclear explosions in south Asia undermined assumptions both about the declining significance of nuclear weapons and the strength of the nonproliferation 'regime'. Prior to these tests, the political and psychological barrier to testing a nuclear weapon and thereby declaring a nuclear capability was considered the strongest part of the regime. Such an event was thought to risk the strongest world condemnation and sanction. Yet, after the Indian and Pakistani explosions, the world's powers saw little purpose in severe sanction, and instead imposed punitive measures that were more of an inconvenience than a threat to the unchastened new nuclear weapons states.[2]

It is tempting to play down the significance of these nuclear tests, especially as it is difficult to know what to do about them. To put the best face on it, the 1998 tests merely confirmed what has been true for many years: India and Pakistan have been building nuclear weapons, as Israel did before them.[3] If India, just as France and China did earlier, decided to conduct thermonuclear testing before the Comprehensive Test Ban made such tests that much more difficult, that was a backhanded recognition of the strength of the international consensus against further testing. India, Pakistan and Israel are the only major non-signatories to the Non-Proliferation Treaty (NPT) of 1 July 1968. Perhaps the Indian and Pakistani tests marked the end of post-NPT nuclear proliferation.

More likely, such a positive perspective of these tests is wishful thinking. One thing is for certain: other would-be bomb-makers in the Middle East and east Asia took note of the May 1998 tests and the mild international reaction to them. The situation calls for a re-evaluation of prevailing assumptions in arms control circles about the spread of nuclear weapons and what can be done about it. A good place to begin is by clearing away some of the fraudulent information that fills discussions on this subject.

ARE NUCLEAR WEAPONS REALLY USELESS?

It has become an arms control cliché that nuclear weapons are useless and, once countries that flirt with the idea of making them realize this, they will not want them. Delegations of arms controllers from Western countries trooped to India and Pakistan for years to explain this patiently to the nuclear unwashed. The Indian nuclear tests in May 1998 made it clear the Indians did not find the arguments convincing. They think nuclear weapons are useful and important to have, not least for enhancing their place in the world. It is hard to disagree; indeed, these weapons have enhanced India's importance as they have done for every possessor, or even suspected possessor.

The five nuclear powers legitimized by the Non-Proliferation Treaty obviously regard their own nuclear weapons as valuable and important. The United States and Russia have taken large steps to reduce their arsenals, but they are in no rush to give them up entirely. Neither Britain, France nor China has agreed to reduce its nuclear arsenal. Nor has Israel – the undeclared nuclear power – agreed to destroy its arsenal.

These countries and others treat any move by yet another state to obtain nuclear weapons as a matter of the utmost importance, as indeed it is. Consider, for example, the impact of an Iraqi or North Korean nuclear arsenal, no matter how small. Significantly, the United States bombed Iraq but treated North Korea with respect. The difference is North Korea really did have the nuclear explosives for a bomb and the capability for producing more, a production capability North Korea skillfully turned into a powerful bargaining chip. In 1994 the United States agreed to provide North Korea with an energy package worth billions of dollars in exchange for freezing its small plutonium production operation.[4] Clearly, countries with nuclear weapons have more weight in the world.

What this shows is that while, in a certain sense, it *is* true the owners cannot do much militarily with nuclear weapons, the opposite is also true. This duality is characteristic of many propositions about nuclear weapons. Years ago, Neils Bohr used the term 'great truths' for such propositions whose opposites were also true. Bringing nuclear weapons into a power equation is the political equivalent of dividing by zero.

WILL A NUCLEAR 'OPTION' SATISFY WOULD-BE NUCLEAR STATES?

Another assumption widely held in arms control circles was that countries like India and Pakistan would not actually manufacture and deploy nuclear weapons – they would be satisfied to maintain the 'option' to obtain weapons. Perhaps, the thinking went, they would do enough so they could make the bombs if they had to, but would not actually take the last few steps. In this way, arms controllers reasoned, the country in question would get the benefit of almost having the bomb without incurring the onus and cost such a program was thought to entail. A more recent variation of this assumption is that, in any case, would-be nuclear states would not go through full-scale testing because of the possible severe world response this would bring. It is important to note the testing was not necessary from a technical point of view.

As for the notion of an 'option', anyone who has thought about it seriously knows such a technological 'option' is not an exercisable option until every single technical step, down to the last one, has been mastered. One simply cannot foresee what technical stumbling blocks may lie ahead. In other words an 'option' is only available if the technology is obtainable and functioning.

For years it has been evident that India and Pakistan both developed and manufactured nuclear weapons, as Israel had before them. Yet for years it was thought indelicate to say so, as if pretending that these countries did not have nuclear weapons would maintain the psychological barriers to test-explosions and weaponization.

India showed that if the conditions were right those putative psychological barriers were no more than plate glass, and Pakistan followed quickly through India's opening. The tests served important purposes. Analysis and simulation may convince technical people but, in the world of international affairs, a successful full-scale test is much more convincing. Do not forget the exultant crowds in the two countries who made heroes of the weapons scientists and their political masters. The misjudgment by Western observers and intelligence agencies regarding the likelihood of Indian tests shows again that wishful thinking is a poor guide to the actions of players in the international power game. There are now reports out of India that the country is thinking about submarine-based warheads.[5]

This experience raises questions about other prevalent assumptions, including the thought that military use of nuclear weapons by these new states is extremely unlikely. These assumptions rest on similar psychological propositions that may, in the excitement and confusion of crisis, be no more than plate glass, either. It does not help that south Asian targets and launch pads are only a few minutes apart.

WHAT HAPPENS TO THE FICTION OF 'FIVE NUCLEAR STATES'?

The NPT was designed to avoid precisely such dangerous situations. It was based on the notion that it was in the interest of all countries to limit the spread of nuclear weapons. One had to draw the line somewhere, even if it was arbitrary. Such line drawing implied a degree of 'unfairness', but this was not, however, to last indefinitely. Under the treaty, the five approved nuclear states agreed not only to eliminate their nuclear arms over the course of time, but also to provide non-nuclear states with assistance in the development of nuclear programs for peaceful purposes. Non-nuclear member states agreed not to pursue military, nuclear programs.

It did not completely work out this way on either side of the bargain. The United States and Russia have made important (and insufficiently appreciated) nuclear reductions in recent years, but the nuclear states as a whole are not yet contemplating eliminating their nuclear arsenals. At the same time, while almost all other countries joined the NPT, some of the holdouts obviously developed nuclear weapons – Israel, India, Pakistan and South Africa.

So long as these states did not carry out detectable tests, the keepers of the NPT were able to maintain the fiction there were still only five nuclear powers. The elimination of the nuclear weapons stockpile in South Africa, and the surrender of nuclear warheads by several former Soviet republics, even suggested a reversal in the proliferation process. The hope was the real world would eventually come around to the world of pretense.

The May 1998 nuclear tests in India and Pakistan have thrown this result into doubt. The five grandfathered nuclear states have said in response they will not give India and Pakistan the status of 'nuclear weapons states' under the NPT.[6] The so-called P5 – who were all nuclear weapons states and permanent members of the Security Council – understandably wanted to avoid the impression that a country can shoot its way into the nuclear club. But, like it or not, India and Pakistan are nuclear weapons states all the same, probably with dozens of bombs each (as is Israel, with many more).[7] India, at least, is likely to retain its nuclear weapons as long as any of the five nuclear weapons states. In time, the declared nuclear powers under the NPT will want the cooperation of India and Pakistan in an agreement to end testing and to control the flow of dangerous technology. To achieve this, the nuclear weapons states will have to acknowledge the new nuclear status outside the framework of the NPT that India and Pakistan have achieved. Or, to put it another way, the supposed need to ensure India and Pakistan act 'responsibly' in avoiding the further spread of nuclear technology gives the declared nuclear powers the rationale for doing away with the troublesome sanctions regime while appearing consistent with the nonproliferation 'regime.'

WEAKNESS OF THE NPT: THE CASE OF NORTH KOREA

As it stands, that 'regime' is a pretty fragile entity. It rests on a Non-Proliferation Treaty that allows for withdrawal upon 90-days' notice. The NPT allows member countries to accumulate nuclear explosives – separated plutonium and highly enriched uranium – so long as the countries promise to use the materials as fuel, not bombs. The difficulty is countries could break such promises and use the materials for military purposes very quickly. Compliance with the NPT is verified by a weak inspection system, and there is no explicit enforcement mechanism.

At least two member countries – Iraq and North Korea – have violated the NPT in important ways. The North Korean case, the more serious of the two, is especially instructive. North Korea refused in 1993 to allow International Atomic Energy Agency (IAEA) inspectors to check on whether it secretly separated bomb quantities of plutonium for nuclear weapons. When pressed, North Korea threatened to exercise the 90-day provision to withdraw from the NPT. This panicked the organizers of the upcoming 1995 NPT Review Conference who feared the effect of a withdrawal on the prospects for extension.[8] The custodians of the NPT were more concerned about extension than enforcement. The United States and its Japanese and South Korean allies also feared triggering North Korean violence. As a consequence, the United States and other countries did not impose sanctions, nor did they insist on elimination of treaty violations by North Korea. Rather, the United States offered North Korea two large nuclear reactors, worth about $5 billion, in return for freezing its small indigenous nuclear program. North Korea agreed, but refused – and still refuses – to allow IAEA inspectors to check on past plutonium diversion.[9] Nor is North Korea cooperating with the IAEA to fulfill the country's other NPT safeguards responsibilities.[10] No one is pressing it very hard to do so, or to clarify North Korea's ambiguous status under the NPT. The inescapable conclusion is that the most flagrant violator of IAEA safeguards in the history of the treaty has received the most generous treatment from the 'keepers'.

WEAKNESS OF IAEA INSPECTIONS

The IAEA inspection system is supposed to deter violations through the threat of detection. Despite the system's obvious deficiencies, for years arms controllers regarded any criticism of it as heresy. In its inspections of Iraq before the Gulf War, the agency missed the country's illicit nuclear weapons program completely. The Vienna-based inspectors were happy to work with blinders on – they were not interested in learning about anything nuclear in Iraq outside the country's declared facilities. The IAEA accepted the peaceful character of the declared facilities at face value, as it does elsewhere, even though they made absolutely no sense in terms of Iraq's energy needs. When, after the Gulf War, defectors revealed Iraq's secret weapons program, the Security Council still had to prod the agency pretty hard to persuade it to get tough with Iraq.

After North Korea joined the NPT in 1985, the agency bureaucracy dithered for five years before starting inspections, a circumstance that may have led North Korea to think it could get away with cheating. To give the IAEA inspectors credit, when they finally got to North Korea in 1992, after the Iraq experience, they tried to do their work professionally.

The agency claims to have changed after the Iraqi experience and says it is now taking a more serious approach to its policing responsibilities. There are some signs this is happening. The IAEA has, however, always suffered from an intrinsic conflict of interest in that its instinct is to protect anything nuclear its member states are doing. This includes fuel-cycle activities involving separated plutonium and highly enriched uranium. In the end, the IAEA is still the product of the 1950s Atoms for Peace program. It continues to put major emphasis on its role of promoting nuclear technology, and remains a reluctant enforcer of the NPT.[11]

WEAK INTERNATIONAL REACTION TO NUCLEAR EXPLOSIONS

Of course, India and Pakistan (and Israel) did not sign the NPT so their tests did not violate the treaty. Still, it was widely thought violating this international norm entailed serious penalties. It turned out that, despite all the talk deploring the Indian and Pakistani explosions, there was not really much the United States and other countries could do in response without undermining other important interests. They quickly saw that to punish India and Pakistan severely would create political and economic problems for themselves they would rather avoid. While the United States imposed some sanctions to avoid the impression India and Pakistan are getting a free ride, in the main it has waived even these measures. Similarly, Russia announced the May explosions would not affect the sale of two Russian nuclear power reactors to India. To add to the difficulties, it is especially awkward for the United States to impose economic sanctions on a relatively democratic India for testing several warheads while the United States is selling nuclear technology to undemocratic China with heavy nuclear armament. One cannot imagine a military conflict between the United States and India, yet it is not so hard to imagine one with China. Would-be bombmakers are bound to note the key to success is to confront the guardians of the NPT with a dilemma.

In many ways, the US reaction to the May 1998 test series was a replay of the events of 24 years ago. India used US-supplied materials to make plutonium for its 1974 nuclear explosion in violation of an agreement with the United States (and a separate agreement with Canada). In spite of this, the United States continued providing nuclear fuel to India's two US-supplied power reactors.[12] The current US administration made clear prior to the explosions that it did not want nuclear issues to get in the way of what it regarded as more important economic and political issues between the two countries. Having turned a blind eye to nuclear developments in south Asia for so long, the United States was not left with any good options once the explosions took place. But if we could so easily rationalize an Indian bomb, and then a Pakistani bomb, will we also rationalize subsequent ones?

In some ways, even though Pakistan responded to India, Pakistan's explosions are more worrisome. India has to be regarded as one of the world's leading countries and could be seen as a permanent member of the Security Council. There are, so to speak, no other Indias. Pakistan, however, is more representative of a wider class of countries that could plausibly attempt to get nuclear bombs, whether by their own means or by purchase or theft. The psychological barriers against this have lowered too.

The effect of the south Asian explosions on North Korea (DPRK) will be especially interesting. It seems likely North Korea had a nuclear weapons program that did not end with the 1994 US–DPRK agreement.[13] The recent tests by India and Pakistan are likely to reinforce the DPRK's determination to carry on with its secret nuclear program. If a large state like India sees the need for nuclear weapons to guarantee its own national security, then North Korea may well see it as even more important for itself.[14] The weak world reaction to the south Asian tests may suggest to North Korea it could get away with even more than it had imagined. Recall that, under the 1994 US–DPRK agreement, North Korea retains its indigenous plutonium production facilities in a mothballed state. It is allowed to do so until the United States supplies the second of the two large power reactors promised to North Korea. As a result, North Korea will retain the means for continued nuclear blackmail for a long time. Nor does the NPT, as it has been interpreted, bar North Korea from accumulating plutonium. The treaty only bars doing so out of sight of IAEA inspectors.

CONTROL OVER 'CIVILIAN' TECHNOLOGY TRANSFERS STILL
VITAL

Keeping countries with nuclear ambitions from accumulating nuclear explosives, legally or otherwise, is still an important goal, even in the case of countries that have some already. There is no need to make it too easy for countries to obtain nuclear bombs. So while it has become fashionable to deride controls on technology exports, such controls, however imperfect, have played an important role in stopping or slowing nuclear weapons developments, including in some worrisome places. The key technologies are those for plutonium separation and uranium enrichment.

Would-be nuclear states invariably emphasize the indigenous nature of their nuclear development. In reality, there is in almost every case a strong dependence on external technology as can be seen in both the Indian and Pakistani cases. Pakistan stole the uranium enrichment technology from the Netherlands and Germany. An enrichment plant at Kahuta is the source of highly enriched uranium for bombs. Pakistan was able to complete its work on the plant only with the active cooperation of European firms. They were happy to have the business and looked the other way, as did some of their governments. The United States did too, during the Afghan war when helping Afghans to defeat the Soviets took precedence over stopping the Pakistani nuclear bomb program.

It has of course been obvious for years that, despite the protestations of Pakistani leaders, the uranium enrichment program was dedicated to military use. Pakistan had no reactors that used enriched uranium. They are apparently now also building a plutonium production reactor. The Pakistanis are widely believed to have received assistance in this area, including actual nuclear weapons designs, from China.[15] If that were so, it would put China in egregious violation of the NPT. It would also indicate Chinese willingness to use selective proliferation as a calculated strategic step, a possibility whose implications are open-ended. Ironically, the only ones who are calling the Chinese on this are the Indians, who are not even party to the NPT.

'PEACEFUL' PURPOSES

India's indigenous nuclear technology is far greater than Pakistan's. India's bombs rely, in part, on nuclear explosives produced in a facility covered by international obligations prohibiting bomb use: the 40 megawatt CIRUS (Canadian–Indian Reactor–US) reactor, supplied by Canada in the 1960s and charged with heavy water from the United

States. Despite contractual obligations to use the CIRUS reactor for 'peaceful' purposes, India used plutonium produced there for its 1974 explosion and has stockpiled it since then for use in weapons. In fact, the reactor has produced over one bomb's worth of plutonium each year since it began operation. The CIRUS reactor and India's other plutonium production facility, the 100 megawatt Dhruva reactor which went into operation in 1985, have produced enough weapons-grade plutonium for perhaps 100 warheads.[16] Over one-third of this stockpile has been produced in the CIRUS reactor.

In response to the charge that India may have used this material in the 1998 tests, India insisted that it did not *need to* depend on CIRUS-produced material because it had plutonium from the Dhruva reactor and from a number of its power plants.[17] Significantly, India did not say that it did not actually use plutonium from CIRUS. Unfortunately, the US State Department, as much as it deplores India's nuclear tests, would apparently rather forget about the CIRUS issue. The department wants to engage India in new agreements. There is not much point, however, in engaging countries in new agreements if one does not insist on respect for existing ones.

CONCLUSION: ONE RULE FOR ALL?

The May 1998 south Asian tests have created a new situation, one in which it is more difficult to maintain the pretenses of the NPT non-proliferation 'regime'. The 'huffing and puffing about test bans and non-proliferation' did not stop India and Pakistan and is not going to stop major states from getting nuclear weapons when their security interests so dictate.[18] US and international nonproliferation efforts had limited success even in dealing with small troublemakers like Iraq and North Korea.

Whatever chance there is to stop this process depends on setting up a much stricter international system of control over all nuclear explosives, civilian and military – going beyond the requirements of the Non-Proliferation Treaty. If that is still possible, it can only happen with the wholehearted support of the large majority of states. Whatever one thinks of India's 'in your face' nuclear policy, it has made clear that the NPT line between nuclear states and non-nuclear ones is ultimately untenable. Support for strict and effective bars to nuclear weapons could only come on the basis of a uniform standard, applicable to all states, including the current official nuclear states, in both the civilian and military spheres. That would mean the official five – all of them – would have to reduce nuclear arms themselves beyond what they currently plan to do; and the unofficial three would have to join them.

So far, there is no sign of either stricter controls over nuclear explosives or sharper warhead reductions in all nuclear weapons states. The likely consequence is more states with nuclear weapons.

NOTES

1 Victor Gilinsky is a Washington, DC-based consultant on energy issues and a former NRC commissioner, 1975–84.
2 'Flanked by giant cardboard posters of a mushroom cloud and two soaring missiles, Prime Minister Atal Bihari Vajpayee tonight marked the first anniversary of India's watershed underground nuclear tests with a muscular, pro-defense speech that formally launched his party's campaign for national elections in September.' Pamela Constable, 'Indian Nuclear Test Anniversary is Hindu Party's Campaign Kickoff', *Washington Post*, 12 May 1999.
3 'Everybody has known for years that India has nuclear weapons. They used to set off their tests by calling them peaceful explosions. The significance of this is that they have sort of put it in our face, but it is not a change in the strategic situation.' Former Secretary of State Henry Kissinger, CNN Money-line, 13 May 1998.
4 Agreed Framework Between the United States of America and the Democratic People's Republic of Korea, Geneva, 21 October 1994.
5 'With Russian help, India plans to build its first nuclear-powered submarine by 2004 and eventually fit it with missiles carrying nuclear warheads, an Indian researcher said Friday.' Ramola Talwar, 'Jane's: India to Build Nuclear Submarine by 2004 with Russian Aid', Associated Press, 26 June 1998. India indicated an interest in nuclear submarines much earlier. See interview with former Indian Atomic Energy Commission chairman, 'Nuclear Submarine', Ranjan Roy, Associated Press, 1 December 1994.
6 'Notwithstanding their recent nuclear tests, India and Pakistan do not have the status of nuclear weapons states in accordance with the NPT.' Joint Communiqué issued by the P5 Foreign Ministers, Geneva, 4 June 1998.
7 'It is faintly absurd and hypocritical for the five permanent members of the UN Security Council to react with such pained outrage to their tests.' Speech by Lady Margaret Thatcher to the American Enterprise Institute Conference, 25 June 1998.
8 The NPT was extended indefinitely in 1995.
9 For a more detailed description of the events up to 1997, see Victor Gilinsky, 'Nuclear Blackmail: The 1994 U.S.–Democratic People's Republic of Korea Agreed Framework on North Korea's Nuclear Program', *Hoover Institution Essays in Public Policy* (Stanford University, CA: 1997).
10 '... we have not made any progress on long standing and important issues of the DPRK's compliance with its safeguards agreement.' Address by IAEA Director-General Dr Mohamed ElBaradei, 'Nuclear Energy in the Service of Development and Peace: The Role of the International Atomic Energy Agency', New Delhi, 19 February 1999.
11 'The agency is guided by three complementary and equally important strategic objectives. These are: to assist Member States in the use of nuclear technology; to promote radiation and nuclear safety; and to ensure *to the extent possible* that pledges related to the exclusively peaceful use of nuclear energy are kept.' IAEA Director-General Dr Mohamed ElBaradei, address at the Japan Atomic Industrial Forum, 'The Future of Nuclear Power: Looking Ahead', Sendai,

12 April 1999 (emphasis added).
12 Henry Kissinger was then secretary of state.
13 Witness US concern over a suspicious North Korean underground site and willingness to pay heavily to inspect it (even after having given North Korea several months to sanitize it). 'Japan Welcomes U.S.–North Korea Nuclear Deal', Reuters, 17 March 1999.
14 The Gulf War must also have impressed the world's troublemakers with the need for an 'equalizer'.
15 Rodney W. Jones, Mark G. McDonough, Toby F. Dalton, Gregory Koblentz, *Tracking Nuclear Proliferation* (The Brookings Institution Press, Washington, DC, 1998), 131.
16 Ibid., 112.
17 Letter to the Editor of the *Washington Post* (unpublished) from Shiv S. Mukherjee, Minister, Embassy of India, Washington, DC, 29 June 1998.
18 Speech by Lady Margaret Thatcher to the American Enterprise Institute Conference, 25 June 1998.

2

Terrorism and Weapons of the Apocalypse

DAVID C. RAPOPORT[1]

INTRODUCTION

On 20 March 1995, *Aum Shinrikyo* startled the world by launching a nerve gas attack in the Tokyo subway. Many felt that terrorists finally crossed a threshold by producing and using an apocalyptic weapon, the 'poor man's atomic bomb' as the literature so often suggests.[2] A second conclusion was that *Aum* confirmed a belief widespread among students of terrorism that religious groups are particularly attracted to these weapons.

The first conclusion, that a threshold has been crossed, runs wildly against the facts. No one in the near future is going to see cities destroyed where tens of thousands die. Conventional explosives, like those used to create the Nairobi or Oklahoma City atrocities, will continue to inflict the overwhelming bulk of the casualties. The plain fact is neither chemical nor biological weapons presently are truly weapons of mass destruction in the way atomic weapons are; and they are certainly not so in the hands of terrorists.[3] Misreading the *Aum Shinrikyo* experience, *inter alia*, could waste tens of billions of dollars.[4]

With respect to the second conclusion, we have closed the book too quickly on who might be attracted to these weapons. The historical record indicates secular groups have sought to use such weapons more often than religious groups. This will likely continue into the future too.

DIFFICULTIES IN DISCUSSING THE PROBLEM

Before we turn to the reasoning, it will be useful to explain why this issue is so difficult to discuss. First, one cannot say much that is either new or certain about the matter, partly because there have been so few incidents, and we know so very little about those events. Groups gathered materials and sometimes made threats to use them but they did not employ them, and we do not know why.[5] Beyond the absence of information, there is a second problem. We are dealing with a frightening and very remote possibility, but one which, alas, can neither be demonstrated nor disproved. Just as there is no logical way to show religious believers they are in error in thinking the world will come to an end, so likewise no way exists to demonstrate terrorists will never use apocalyptic weapons. Because of this uncertainty, the issue moves out of the academic realm gaining serious and potentially pernicious consequences.

Elsewhere I have discussed religious believers who want an apocalypse to occur in order to redeem the world.[6] Here I want to talk about two other types: those who fear the apocalypse or simply see it as an unprecedented catastrophe, and those who exploit that anxiety for their own mundane purposes. Apocalyptic expectations have consequences because of certain propensities in human nature. If you want people to pay attention to uncertain but dangerous matters, you *must* exaggerate. The fact was driven home to me for about the twentieth time in late July 1998. The Discovery Channel was planning a program on terrorists and weapons of mass destruction. The producers discussed details with me in several conversations, and I thought the deal for my presentation was nailed down. A week later London called asking, 'By the way what is your general view of the problem?' 'A frightening thought,' I said, 'but not a serious possibility now.' 'Oh dear!' came the response, and a pregnant silence ensued. That ended the call, and I am still waiting for the baby.

Another way to think about our propensity to exaggerate disaster is to ask yourself, which position would you as an analyst prefer to be in? Is it better for your reputation to predict that grim events will happen and be wrong, or is it better for your professional credentials to be optimistic about disaster and equally wrong. All things being the same, the consequences of error would be much greater for the optimist and, therefore, the prudent analyst will be grim. This is the logic that insurance policies are based on, a profitable economic activity. There are other consequences of the propensity to prepare for the worst, beyond good business for insurance sellers. Consider a 7 August 1998 front-page story in the *New York Times* that described the workings of a panel which recommended the government spend $420 million over five years ($51 million in the first year) for vaccines and antibiotics against a possible terrorist attack.[7] Scientists, business executives and policy makers completed the task in record time because they could overwhelm 'doubters' and 'side-step objections'. The panel made bad and costly decisions, and it is necessary to reconsider the whole problem again. 'Cheaper more effective vaccines' seem likely in the 'next few years' and, in any case, the facilities to produce the initial vaccines ordered are not available.

The major problem in dealing with biological and chemical attacks is that so many different toxins and pathogens can be used, and, since a vaccine for one is not useful for another, it is economically impossible to stockpile for all potential agents. The story noted also that, since there is money to be made, problems were exacerbated by those with conflicting interests. No wonder a well-known analyst of terrorist activity, Larry Johnson, noted in *US News and World Report*,[8] that this particular anti-terrorism anxiety is the 'latest gravy train': one which academics, government bodies and business corporations are all eager to board. It is one thing to buy insurance with your own money; it is another to urge insurance with someone else's money, especially if the insurance salesman will make a personal profit on what he sells and that fact is not obvious to the purchaser who thinks the advice is impartial.

A second psychological disadvantage associated with this issue stems from the conflict between serious students of terrorist experiences and those from the physical sciences. Physical scientists are more impressed with the dangers because they are more clearly aware of the potential of chemical and biological agents and the ability of science to increase the powers of those agents. In addition, the authority of physical scientists is intimidating, especially to the untrained.

Nonetheless, those of us who have been in terrorist studies for a long time are likely to be skeptical for the simple reason that we know there have always been enormous gaps between the potentiality of a weapon and the abilities and/or will to employ it. Terrorists, in particular, operate in contexts of enormous uncertainty and anxiety; accidents fatal to the terrorists are plentiful, and to avoid them terrorists seek simple weapons that are easy to transport and assemble.[9]

CONFLICTS BETWEEN CONVENTIONAL WISDOM AND EXPERIENCE

Since the 1960s, when terrorism re-emerged as a serious concern, there has been an unhealthy tendency to exaggerate the importance of technology in explaining the phenomenon, a tendency which is reflected in our explanations of all violent struggles.[10] Because of that tendency, many have been mystified that terrorists have not been interested in the various chemical and biological toxins and pathogens readily available since the First World War. The conventional explanation for this restraint, or mystery if you like, is that terrorists have been political animals who know full well that these weapons would alienate their potential constituencies.

However, in recent years the nature of terrorism has changed because religious objectives replaced secular or political ends for many groups,[11] and many commentators are certain religious terrorists will be attracted to chemical and biological weapons as moths are to a flame. Why? Because religious terrorists are only interested in serving their deities and are oblivious to human constituencies. And there are other reasons too. Religious believers have much less concern for their lives in this world; they will accept risks secular terrorists refuse to take, and they are, we often read, consumed by the idea of sheer destruction. The revelation that *Aum Shinrikyo* was a religious group seemed definitive proof of this connection between religion and chemical and biological weapons, a connection which creates a doomsday problem for us all. But a closer look both at the historical record and at the *Aum* experience suggests a much more ambiguous picture.

The historical record: states

Who has used chemical weapons, why and to what success? Undeniably, the principal users have been states; and, while there are significant differences between states and terrorist groups, there are some generally ignored parallels in their experiences well worth pondering.

In the twentieth century, chemical weapons were used by both sides in the First World War and by Italy against the Ethiopians in the 1930s. More recently, Iraq employed them first against Iran, and then against Iraqi Kurds. Egypt's Nasser employed them in Yemen, and Libya under Qaddafi experimented with them in Chad. Perhaps 30 states today have chemical weapons.[12]

States have used chemical weapons, but they did so rarely, a potentially very significant fact, and one to which we shall return after considering the military circumstances encouraging states to use them. The evidence is that the temptation is greatest in situations where a military stalemate has developed, a deadlock which desperate belligerents want to break.

Ironically, despite the belief that they may be a decisive weapon, they do not seem to be very effective on the battlefield, especially when appropriate defensive measures are available. The weapons have blunted an offensive; but it is very difficult to find that tactical advantage being transformed into a decisive strategic one, because, in the cases familiar to us, the original stalemate and/or war of attrition continued.[13] This pattern, so often repeated in history, occurred again in the best documented recent use of chemical weapons during the long Iran–Iraq War.

> Iraq employed this weapon only in vital segments of the front and only when it saw no other way to check Iranian offensives ...

[C]hemical weapons ... had a negligible impact on the war limited to tactical rather than strategic [effects].[14]

Iraqi gases killed 5,000, but the Iranians suffered 600,000 dead altogether. Gas, thus, killed less than 1 per cent.[15] By far the deadliest experience with gas occurred during the First World War, but still it accounted for only 5 per cent of the casualties and those gassed were more than 10–12 times likely to recover than those wounded by traditional weapons.[16] These facts help us appreciate the supreme irony Amos Fries and Clarence West propose after examining the First World War experience: 'Instead of being the most horrible form of warfare, it is the most humane, because it disables far more than it kills, i.e. has a low fatality ratio.'[17]

It is also worth remembering that Iraq's use of chemical weapons against Iran was a violation of international law, but oddly, in view of present American concerns, Iraq was not named as a culprit in United Nations resolutions. Apparently, at that time, the matter did not seem very important.[18] The West developed a different view after the Gulf War, and in 1997 Secretary of Defense William Cohen indicated US military superiority was so great potential adversaries, unable to compete in conventional arms, may feel compelled to use apocalyptic weapons in a struggle against the United States.[19]

Why did Saddam Hussein decide not to use gas in the Gulf War? The conventional wisdom is that he feared the nuclear response that was threatened. That certainly may be correct. But it is also true, and possibly more pertinent, that the experiences in the Iranian War could not make him confident that his chemical weapons had military value, and the potential significance of this fact is much overlooked.[20]

Consider, too, another fact relevant to the argument. Chemical weapons were used more often after the Second World War than during the inter-war period. There are no technological improvements to explain this difference but there are some good relevant military reasons. After 1945 more wars of attrition were fought; and they have been fought largely between Third World armies which generally lack serious offensive capabilities. Most can fight only in trenches, and trench warfare is always attrition warfare.[21]

States have been the principal users of biological weapons too, and although available for a much longer period of time than chemical weapons they have probably been used less often. The Republic of Venice used biological weapons in the fifteenth and sixteenth centuries, as did the English in the French and Indian War (Seven Years War). Venice was attracted largely because poison seemed ideal for assassination strikes; the illness induced was likely to be considered as a product of natural causes thus making Venetian involvement easier to conceal. The English, on the other hand, were interested in the potential for large-scale destruction when they attempted to spread smallpox among the Indian tribes supporting the French. Later, the weapons were used for both ends. It is difficult, oddly, to find states using biological weapons for religious purposes, and this is true in spite of the fact religious wars are traditionally reputed to be the most ferocious. The fact should also be interesting for those concerned with possible use by terrorists because it is assumed religious terrorists are 'naturally' attracted to those weapons.

Japan's military efforts offer the most modern, comprehensive, and interesting examples of chemical and biological activities, but we can only discuss the second here.[22] Starting in 1932, Japanese scientists experimented with many different biological weapons, and created production facilities with 'a potential for creating sufficient bacteria to kill the world's population several times over', and the experiments on prisoners killed some 3,000.[23] Japanese records describe 11 attempts to use the weapons spreading 'germs of cholera, dysentery, typhoid, bubonic plague, anthrax disease, and paratyphoid' through water supplies and air drops from the 1930s to the end of the war.[24]

Considering the reputed potentialities of Japanese materials, they were used very infrequently, most likely because they did not live up to expectations or were very impractical weapons, producing relatively few casualties against armed forces. There were also difficulties in controlling diseases generated, and the cost could be as great to the attacker as to the attacked. In the assault on Chekiang (China 1942), Japanese toxins occasioned 10,000 Japanese casualties, including 1,700 deaths. The Japanese program's principal defect, a problem common to all efforts so far, is an ineffective delivery system, a usable shell, bomb, or spray.[25]

Biological and chemical weapons have similar military rationales. An adversary believing himself to be at a great disadvantage at a crucial moment is sorely tempted to consider chemical and biological weapons. The British in western Pennsylvania (1754) had few troops and inadequate supplies. The historian Francis Parkman noted that

> terror reigned supreme ... The Indian scalping-parties were ranging everywhere, laying waste the settlements, destroying the harvest and butchering men, women, and children, with ruthless fury.

If Fort Pitt was lost, the frontier would be forced back some 200 miles to Lancaster, 'forfeiting many years of colonization'. Desperation inspired the British to try to create a smallpox plague among the Indians.[26]

The Japanese initially developed their biological program because they anticipated that a much larger Soviet Union would try to expel them from recently conquered Manchuria. The major Japanese biological strike (Chekiang) came after the Doolittle Raid, the first attack on the Japanese homeland and a very serious psychological blow. The Japanese hoped to destroy the area containing Allied airfields. When that strike backfired and generated so many self-inflicted casualties, the biological program was virtually abandoned.

The limited value or effectiveness of chemical or biological weapons in wars of the past seems the most compelling reason they were not used much, a possibility usually ignored, or at least obscured. Discussions of the weapons take their deadliness for granted. Most offer two reasons only to explain why attacks are so infrequent, namely the intense moral revulsion they arouse and the fact that the states threatened are able to retaliate with similar weapons.

Technological innovations, like the ballistic missile, could render the issue of military ineffectiveness moot. Still, for most countries missiles are very expensive and unreliable. General Norman Schwartzkopf says the Scud missile in the Gulf War was the military equivalent of a mosquito.[27] The fact is that weapons designed solely to inflict casualties and not break organization – the object of battle – cannot be decisive as a military weapon.[28] In any case, the issue of what history can and cannot teach us should be joined, and rarely is.

The historical record: non-state actors

Now let us look at the experiences of non-state actors, especially those of terrorist groups. We will treat chemical and biological attacks together. As noted above, states have not used these weapons often, a pattern which is even more striking when we examine terrorist groups. According to a Central Intelligence Agency report, 40,000 international terror incidents occurred between 1968 and 1980, but only 22 had chemical or biological elements. For every 2,000 incidents, nearly one chemical or biological event occurred. The casualties are also fewer per incident.[29] Another surprise: by far the overwhelming number of attempts are inspired by criminal purposes, and of those which served public ends most were political and very few religious.[30]

One striking example of a non-state actor was a group of about 150 Jewish partisans from Poland. In the aftermath of the Nazi defeat, this group of survivors sought to avenge the Holocaust before the Allies decided to prosecute Nazi war criminals. A plan to poison the water supplies of four German cities, killing 2 million Germans, was frustrated at the last moment by British intervention. Next, an effort to poison the bread of nearly 40,000 interned SS men was made;

although 1,000 were poisoned, apparently none died. Attacks ceased when the Allies announced plans to prosecute Nazi war criminals.[31]

In 1978 the Palestine Liberation Organization (PLO) began to poison Israeli oranges in European markets, injuring 12 and seriously damaging the Israeli economy. But then the activity stopped, and we do not know why. There are some claims that in the same period the PLO in Lebanon trained the German Red Army Faction (RAF) and others to use chemical and biological weapons. *Stasi* (East German intelligence) apparently was also training groups at the same time. The RAF stole a cache of mustard gas and promised to poison water supplies; and in November 1980, in an RAF apartment in Paris, French police discovered a miniature factory where both a botulism culture and notebook with instructions about how to spread bacterial disease had been produced.[32]

In 1984 a *Fatah* official threatened chemical attacks against Israel. At the same time the Covenant, Sword and Army of the Lord (CSA), a right-wing religious terror group in Arkansas, procured 30 gallons of cyanide. A neo-Nazi group, Order of the Rising Sun, produced 80 pounds of typhoid bacillus. *Rajneeshee*, a Hindu religious group in Oregon, poisoned 750 but none died. It still is unclear why the RAF, Palestinians, and neo-Nazi groups never used the materials they had and/or threatened to use. Were they restrained by moral, political or organizational concerns? We do not know, and a number of the instances have not been seriously examined.[33] Beyond the activities we know happened, there is an unknown, indeed unknowable, number of other groups which for some reason or another aborted their plans.

AUM SHINRIKYO

Given our anticipation of what nerve gas might do, knowledgable persons should have been very surprised that so *little* damage had occurred. And we should be surprised also that other groups have not yet followed suit. A 'copy-cat' phenomenon usually follows apparently novel acts of violence, and that fact led a CIA National Intelligence Estimate (1984) to predict that, although chemical and biological weapons were not yet popular among terrorists who were still terrified of them, 'one successful incident would significantly lower the threshold of restraint'.[34]

Looking more closely at the *Aum* experience, several unique features suggest *Aum*'s attack is not the decisive turning point conventional wisdom has been expecting. *Aum* contained 20 scientists with graduate degrees, and its laboratories were so good that the chief chemist said he left the university because *Aum*'s facilities were better.[35] *Aum* apparently began its efforts in 1990, five years before the notorious subway attack. Its assets were valued at $1 billion and it had 50,000 members world-wide. Because *Aum* was a religious group, Japanese law placed serious obstacles on police inquiries even though *Aum* members had murdered several individuals, including members of the group. Finally, with no previous experience of groups exploring chemical or biological agents, the police ignored complaints about awful odors coming from the main commune. Despite all these advantages, which no terrorist group ever had or perhaps ever could have, *Aum*'s record as a terrorist group was poor.

The subway incident captured our attention. But *Aum* made nine attempts before and then two attempts after the major subway incident. Twelve attacks but none succeeded, and ultimately *Aum* itself was crushed. All this suggests that successful chemical and biological efforts are much more difficult than conventional wisdom suggests, at least now, and that the 'poor man's atomic bomb' remains costly and unreliable. Perhaps *Aum*'s failures will discourage others; if not, prospective users are unlikely to match *Aum*'s effort, let alone exceed it.

There are other pertinent details. In the first eight attempts, *Aum* tried to use biological toxins believed to be more destructive than chemicals. A gas thought to be deadly was developed in 1990, and *Aum* sent three trucks to attack the US installation in Yokohama, the naval base at Yokuska, and Narita International Airport. But the three trucks caused no damage, and nobody even *noticed* the incidents because the gas *Aum* developed was not lethal.

Aum next attempted to develop an anthrax bomb and released it on two separate days, first from a truck and then from a Tokyo skyscraper. Again, nobody noticed, no damage was reported; despite the expectation of its scientists, *Aum* failed to create a deadly weapon. After four such attacks, *Aum* abandoned biological weapons altogether. It turned to chemical weapons, and made two sarin gas assassination attempts. An *Aum* scientist was the only casualty. The lesson drawn was to dilute the gas to protect *Aum* members. Despite the common wisdom that religious believers are indifferent to personal safety needs, *Aum* was very concerned with such details and developed anti-sarin pills as well.

Prior to the big subway attack, there was a strike against a court building to prevent a case against *Aum* from being heard. *Aum* hoped to kill three judges but it only injured them, as an unexpected wind blew the gas in another direction to kill six and injure 600. *Aum* next tried an aerosol sprayer attack on the subway, on 15 March 1995, but the person filling the container became conscience stricken and put water instead of sarin gas into it. Five days later the big subway attack came which riveted Japan for nearly a year, getting more attention than the Kobe earthquake, which preceded it and killed approximately 6,000 people. Finally, *Aum* rushed into both subway attacks before the group was ready to attack in order to divert the police on its trail. The two initial subway attacks were followed by two more subway assaults, one with cyanide, but both were aborted. A US congressional sub-committee opined that if an undiluted dose was used in the 20 March attack, 10,000 people might have died.[36] Perhaps, but *Aum* felt the dilution was necessary to protect its carriers, and like so many terrorist organizations it was in flight when it struck, a circumstance where accidents and misjudgments are common and a circumstance which provided another reason to dilute the poison. It is striking, too, that every death was occasioned by direct contact with the liquid and none by the gas.

It is unlikely that *Aum* was exceptionally inept. Estimates of Irish Republican Army (IRA) casualties produced by accidents, as opposed to those inflicted by security forces, range from 40 to 56 per cent, and this happens when comparatively easy to use explosives are employed over and over again and handled, thus, by veterans.[37] Remember, too, the IRA has been active longer than any comparable group, and there-fore, presumably, is efficient.[38]

In an essay I wrote many years ago I tried to explain the paradox of why ancient terrorist groups were more destructive and durable than their contemporary counterparts. One reason was the simplicity of the weapons which made decisions easier, and accidents less likely in situations of great uncertainty. It is pertinent perhaps, too, that, of the many delivery methods devised by *Aum*, the most effective was the most primitive, namely releasing the gas by using sharpened umbrellas to penetrate the plastic containers. What is true for terrorists has some relevance for soldiers too. How else can we explain that artillery rounds were responsible for most casualties in all the wars of the last two centuries.[39]

What does the *Aum* experience tell us about the difference between religious and secular groups? Not as much as some would believe. Certainly, secular groups have been attracted to these weapons. The Avengers failed, but genocides may provoke more disastrous reactions in the future.[40] The PLO and RAF seemed to be on the verge of using chemical and biological weapons just because their other weapons failed.

There was, however, an interesting unique odyssey in *Aum*'s development. It did not react to a devastating atrocity and did not try other weapons first. It began as a political party, and, after a humili-ating defeat in the 1989 parliamentary elections, it immediately began to experiment with biological pathogens as its first weapon. One might even say that it was obsessed with pathogens and toxins. If so, why?

Most have said that such activity is especially attractive to religious elements who have no restraints on their destructive appetites. Perhaps, but something else was more crucial. *Aum* worshiped Shiva, the Hindu god whose consort Kali inspired the Thugs, perhaps the most deadly terrorist group in history. As stranglers, the Thugs killed without shedding blood believing that those who died this way would go to paradise, a doctrine which made killing easier for the killer. This doctrine is found in *Aum* too. If this is the source of *Aum*'s fascination with gas, then it is not religion *per se*, but rather the type of religion that is most critical here, and presumably in other cases too.[41]

IMPLICATIONS AND CAVEATS

Scholarship

There are few facts and cases available, and *all* speculations on apocalyptic weapons are on shaky grounds. Still, we can know more. We had to wait until 1998 before we got the first good efforts to analyze reported cases from open sources, when Seth Carus and the Monterey Institute of International Studies both found various instances with conflicting or incomplete evidence.[42] Chemical weapon efforts analyzed are largely in the United States. Even in cases we know something about, there are gaps particularly with respect to why individual groups have been attracted to apocalyptic weapons, and why they decided to abandon materials once gathered.

Terrorism, furthermore, has a long history stretching back at least to the first century, and the weapons employed have varied from period to period. But we have no account of how and why new weapons become part of the terrorist arsenal, how quickly innovations are transmitted to various groups and what the obstacles to the transmission might be. Changes in tactics represent a virgin field for inquiry.[43] Finally, we have barely begun to scratch the surface on target selection.[44]

Priorities and money

Nonetheless, there are good reasons to think terrorists cannot produce doomsday catastrophes – yet. *Aum* had extraordinary time, much money, many scientists, and wonderful cover. Still, in 12 attempts it only occasioned 13 deaths, including two *Aum* members, while hospitalizing 1,200. Compare this record with a 1984 CIA report which said the 'clandestine production of chemical and biological weapons for multiple casualty attacks raise no greater technical obstacles than does the clandestine production of chemical narcotics or heroin'. The statement was repeated on 15 November 1998 by Secretary of the Navy William Danzig who went on to say that 'a single leased airplane disbursing a biological weapon can kill more people than died world-wide in any month in World War II'. One wonders who is living in what world.[45]

Since 1970, 12 chemical and biological attacks have occurred in America, producing one fatality and 772 injuries, almost all minor.[46] Seth Carus' study of biological attacks world-wide contains interesting information. Excluding military efforts, 70 biological attacks, including 18 terrorist, have occurred since the beginning of the twentieth century, occasioning nine deaths and 985 casualties. Forty-five of those attacks have occurred in the last decade which indicates great interest now in biological weapons however unimpressive the demonstrated capacities to use those weapons are.[47] Certainly capacities can become better, but so can countermeasures. Japanese police now investigate religious groups, now anticipate chemical and biological conspiracy possibilities, and apparently abandoned traditional propensities to negotiate endlessly.[48] States can supply terrorists with materials. But states have so much to lose by giving such power to agents they cannot control that this is a very remote possibility, and not one that has been attempted.

The question is how much should one spend for remote possibilities, when other perhaps more pressing and certainly more real dangers exist? A program to prepare every defense for every possible chemical or biological strike can be very expensive and irrelevant. One can stockpile vaccines and antibiotic treatments for ten toxins only to discover that one we have not prepared for is the one being used. The 1998 attack on the US embassy in Nairobi taught us that the government did not have enough money to protect all embassies; and it seems that attacks with explosives are not only more likely but more deadly too. Before throwing more money at the problem, clear priorities should be established for US counter-terrorism policies.

Panic and confusion

The absence of clear direction leads to confusion and sometimes panic. In the 1996 Olympics, everyone was preparing for chemical and biological attacks, and it is conceivable this pre-occupation hampered the ability to handle the conventional bomb explosion which did occur. The odd, unprofessional behavior of FBI agents in a February 1998 Nevada press conference announcing they had arrested persons with anthrax – which lab tests the next day revealed to be a vaccine – suggests that the agents had panicked. If government agents panic when apocalyptic weapons are suspected, how can we expect the population to remain calm? Television interviews where public officials describe how many people a vial of anthrax will kill terrify, but do they enlighten? Simulated exercises in which tens of thousands die do not provide the basis for sound useful policies. Worst-case scenarios which highlight only potential vulnerabilities are bound to have effects on those who wish to terrify and those who can be petrified. In Los Angeles, in the last two months of 1998, 20 anthrax threats, costing over $100,000 each, were made: a virtual epidemic which could intimidate a public and then make it blasé to all reasonable possibilities. One doubts whether this is the 'copy-cat phenomenon' anticipated by government authorities.

We lack a sense of history, or at least a belief that something can be learned from experience. Without that link to experience, our sense of proportion dissipates. This gap is a problem which pervades those strange people who think one needs an apocalypse to get to paradise and it is evident too among ordinary people who simply see apocalypse as hell itself.

NOTES

1 David C. Rapoport is Professor Emeritus of Political Science at the University of California, Los Angeles, and Editor of the *Journal of Terrorism and Political Violence*. Professor Rapoport is also Founding Director of the Center for the Study of Religion at UCLA.

2 One government study, for example, claimed that in some scenarios involving chemical and biological weapons 'the level of sophistication required may be lower than was the case for sophisticated bombs that have been used against civilian aircraft'. Office of Technology Assessment, *Technology Against Terrorism: The Federal Effort* (Washington, DC: Government Printing Office, 1991), 57.

3 It is not clear to me why and how chemical and biological weapons, which have been available for some time, have recently been designated 'weapons of mass destruction' along with nuclear bombs. Certainly, the history of the three weapons indicates clearly that they are vastly dissimilar with respect to destructive capabilities. I have, therefore, avoided using the term weapons of mass destruction when referring to chemical and biological toxins. See John and Karl Mueller's perceptive and provocative essay, 'Sanctions of Mass Destruction', *Foreign Affairs*, 78, 3 (May/June 1999), 43–53. The Muellers compare casualties inflicted by various weapons and show how the recent reshaping of language cannot be justified by our experiences.

4 Two other factors contribute to the anxiety: the knowledge of how insecure the former Soviet Union's chemical and biological weapons are, and difficulties with Saddam Hussein. A third factor could be the influence of a science fiction novel *The Cobra Event* over President Clinton if a *New York Times* story is right. See William Broad and Judith Miller, 'Thwarting Terror: A Special Report: Germ Defense Plan in Peril as Its Flaws Are Revealed', *New York Times*, 7 August 1998.

5 Jeff Simon's essay *Terrorists and the Potential Use of Biological Weapons* (Santa

Monica, CA: RAND Corp, 1989) is still unsurpassed. It is striking that Ron Purver's careful and useful discussion of the literature does not contain a single statement by either a potential or actual user. See his 'Understanding Past Non-Use of CBW' in Brad Roberts (ed.), *Terrorism With Chemical and Biological Weapons: Calibrating Risks and Responses* (Alexandria, VA: Chemical and Biological Arms Control Institute, 1997), 65–74.

6 David C. Rapoport, 'Messianic Sanctions for Terror', *Comparative Politics*, 20, 2 (January 1988), 195–211.

7 See William Broad and Judith Miller, 'Thwarting Terror: A Special Report: Germ Defense Plan in Peril as Its Flaws Are Revealed', *New York Times*, 7 August 1998.

8 Cited by Ehud Sprinzak, 'The Great Superterrorism Scare', *Foreign Policy* (Fall 1998), 117. Sprinzak sent me his essay in proofs just as mine was being finished, and our arguments overlap.

9 David Ronfeldt and William Slater's interesting study of the late nineteenth-century Anarchist fixation with dynamite certainly runs against the argument that terrorists prefer cheap, safe, easy-to-transport and assemble weapons. But that fascination did ultimately wear off; and it was initially generated because dynamite was so cheap, not used by criminals, and reliable if one was prepared to give one's own life in the process. The Ronfeldt–Slater argument that this fascination will repeat itself with new technology has not been borne out, and the trend, except in the case of Islam and Sri Lanka, has been to expand the distance between the assailant and weapon to protect the former. See *The Mindsets of High-Technology Terrorists: Future Implications From an Historical Analog* (Santa Monica, CA: RAND Corporation, 1984).

10 David C. Rapoport, 'Fear and Trembling: Terrorism in Three Religious Traditions', *American Political Science Review*, 78, 3 (September 1984), 658–77 attempts to expose the technological determinism myth, by arguing that the modern view of terrorism as a novel, recent phenomenon, attributable to post-Second World War developments in communications, transportation and weapon technologies is fundamentally flawed. Organized terrorist campaigns go back at least to the first century and, contrary to conventional wisdom, earlier organizations were more durable than modern ones, a durability enabling them to wreak more physical and political destruction too. Differences between various historical groups were not due to technologies so much as to differences in doctrine, organizational structure and intended audiences.

11 I may have contributed to this misconception when I noted in 'Fear and Trembling' (see note 10) that one could not understand religious terror without remembering that the deity is one of several audiences. This point, alas, was misinterpreted by my good friend Bruce Hoffmann in an influential essay to mean that the deity, who never prescribed limits, was the *only* audience. See his *'Holy Terror': The Implications of Terrorism Motivated by a Religious Imperative* (Santa Monica, CA: RAND Corporation, 1993), 78ff. See also his *Inside Terrorism* (London: Victor Gollanz, 1998), Chapter 4.

12 American government sources have alleged that the Soviets used chemical and biological weapons against Muslim fundamentalists in Afghanistan. But some reputable sources are unconvinced. See Stockholm International Peace Research Institute (SIPRI) Year Book 1985, *World Armaments and Disarmaments* (London: Taylor & Francis, 1985), 5, 169, 173, 180.

13 See SIPRI, *The Rise of CB Weapons* (New York: Humanities Press, 1971), 121–44. It is often extremely difficult to verify and elaborate allegations concerning the use of chemical and biological weapons for obvious reasons; with rare exception users have tried to hide their tracks, and others find

political advantage in making and exaggerating allegations. See, for example, the problems associated with Japanese use; Andy Thomas, SIPRI, *Effects of Chemical Warfare: A Selective Review and Bibliography of British State Papers* (London: Taylor & Francis, 1985), 65–7. We know most about the Iran–Iraq War; and, therefore, when one realizes how little we know about gas there, the result should be humbling. See the careful study by Gordon Burck and Charles Flowerree, *International Handbook on Chemical Weapons Proliferation* (New York: Greenwood Press, 1991), 31–152.

14 Efraim Karsh, *Iran–Iraq War: A Military Analysis*, Adelphi Papers, No. 220 (London: ISSS, 1987), 57. Karsh also says that 'Iraq's use of chemical weapons was incremental and heavily circumscribed. Iraq did not employ lethal gas before it had indicated its intentions both by using tear gas first and by continuous and persistent warnings ... to leave the door open for an Iranian retreat.' An interesting feature of the commentary on the Iran–Iraq War is that the use of chemical weapons received little attention at the time. Shahram Chubin and Charles Tripp's *Iran and Iraq at War* (Boulder, CO: Westview Press, 1988) has six references to it in some 300 pages; altogether the material is less than a paragraph. Most information deals with international reaction. The military significance of chemical weapons is suggested by the comment on page 80, 'Iran maintained considerable restraint. It saw no need to imitate Iraq's panicky and cynical use of chemical weapons.'

15 Thomas McNaugher argues that, of the 27,000 gassed through 8 April 1987, only 262 died. 'Ballistic Missiles and Chemical Weapons: The Legacy of the Iran–Iraq War', *International Security*, 15, 2 (Fall 1990), 31. US Department of State James Rubin on 16 March 1998 indicated that 20,000 died, but did not explain why the estimate was so different from previous ones. Internet: http//secretary. state.gov/www/briefings/statements/1998ps980316a.html

The context, of course, changes when an army strikes a defenseless population. Still, I have not yet found a clear picture of the various impacts of different weapons employed against the Iraqi Kurds in 1987–88. A *Human Rights Watch Report* speaks of 'tens of thousands dead', but does not estimate the importance of the different weapons. 'The Iraqi Government in its Own Words' (February 1994), 13. Earlier analyses indicated that too much time had elapsed to detect chemical traces. Nonetheless, as indicated in the preceding paragraph, a State Department spokesman nearly a decade later felt sufficiently confident to state without explanation that 5,000 were killed by gas in the attack on Halabja.

16 Reference to chemical and biological statistics vary widely even in well-known documented instances. P. Williams and D. Wallace estimate that in the last six months of the First World War gas accounted for one out of six casualties, or between 16 and 17 per cent. See *Unit 731: Japan's Secret Biological Warfare in World War II* (New York: Free Press, 1989), 9. See McNaugher, 'Ballistic Missiles', 19, for statistics regarding the disparity between casualties and deaths from gas as opposed to those from traditional weapons.

17 Cited by Jessica Stern, 'Will Terrorists Turn to Poison?', *Orbis* (Summer 1993), 397. Eliot Cohen makes a similar argument in an impressive article on high technology weapons: 'Indeed, some high technology weapons probably decrease lethality.' See 'Distant Battles: Modern War in the Third World', *International Security*, 10, 4 (Spring 1986), 159.

18 See Burck and Flowerree, *Chemical Weapons Proliferation*, 13.

19 'As the new millennium approaches, we face the very real and increasing prospect that regional aggressors, third-rate armies, terrorist groups and even religious cults will seek disproportionate power by acquiring and using

[weapons of mass destruction].' William S. Cohen, 'In the Age of Terror Weapons', *Washington Post*, 26 November 1997. Jessica Stern drew my attention to the document. The argument reflects, of course, our ever-present assumption that superior technology is decisive in violent confrontations. Jessica Stern discusses Secretary Cohen's statements in *The Ultimate Terrorists* (Cambridge, MA: Harvard University Press, 1999), 7.

20 We do not know why he was restrained. Nuclear responses were threatened but were they credible in these circumstances? See Keith B. Payne, 'Deterring the Use of Weapons of Mass Destruction: Lessons From History', *Comparative Strategy*, 14, 4 (1995), 353–5. If the Allies did intend to use nuclear weapons, the outrage chemical weapons generated, not their effectiveness, would have made the threat meaningful.

Anticipated terrorist action by Iraqi-supported elements against civilians did not materialize either. If either action had occurred, the Allies would probably have expanded their military aim to remove the government and/or try Hussein for war crimes. Weapons which enrage but do not create significant military damage are counter-productive, that is to say they do more damage to assailants than to victims.

21 See Cohen, 'Distant Battles'. Libya used gas as 'a desperation measure' when its forces were expelled from northern Chad. But most of the gas 'missed the Chadian forces and apparently floated over Libyan lines.' *Christian Science Monitor*, 5 January 1988. A British assessment of the Japanese use of mustard gas in a 1941 battle against the Chinese who had no protective clothing is worth citing too. 'This was a battle in which the Japanese had suffered a reverse – and they used gas to help restore the situation. Remember that the same thing may happen on our front one day when we are pushing them back.' Quoted in Thomas, *Effects of Chemical Warfare*, 66.

22 'According to a document prepared by a younger brother to Japanese Emperor Hirohito, the Japanese military attempted to poison members of the Lytton Commission, [established] by the League of Nations ... to investigate Japan's conquest of Manchuria, by serv[ing them] fruit "laced" with cholera.' W. Seth Carus, *Bioterrorism and Biocrimes*, Working Manuscript (Washington, DC: National Defense University, December 1998), 82. (Carus' study of non-state groups is the best available.) The Venetian experience usually produced results similar to those of the Japanese.

23 Williams and Wallace, *Unit 731*, 23.

24 China, on the other hand, reported some 900 incidents on its soil before 1941. It is not clear how the discrepancy could be so great. See Williams and Wallace, *Unit 731*, 94.

25 Christopher, *et al.*, 'Biological Warfare: An Historical Perspective', *Journal of American Medical Association*, 278, 5 (6 August 1997), 413 and Williams and Wallace, *Unit 731*, 68–70. The evidence concerning enemy casualties inflicted is very unclear but does not seem to be great. In most attacks the casualties given by the Japanese were around 100. Sheldon Harris in *Factories of Death: Japanese Biological Warfare 1932–45 and the American Coverup* (London: Routledge, 1994) believes that the casualties were higher and gives a grand total of some 200,000. But this is very doubtful, and Harris provides little evidence, acknowledges that we have no real hard information and that the problems in the delivery process proved insuperable.

Raymond Zilinskas makes an interesting and persuasive argument that biological toxins have been even less useful to states than chemical ones, but then he goes on to argue that terrorists will find more uses for biological materials than states have. I do not find his reasoning on this point convincing.

See his 'Terrorism and Biological Weapons: An Inevitable Alliance', *Perspectives in Biology and Medicine*, 34, 1 (Autumn 1990), 44–71.

26 Parkman is cited in the excellent account of James A. Pourpard, Linda A. Miller and Lindsay Granshaw, 'The Use of Smallpox as a Biological Weapon in the French and Indian War of 1763', *ASM News*, 55, 3 (1989), 122–4. The reason for distinguishing between French and Indians is not clear, but the native population was known to be vulnerable. It is commonly believed that the English tried to release a plague against the American forces during the Revolutionary War and the soldiers in the Continental Army were inoculated.

Earlier, the French – desperate to stop the Miami Indians from trading with the English in 1732 – apparently poisoned some 300. Joseph L. Peysner, 'It Was Not Smallpox: The Miami Deaths of 1732', *Indiana Magazine of History*, LXXXXI (June 1985), 159–69. My thanks to Professor Robert White for sending me the reference.

As in all other cases of chemical or biological attacks, accurate information about spreading smallpox in the native population is difficult to get. Many allegations are made about the French, Spanish and English practices. See E. W. and A. E. Stearn, *The Effect of Smallpox on the Destiny of the Amerindian* (Boston, MA: Bruce Humphries, 1945). A case of a trader spreading smallpox to avenge an apparent wrong is described by D. R. Hopkins, *Peasants and Princes* (Chicago, IL: University of Chicago Press, 1983), 236.

27 H. Norman Schwartzkopf, *It Doesn't Take a Hero* (New York: Bantam, 1992), 417. General Schwartzkopf is referring to missiles with conventional warheads. Obviously, missiles armed with nuclear weapons are a different matter. But with respect to chemical and biological weapons, the issue is how many of these expensive missiles does one need to create serious damage, and while estimates vary they seem beyond the means of states who are potential adversaries, and certainly beyond the capacities of terrorist groups.

28 Does the 'Vietnam Trauma', a prominent feature of the American psyche, make us so casualty averse that the conventional object of battle – break organization – is no longer pertinent? I think that 'casualty aversion' becomes a crippling problem only when the war cannot be justified and one must depend on conscripts. There was no casualty aversion problem in the Second World War. See David C. Rapoport, 'A Comparative Theory of Military and Political Types', in Samuel Huntington, *Changing Patterns of Military Politics* (Glencoe, MN: Free Press, 1962), particularly 74–7.

29 Joseph Pilat discusses the CIA report in 'World Watch: Striking Back at Urban Terrorism', *NBC Defense and Technology International*, June 1986, 30.

30 Jessica Stern's analysis of a RAND database of incidents involving chemical and biological materials from 1968 to 1987 indicates that 60 per cent served criminal, 21 per cent terrorist, 7 per cent protester, 4 per cent state, 0.5 per cent religious, and 8 per cent unknown ends. See Stern, 'Will Terrorists Turn to Poison?', 406.

31 The Germans reported that several thousand died, the Americans said there were no deaths, and the Avengers claimed 1,000 deaths. Each party had an interest in giving its own statistics, and, as far as I know, there is no definitive account. If the Avenger estimate is correct, the attack is the most deadly ever by a non-state group. The Avengers are described by Michael Elkins, *Forged in Fury* (New York: Ballantine Books, 1971) and Michael Bar Zohar, *The Avengers* (New York: Hawthorne Books, 1967). The war trials did not occur because of the Avengers; still, once the trials were announced, the basic rationale for the group disappeared. Carus notes that there is not enough information available to establish the true casualty statistics, and Ehud Sprinzak tells me that the

American claim that no deaths occurred seems accurate.

32 Information concerning the Paris incident comes from a variety of sources: government officials, newspapers and books. But the details are not always identical and cannot be verified from open sources. See Carus, *Bioterrorism and Biocrimes*, 72. Carus also indicates that information concerning other incidents specified in this paragraph is too meager to analyze.

33 Presently, we have no analysis of chemical attacks outside the United States. Carus, *Bioterrorism and Biocrimes* examines all biological attacks by individuals and non-state groups. A CNS Monterey Institute of International Studies study, *Terrorism in the U.S.A. Involving Weapons of Mass Destruction* (Monterey, 1988) looks at chemical and biological efforts in the United States. Both studies are good and demonstrate how difficult it is to be definitive about many cases.

34 Jack Anderson, 'Chemical Arms in Terrorism Feared by the CIA', *Washington Post*, 27 August 1984. B. David, 'The Capability and Motivation of Terrorist Organizations to Use Mass Destruction Weapons', in Ariel Merari (ed.), *On Terrorism and Combating Terrorism* (Frederick, MD: University Press of America, 1985), 150–1. Not much time has elapsed since the 20 March 1995 incident, and so perhaps the thesis has not yet been truly tested.

35 Murray Sayle, 'Nerve Gas and Four Noble Truths', *New Yorker*, 1 April 1996, 71.

36 Most US analysts initially thought that *Aum* either used a poor quality sarin or had not developed a proper distribution system. For reasons related, I think, to our misunderstanding of religious terror, we found it difficult to believe that *Aum* members were concerned with their own lives.

Early newspaper reports exaggerated *Aum* accomplishments and the most misleading was the claim that *Aum* had developed biological weapons. That claim and others were repeated in David Kaplan and Andrew Marshall's *The Cult at the End of the World* (New York: Crown Press, 1996). See Milton Leitenberg, *Biological Weapons Arm Control*, PRAC Paper 16, College Park, CISS, School of Public Affairs, University of Maryland, May 1996. See also a second Leitenberg piece, 'The Widespread Distortions of Information on the Efforts to Produce Biological Warfare Agents by the Japanese *Aum Shinrikyo* Group: A Case Study in the Serial Propagation of Misinformation', in *Journal of Terrorism and Political Violence*, 11, 4 (Winter 1999), 149–58.

37 The 56 per cent estimate is based on data collected by Robert and Terry Falkenberg White and covers a five-year period. 'Revolution in the City: On the Resources of Urban Guerrillas', *Terrorism and Political Violence*, 3, 4 (Winter 1991), 100–32. Some accidents, of course, may be due to British intrigues. But J. Bowyer Bell, a very reliable, long-time student of IRA tactics notes, 'Other than carelessness that comes from familiarity and limited original training, the necessity for speed and the quality of the weapons are major reasons for premature explosions.' *The Gun in Politics* (New Brunswick, NJ: Transaction, 1987), 51.

38 How typical is the IRA experience with respect to 'accidents'? We have no data to compare groups systematically. However, anyone familiar with the history of modern terrorism since the beginning in the nineteenth century will agree that the experience seems to be common.

39 'The great killer in all of the wars under discussion has been [a product of] the simplest of technology, the artillery round, which is not greatly different from its ancestor in World War I (with the possible exception of cluster bomb units, which, however, do not differ greatly in *conception* from the shrapnel shell at the beginning of the war). The high technology Exocet missile, for example, caused only a handful of casualties in the Persian Gulf War.' Cohen, 'Distant

Battles', 158–9, original emphasis.

The comment of a prominent anthropologist is worth citing in this connection. 'Citizens of modern states tend to believe that everything they do is more efficient or effective than the corresponding efforts of primitives or ancients ... Therefore, it comes as a shock to discover that the proportion of war casualties in primitive societies almost always exceeds that suffered by even the most bellicose or war-torn modern states.' L. Keeley, *War Before Civilization* (New York: Oxford University Press, 1996), 88.

40 On the other hand, the Armenian reaction was different. Armenian groups initially tried to kill Turkish officials they thought responsible; and when the latter died any Turkish official might be fair game.

41 For a good discussion of *Aum*'s theology, see Manabu Watanabe, 'Religion and Violence in Japan Today: A Chronological and Doctrinal Analysis of *Aum Shinrikyo*', *Terrorism and Political Violence*, 10, 4 (Winter 1998), 80–100. Watanabe does not consider a possible Thug connection.

42 See Carus, *Bioterrorism and Biocrimes* and CNS, *Terrorism in the U.S.A.*

43 Martha Crenshaw's perceptive 'Incentives and Disincentives for Nuclear Terrorism' contains an interesting discussion of what we do not know about these matters (APSA unpublished paper, 1997).

44 See C. J. M. Drake, 'The Role of Ideology in Terrorists' Target Selection', *Terrorism and Political Violence*, 10, 2 (Summer 1998), 53–85.

45 See Anderson, 'Chemical Arms' and Richard Danzig, 'The Next Super-Weapon: Panic', *New York Times*, 15 November 1998. Danzig says of biological weapons, 'Neither their production nor their delivery requires large, expensive, or visible systems. Potent biological weapons can be made in a room and held in a vat.'

46 The figures are compiled from the materials in the Monterey Institute Report, *Terrorism in the U.S.A. Involving Weapons of Mass Destruction*.

47 See Carus, *Bioterrorism and Biocrimes*, 12 and 26. Diseases like the Black Plague which afflicted medieval Europe or the influenza epidemic in the early twentieth century killed more people than did weapons during the same periods. But, fortunately, we do not know how to create epidemics we can control.

48 See Taiji Myaoka, 'Terrorist Crisis Management in Japan: Historical Development and Changing Responses 1970–97', *Terrorism and Political Violence*, 10, 2 (Summer 1998), 31.

3

The Next Strategic Threat: Advanced Conventional Weapons Proliferation

TIMOTHY D. HOYT[1]

INTRODUCTION

Policy makers and specialists who worry about proliferation focus on specific, predictable threats, reflecting their visions of the most menacing forms of strategic war. Increasingly, discussions of nonproliferation policy include not just nuclear, but also biological and chemical weapons and the ballistic missiles which might be used to deliver them. This focus produces a natural overlap between arms control and nonproliferation policies – an overlap which is useful analytically, but which may not reflect the changing nature of the strategic threat faced by the United States in the twenty-first century.

This chapter examines several cases which do not breach current nonproliferation guidelines, but which pose potentially significant strategic obstacles to future US military missions. These cases suggest that nonproliferation policy should not, and indeed cannot, focus exclusively on so-called 'weapons of mass destruction'. Nonproliferation policy must begin to reflect the difficulties of controlling 'soft' technology – knowledge, processes, software – as well as the heavy machinery and production technology currently dealt with through export controls. New methods of punishing and dissuading proliferating entities may provide increased leverage in some of these areas of concern. Policy makers must reconnect nonproliferation policy with military perspectives on emerging strategic threats to US national security interests. In other words, the United States must re-evaluate the meaning of strategic threats, and incorporate those assessments into its nonproliferation and arms control efforts.

NONPROLIFERATION: THE ORIGINS OF CURRENT POLICY

Early efforts to control the spread of 'strategic' weapons focused on specific and predictable threats, and the most menacing forms of potential war. It is hardly surprising, therefore, that nuclear weapons have been a serious concern for the United States since the beginning of the Cold War. The prevailing vision of the most threatening form of strategic war helped define the nature of nonproliferation efforts. The Baruch Plan, for example, attempted to establish international ownership of all dangerous nuclear activities, reflecting the prevailing fear that in a nuclear environment the aggressor would always win. 'Atoms for Peace' used the NSC-68 definition of strategic threat (a knockout blow against 100 US cities) to suggest a dual-track nonproliferation effort: the establishment of a fissile bank which would limit Soviet fissile stockpiles below the danger threshold of 100–200 warheads, and inspection efforts which would guard against substantial diversions of nuclear material that might allow other states to rapidly reach that danger threshold.

Nonproliferation efforts since the late 1950s have focused on the danger of catalytic or accidental wars between smaller nuclear powers which might escalate into global cataclysm. These efforts focus on limiting the supply of critical, safeguardable technologies used in the production of nuclear weapons or the missiles that carry them.[2] Some, like the Nuclear Non-Proliferation Treaty (NPT), are multilateral treaties signed by virtually all the states in the international system.[3]

Treaties have advantages and disadvantages. Treaties are the most binding of all international agreements, but the nature of the treaty-making process is such that signatories wish to ensure they are not bound by any conditions not specifically spelled out in the treaty itself. This makes the creation of a treaty time-consuming and highly political. In an effort to come up with more comprehensive and rapid responses to proliferation problems in the late 1970s and early 1980s, the major industrialized powers began creating 'regimes'. These include the Nuclear Suppliers Group, which constrains the sale of nuclear fuel to states with reactors which are not under International Atomic Energy Agency safeguards and inspections; the Australia Group, which polices the transfer of chemical weapons, production technology and precursor materials; the Missile Technology Control Regime (MTCR), which constrains the sale of technology that can be used for long-range missiles or for space launch vehicles; and, later, the Wassenaar Arrangement, which focuses on conventional weapons and dual-use technologies. Each regime attempts to constrain dual-use technologies that can also create strategically significant military capabilities.[4]

The collapse of the Soviet Union fundamentally altered the threshold of strategic threat to both the United States and the international community. In the late Cold War era, analysts viewed the proliferation of nuclear, biological and chemical (NBC) weapons as a threat because regional conflicts between NBC-armed opponents might escalate, deliberately or accidentally, into a superpower nuclear exchange. The emerging international system exhibits abundant violence and proliferation, but this violence is divorced from the menace of superpower confrontation.[5] Defining current US nonproliferation policy based on the Cold War context of superpower competition is misguided. Lacking any true peer competitor, how can the United States best assess and anticipate strategic threats?

STRATEGIC PROLIFERATION: A PRACTICAL DEFINITION

The definition of 'strategic proliferation' used by the Office of the Secretary of Defense (OSD) in the early 1990s provides a useful starting point for analysis. According to OSD, a weapon or weapons-related technology was of concern if it fulfilled three criteria.[6]

First, did it enable another state to inflict high-leverage strategic harm against the United States or its friends? This could be, in the case of NBC weapons, the ability to destroy cities or cause mass casualties. High-leverage strategic harm could also refer, however, to a successful attack on the US Navy, for example, or the ability to prevent the United States from intervening in a particular region.

Second, did the United States lack effective defenses or countermeasures against this capability? Here, for example, the issue of ballistic missile proliferation clearly applies. The Gulf War indicated the limitations of current US defenses and countermeasures against mobile ballistic missiles. Another weapon of concern might be the Russian SS-N-22 Sunburn anti-ship missile, which according to some analysts may be able to defeat existing US Navy point defense systems due to its speed, or land attack variants of other anti-ship cruise missiles or unmanned aerial vehicles (UAVs).[7]

Third, does the mere acquisition of the weapons technology under consideration lead other states to question the identity of the leading power in the region? Ballistic missiles and chemical weapons contributed substantially to the perception that Iraq had become the leading Persian Gulf power in the late 1980s. The political impact of certain weapons can be quite substantial. Allies may fear the United States will be deterred by an adversary possessing NBC weapons and delivery capability. Weapons which make US regional partners reconsider the reliability of US security guarantees have substantial strategic and political impact.

NBC weapons, and particularly nuclear weapons, still constitute weapons of proliferation concern. These weapons can inflict high-leverage strategic harm, are resistant to some degree to existing defenses, and offer significant political leverage to states which possess them.[8] Similarly, certain types of ballistic and cruise missiles, particularly those with high accuracy or ranges greater than 300 kilometers, are issues of great concern. These missiles can carry NBC weapons or advanced conventional munitions to enemy capitals in regional conflicts, or possibly negate the US ability to project force from the sea or from regional airfields.

Current nonproliferation policies continue to reflect the assumptions and approaches of the Cold War. Efforts to impact the supply side of the proliferation trade focus on broad technology and export controls, while demand-side questions are dealt with in terms of broad multilateral treaties. These efforts are important, but in the post-Cold War environment they may not be sufficient. The examples of Iraq and North Korea show that these controls and regimes can be broken and violated by determined adversaries. India and Pakistan, after years of maintaining 'virtual arsenals', chose to breach the international norm against nuclear weapons testing in May of 1998.[9] These events suggest a decline in the efficacy of traditional means. In addition, lower-level technologies are much more widely available – despite the Wassenaar Arrangement and other efforts, the conventional arms trade and indeed the sale of defense manufacturing technology remains largely a commercially driven market.[10]

US security policy requires its military to be capable of intervention in regional conflicts. There are many weapons and technologies currently available on the international market which, alone or in combination, threaten the US ability to intervene. These lower-echelon threats are not covered by current nonproliferation policy, but constitute a significant threat to US interests. This chapter will examine several cases of lower-echelon strategic proliferation, detailing the means by which they circumvent existing nonproliferation thresholds and represent a potentially significant threat to US interests. The case studies examine three different aspects of the strategic proliferation problem: the establishment of independent and autonomous industries producing strategic weaponry; the ability of weaker states to procure conventional capabilities with strategic implications via the international arms market; and the transfer of strategic technology and know-how through commercial transactions.

INDIA'S *PRITHVI* SURFACE-TO-SURFACE MISSILE

The Indian government began the Indigenous Guided Missile Development Program (IGMDP) in the early 1980s. The objective of the program was to design and produce locally a family of military missiles more quickly and efficiently than previous Indian indigenous military production efforts had done. For the first time, the national-ized defense industrial sector accepted significant input from both private sector corporations and academic and educational research institutions.[11]

The highest priority development was the *Prithvi* tactical missile. The program made use of information obtained in a previous research effort, code-named 'Project Devil', from the 1970s. Project Devil was an effort to reverse-engineer the Soviet liquid-fueled SA-2 anti-aircraft missile. The ultimate objective of the project remains unclear: some sources believe it was intended to create a surface-to-surface missile, but others argue the objective was to master basic missile technology and obtain the ability to produce the SA-2 – or parts of it – locally.[12] The end results of Project Devil were two liquid-fueled motors, which formed the basis of the *Prithvi* design.

The *Prithvi* is a single-staged missile with a range of 40–250 kilo-meters, but more advanced versions are reportedly near deployment.[13] Two versions have already been fielded: the *Prithvi* 1, with a 150 kilo-meter range and a 1,000 kilogram payload, which is used by the Indian Army; and *Prithvi* 2, with a 250 kilometer range and 500 kilogram payload.[14] The *Prithvi* 3, also reportedly known as the *Dhanush*, is under development. This solid-fueled missile will have a range of 350 kilo-meters, exceeding the Missile Technology Control Regime guidelines, and may be deployed in a naval version.[15]

The *Prithvi* 2 can cover virtually all meaningful targets in Pakistan from bases in Indian Punjab. India began testing the *Prithvi* in 1988, and according to some reports this started a missile arms race on the subcontinent, prompting Pakistan to obtain Chinese M-11 missiles. Amidst reports that India was deploying *Prithvi* 1 missiles in forward positions causing a minor crisis in 1997,[16] international experts praised the *Prithvi* as cost-effective and sophisticated.[17]

Unlike the products of Iraq's ballistic missile program, the *Prithvi* is neither derived from the Soviet Scud nor a direct violation of the MTCR (until the *Prithvi* 3 is deployed). The MTCR was devised to prevent the use of the Scud as a technology base for long-range missiles, and the 300 kilometer range restriction reflected both the known capabilities of the Scud and the close distances between capital cities and other major targets in south Asia and the Middle East. It now appears, however, that even less-sophisticated and capable surface-to-air missiles can provide the necessary knowledge base for eventual surface-to-surface missile development. South Korea utilized the Nike-Hercules to produce a tactical missile, while the *Prithvi*, several Iraqi missiles and the Chinese CSS-8 all trace their lineage to the SA-2.[18] *Prithvi* represents a capable, multipurpose tactical missile. It can carry several types of warheads, including cluster munitions, fuel-air explosives, high explosives, and NBC warheads. According to Indian reports, it is also a very accurate missile.[19] *Prithvi* also serves as a building block for other missile systems. A shortened *Prithvi* motor forms the second stage of India's *Agni* I intermediate range ballistic missile (IRBM), and the *Prithvi* 3 may form the second stage of the recently tested *Agni* II IRBM.[20] As a result, the *Prithvi* now represents the evolution of a significant proliferation problem. *Prithvi* provides significant conventional capabilities because of its high accuracy and advanced warheads. It contributes to strategic instability on the subcontinent, as the launcher itself is very vulnerable, and its short-range and low-warning time may encourage Pakistan to pursue asymmetric or pre-emptive military strategies. It also provides a building block for longer-ranged and multi-staged missiles. Compared to the illusive Scud of Gulf War fame, *Prithvi* has greater accuracy, similar mobility and a much wider range of potential combat uses ranging from conventional strikes on airfields and tank concentrations to nuclear attacks.[21]

Just as importantly, however, the case of the *Prithvi* demonstrates the weaknesses inherent in the Missile Technology Control Regime (MTCR). MTCR cannot prevent a state building a missile industry – but it *can* buy time for diplomacy to take effect, if possible, or for preparation of appropriate coercive tools to punish violators. A state which is willing to commit significant resources over time can undercut MTCR by creating and upgrading a tactical missile – a missile which can, over time, be developed into a much longer-ranged system that eventually exceeds MTCR limitations. The primary obstacles to such endeavors are financial resources, project management and systems integration.[22] As the case of the *Prithvi* demonstrates, given sufficient determination and even modest levels of funding, in a period of roughly 15 years India was able to create a sophisticated 300plus kilometer range missile from an obsolescent surface-to-air missile.

Relying on the MTCR as a sufficient restraint, therefore, will not *solve* the long-term problem of long-range missile proliferation. Other methods must be found to coerce or punish proliferating entities, whether at the state or firm level. This requires a much more focused approach. In May 1998, just after the Indian nuclear tests and the imposition of sanctions by the United States, the Commerce Department allowed the shipment of software for designing printed circuit boards to Bharat Dynamics Limited (BDL). BDL is one of India's defense public sector units, and plays a major role in the development and production of Indian military missiles. The British government's list of proliferation risks included BDL; sadly, the US list did not. BDL assembles both the *Agni* and *Prithvi*, and with improved circuit boards they are likely to have improved accuracy.[23]

AREA DENIAL CAPABILITIES: A NEW STRATEGIC PROBLEM

The United States relies on power projection to deter aggression, secure access to natural resources, fulfill alliance commitments, and – ultimately – to ensure regional and global stability. According to the Joint Staff, 'power projection, enabled by overseas presence, will likely remain the fundamental strategic concept of our future force'.[24] The proliferation of NBC weapons and long-range missiles presents a number of obstacles to the successful pursuit of this strategy. In addition, however, a combination of sophisticated conventional weapons and technologies that currently lie 'under the radar' of major arms control regimes and treaties complicates US force projection operations.[25]

One of the most disturbing examples of this gradual acquisition of area denial capability has occurred in Iran. A decade ago, Iran's position as the dominant military power in the Persian Gulf was shattered by a combination of Iraqi ballistic missile bombardments, conventional ground force assaults, and aggressive US Navy convoy escorts that shattered Iran's naval capabilities. Over the ensuing years, analysts nervously monitored Iran's apparently ambitious military modernization efforts, focusing on high-visibility efforts to obtain latest generation strike aircraft, bombers and interceptors from the former Soviet Union.[26]

In the past five years, however, Iran's naval capabilities have experienced a resurgence based primarily on the acquisition of lower-visibility, and in many cases lower-technology, weapons and forces. Relying on cheap weapons readily available on the international arms market, Iran generated a significant sea-denial force at the mouth of the Persian Gulf. Combined with Iran's existing arsenal of Scud-C missiles and chemical weapons, the United States and its allies now face serious possible complications in the event of a conflict in the region. These complications are only compounded by Iran's continuing pursuit of biological and nuclear weapons, and its cooperation with Russia, North Korea and Pakistan in the production of intermediate range missiles.[27]

The most important and sophisticated purchase made by Iran was the acquisition of three *Kilo*-class conventional attack submarines from the former Soviet Union. The *Kilo* is one of the quietest, most sophisticated conventional submarines in the world. In addition to its normal armament of wire-guided torpedoes, Iran has sought wake-homing torpedoes from Russia, which constitute a serious threat to US and other military vessels in the region. The *Kilo* also provides a significant covert mine-laying capability. While Iran reportedly had difficulty deploying its submarine force in the mid-1990s, these difficulties appear to be easing.[28]

Iran has also rebuilt its surface fleet, which was shattered in 1988 in a futile effort to engage the US Navy. In addition to six large surface combatants, Iran has purchased as many as 20 *Huodong* fast attack craft from China. The *Huodong* is an upgraded version of the old Soviet *Komar*-class missile boat. In the narrow waters of the Strait of Hormuz, and the entrance to the Gulf of Oman, these vessels pose a significant threat.[29] Iran also maintains a fleet of Boghammer speed boats and other irregular light attack craft which complicate operations in narrow waters.[30]

Iran has also deployed four different anti-ship missiles, in sea, air and land-based modes. The venerable HY-1 Silkworm and its more modern HY-2 Seersucker variant are deployed on land-based mobile launchers, providing the same kind of 'shoot-and-scoot' capability Iraq used effectively in the Gulf War. Additionally, Iran deploys the C-801, a reverse-engineered MM-38 Exocet, and the much more dangerous C-802, a sea-skimming missile deployed on *Huodong*-class missile boats and mobile shore launchers. The C-802 has also reportedly been tested in an air-launched version, and the missile's very existence spurred a major US diplomatic initiative in 1997–98.[31]

During the Iran–Iraq War, Iran repeatedly threatened to block the Strait of Hormuz. In response to Iraqi air strikes on Iranian oil facilities, Iran laid over 200 anti-ship mines and used speedboats and other light craft to launch small arms attacks on commercial traffic in the Gulf. At a cost of approximately $1,000 each, these mines caused over $100 million worth of damage, including the sinking of two small ships and the damaging of ten others (including the USS *Samuel B. Roberts*, a frigate).[32] The Coalition's apparent unwillingness to assault the heavily mined approaches to Iraqi-occupied Kuwait in 1991 reinforced Iran's belief in asymmetric, unconventional approaches to naval warfare. Their arsenal now contains over 2,000 mines, a number of mini-submarines, and the *Kilo*-class submarines, which can carry two dozen nautical mines instead of torpedoes.[33]

Iran's naval buildup now represents a significant threat to US (and international) interests. According to the Office of Naval Intelligence, the combination of C-802 missiles and the *Kilo*-class submarine provide Iran 'with a capability to threaten naval forces and merchant shipping and affect passage through the Strait of Hormuz'.[34] It is remarkable that Iran has been able to acquire such a significant capability with so little attention and at such marginal cost through means which fall just under the threshold of existing arms and export control regimes.

Many of these weapons have raised enough concern to garner international treaties or regimes controlling their distribution. Efforts to control the use and possession of submarines date back to the Hague Convention and the Washington Naval Limitations Treaty, but these efforts lapsed during the Cold War due to the demonstrated strategic utility of the submarine. Cruise missiles of the C-801 and C-802 variety do not violate MTCR guidelines, but the decision by the Clinton administration to certify China as a 'non-proliferating state' in the fall of 1997 hinged in part on their readiness to end cruise missile transfers to Iran.[35] Finally, while landmines have recently become the object of international revulsion, it is ironic that the much more strategically threatening use of similar weapons in the Iran–Iraq and Gulf Wars has not spurred efforts to ban naval mines.

The end result is that Iran has developed a low-technology military capability with strategic dimensions. The potential to block, or at least interfere with, traffic through the Strait of Hormuz raises serious concerns along the southern Gulf coast. Combined with the threat of missile strikes on oil facilities, existing US bases, and airfields in the Persian Gulf region, Iran theoretically possesses the capability to seriously degrade US military operations early in a conflict or crisis.

The Iran case represents a disturbing trend in weapons proliferation. Some of Iran's military capabilities (or intended military capabilities) clearly fall under the rubric of existing international nonproliferation regimes, such as the attempts to revive the Bushehr nuclear power station, acquisition and production of long-range missiles with North Korean and (probably) Pakistani cooperation, chemical and biological warfare programs, and efforts to import Russian expertise into its missile and unconventional weapons programs, and the chemical and biological warfare programs themselves. Acquisition of these capabilities has been slowed, but not halted, by broad nonproliferation efforts. At the same time, Iran has pursued a series of lower-technology capabilities which fall well under the threshold for nonproliferation, but which constitute a strategic threat. These capabilities are weighed and monitored in the United States by the armed services, whose role and influence in fighting proliferation is limited to defenses, countermeasures, and damage limitation measures.[36]

The fact is, however, that the overlap of these two 'ends' of the proliferation threat is more serious than either part alone. The combination of a notional NBC threat and a minimal sea-denial capability represents a much more profound strategic problem than the sum of its parts. This combination is not unique to Iran: it represents a potentially formidable form of asymmetric response to US dominance in conventional arms. 'Rogues' are not the only states pursuing such a combination of capabilities. Those medium-sized powers which are unable to purchase or field the full set of new military capabilities and technologies envisioned in the so-called revolution in military affairs[37] are also interested in those capabilities. Accordingly, nonproliferation policy needs to incorporate conventional military planning to a much greater degree in order to anticipate ranges and combinations of strategic threats.

SOFT PROLIFERATION: TECHNOLOGY TRANSFER TO CHINA

In 1987, as part of a Cold War effort to court China, Washington permitted Beijing to bid on the launch of US commercial satellites. This agreement reflected both economic and political concerns: the *Challenger* disaster had set back US commercial satellite launch capability, and the US also sought means to increase political and commercial links with China. The Reagan administration did not ignore the problem of Chinese missile transfers – the sale of CSS-2 missiles to Saudi Arabia in 1988 was a matter of great concern – but it did treat the problem as unrelated to commercial satellite launch programs. This political decision has haunted US nonproliferation efforts for over a decade. The firm which sells Chinese space launch services, Great Wall Industries, has twice been sanctioned under US law for export of the M-11 missile to Pakistan.[38] Sanctions were lifted due in no small part to lobbying efforts by US satellite firms.[39]

Commercial satellite producers have strong incentives to support a successful Chinese satellite launch industry. Satellites cost hundreds of millions of dollars to produce, and are often heavily financed. While the launcher suffers a loss of income ($25–$85 million in hard currency) when a launch fails, the satellite provider suffers relatively greater harm. Not only does it lose a satellite valued at hundreds of millions of dollars, but it also faces increased insurance premiums and lost revenues resulting from delays in replacing the satellite.[40]

The Clinton administration aided the lifting of controls on satellite launches, eliminated systematic government monitoring of pre-launch conversations between US contractors and Chinese firms, and moved the responsibility for monitoring and licensing satellite technology from the Department of State to the Department of Commerce.[41] This technology transfer has potentially serious military ramifications, improving Chinese missile reliability and aiding Chinese command, control, communications and intellegence (C³I) efforts.

Beginning in 1992, Loral Space & Communications, Hughes Electronics and other satellite makers began strenuous efforts to reduce the chance of error and launch failure in Chinese satellite launchers. They worked extensively with the Chinese Academy of Launch Vehicle Technology (CALT). The initial failure of the Hughes Optus B 1 in April 1992 prompted Hughes to review the attitude control system of the Long March booster. This attitude control system, by Chinese admission, is similar to the one used on the M-series of solid-fueled military rockets, 'demonstrated' off the shores of Taiwan during the 1995–96 crisis. Assistance to a commercial launcher, therefore, helped confirm the performance of military missiles later proliferated abroad and used to threaten US allies. The relaunch of the Optus B 1 in August 1992 was successful. Review of the failed launch of the Optus B 2 in December 1992 prompted another extensive review, in which Hughes confirmed that China's indigenously designed payload faring was adequate. This increased China's ability to launch both commercial and military satellites.[42]

Loral responded to a disastrous launch accident in February 1996 with a series of measures which have been called 'major breaches of information' in a confidential report issued by the Defense Technology Security Administration.[43] These included volunteering information about alternative causes which may have caused the electronic flight control system to fail, and suggesting that the Chinese use diagnostic techniques which could allow detection of flaws in the guidance system of any kind of missile, including military missiles carrying nuclear weapons. These violations occurred as part of Loral's participation in an industry team, established at the insistence of international insurers, to assess the 15 February 1996 disaster. This commission gave its findings to the Chinese without prior approval or oversight from the US government.

Hughes Space and Communications supplied China with important technological insights in 1995. Without proper authorization, Hughes scientists provided crucial formulas and mathematical modeling techniques necessary for calculating launch angle, shape of the nose cone, and other factors. These techniques are applicable both to space launch vehicles and to military missiles.[44]

Martin-Marietta's coupled load analysis on China's satellite kick motor, performed after the successful launch of the AsiaSat II satellite in May 1995, also had ominous military implications. The solid rocket kick motor in question had only been tested once. In order to risk the launch, Martin-Marietta insisted on completing coupled load analysis on the motor for the Chinese, as well as witnessing and verifying various kick motor tests. Martin Marietta's assistance could aid China's development of post-boost vehicles for military missiles, which degrade the effectiveness of missile defense systems. In 1997–98, four successful launches of Motorola Iridium satellites built by Lockheed demonstrated that China's new kick motor and satellite dispenser could effectively launch multiple satellites. This technology is interchangeable with the multiple-independently targetable re-entry vehicles (MIRVs) used on inter-continental ballistic missiles.[45] US MIRVs, for example, were originally derived from commercial multiple satellite dispensers. The accurate and timely dispersal of satellites into discrete orbits also has positive impacts on missile accuracy and reliability. Since the Loral disaster of 1996, no Chinese space launches have failed.[46]

Why is this form of proliferation so difficult to control? It involves the transfer of technological software and knowledge, rather than the actual transfer of production facilities, weapons designs or components. The transfer of such capabilities is actually entirely understandable from a business perspective: with the financial risk involved in each satellite launch, it is only natural that a commercial firm would want to maximize reliability and efficiency. Traditional arms control and nonproliferation measures, however, have focused on 'safeguardable' technologies such as large nuclear installations which are noticeable and relatively easy to control. Technology, however, has other components. In the words of Martin Van Creveld, 'Technology is best understood as an abstract version of knowledge, an attitude towards life and a method for solving its problems.'[47]

The transfer of knowledge, or of procedures, also means the loss of control over a technology. This is most clearly seen in the example of Iraqi nuclear capability. While Iraq's nuclear infrastructure has been largely dismantled, the vast amount of research carried out and the existence of 7,000 scientists and almost 20,000 skilled workers who were involved in the program virtually guarantees that a policy based solely on export and technology controls will fail in the long run. Similarly, transfer of knowledge, and the processes by which top US firms maximize quality control, efficiency and reliability means that the United States can no longer control dissemination of that knowledge or the means to which it is put.[48] In most commercial industries, this is a natural, rather than an alarming, trend. In satellite and launcher technology, as well as in other strategic dual-use technologies, it can be argued that the product cycle is not the best means of doing business.[49]

According to press reports, Russia has transferred entire SS-25 mobile missile systems to China. It is not clear, however, that China gets more out of direct transfer than it gains from the teaching provided by willing US commercial satellite producers in the interests of mutual profit. China's most successful defense industrial sectors are those, like the M-series of rockets, where they are not reliant on direct transfers of technology. Conversely, those sectors where China has deliberately attempted to maximize direct technology transfer through importation and reverse engineering, particularly in the aircraft and tank industries, are among the least competitive.

How have these transfers impacted Chinese military capability? The lessons are not clear, particularly with the recent reports of successful Chinese espionage.[50] It appears at a minimum, however, that they have assisted in improving sub-components of existing Chinese military systems, particularly warheads and attitude controls, and have also improved the reliability of the Long March satellite booster, which is based on a Chinese ICBM design. They provide knowledge and technology for Chinese C³I efforts, as well as providing increased reliability for China's own military space programs. They circumvent the Missile Technology Control Regime, because the software transferred appears to be at least as important as the hardware controls imposed by MTCR. Finally, commercial transactions provide strong incentives to ignore Chinese violations of MTCR and other nonproliferation efforts.[51]

CONCLUSION

The nature of the strategic threats to US and international security today differs substantially from the Cold War era. New concerns include regional military balances, US access to the periphery, threats to trade and economic access, and non-state actors. These 'strategic' threats are orders of magnitude lower than those of the US–Soviet competition, but they provide the framework for analysis of current and potential proliferation threats to US and global interests.

The cases examined indicate that these 'strategic' threats, posed for the most part by regional or aspiring powers, circumvent existing export controls and nonproliferation regimes. The nonproliferation net has been developed to catch very large and dangerous fish. The new breed of threat slips through this net with only modest difficulty.

What particular issues of concern exist? The first is that technology denial, while an important tool, is not permanent. Knowledge gained through experimentation, espionage and other means is not an eradicable commodity. India's *Prithvi* missile, derived using knowledge from a variety of civilian and military programs, has become a substantial proliferation threat. Iraq's nascent nuclear weapons design capability remains in the form of 20,000 scientists and technicians, even though the country has temporarily been deprived of much of its industrial base. Transnational cooperation in ballistic missile development continues despite the MTCR, and under-industrialized North Korea has become the world's leading exporter of ballistic missiles.

The second issue is that the sum of systems which can be traded, legitimately or covertly, under existing thresholds may well exceed the value of the parts. Iran's sea denial capability, based on uncontrolled technology, is substantial, and made even more dangerous by the synergistic threat of ballistic missiles and unconventional weapons. The moderate technological assistance provided by US firms to the

Chinese commercial space launch industry appears to have substantial potential military impact in the missile, space and communications arenas.

To fight strategic proliferation, the United States needs to anticipate strategic threats. To do this requires an adequate definition of what a strategic threat is, and argues strongly for allowing the military, currently assigned the peripheral 'counterproliferation' mission, a greater role in determining the direction and scope of US nonproliferation policy. The OSD definition of 'strategic threat' from the 1990s may provide a useful starting point for this discussion. It is crucial, however, that nonproliferation consider more than the usual laundry list of so-called 'weapons of mass destruction'. New technologies of concern include supercomputers and information warfare capability, long-ranged cruise missiles, development of stealth technology by adversaries, satellites and space monitoring systems, and space denial capability which would deprive the USA of vital space-based assets, to name just a few.

In addition to thinking creatively about how to define the threat, and modify our existing policies to manage new problems arising from this definition, we must also think about new methods of influencing proliferating entities. Financial sanctions, while hardly a popular measure, provide a means of leveraging firms and states responsible for strategic proliferation by attacking their fiscal assets.[52] Previous administrations have attempted to prevent proliferation by providing conventional weapons or extending the US nuclear umbrella. With the decision to deploy a national missile defense system, and continuing research and development on theater missile defense systems, the option of providing *defensive* weapons or extending a *defensive* umbrella to states threatened by proliferation or regional proliferators may be a powerful diplomatic tool.[53]

To fight the new dimensions of strategic proliferation, the United States can no longer afford to rely solely on the permeable barriers of export controls and multilateral treaties. Many of the emerging threats arise from transfer of dual-use commercial technologies, from the flow of knowledge and education across national borders, or from the synthesis of multiple weapons and systems. Detection of these emerging capabilities requires sophisticated net assessment and close cooperation between the intelligence, policy and military communities. We must define the most pressing strategic threats, and reconsider the ways in which we use our strengths – political, military, and economic – as leverage against the weaknesses of key proliferating adversaries. This represents the beginnings of a competitive strategies approach to nonproliferation, something analysts have talked about for a number of years.[54] Fighting the proliferation problems of the twenty-first century with the policies of the 1970s will inevitably lead to decreased security, frustration and failure.

NOTES

1 Timothy Hoyt is Visiting Assistant Professor in the National Security Studies Program at Georgetown University. He would like to thank Michael Barletta, Kory Sylvester, Henry Sokolski and Amanda O'Neal for their comments and assistance. An earlier version of this chapter was presented at the 1998 annual meeting of the American Political Association in Boston, MA.
2 Henry Sokolski, 'Nonproliferation: The Last 50 Years', presented before an APSA-ISAC Short Course, 'Strategic Weapons Proliferation and Super-terrorism', at the annual meeting of the American Political Science Association, 27 August 1997, Washington, DC. See chart entitled 'US Nonproliferation Initiatives and Their Strategic Premises', 2.
3 The non-signatories to the NPT are India, Pakistan, Israel and Cuba. The first three are considered to be nuclear powers, and both Pakistan and India have tested nuclear weapons.
4 Richard Speier, 'A Nuclear Nonproliferation Treaty for Missiles?' in Henry Sokolski (ed.), *Fighting Proliferation: New Concerns for the Nineties* (Maxwell Air Force Base, AL: Air University Press, September 1996), 57–72.
5 Rodney W. Jones, Mark G. McDonough with Toby F. Dalton and Gregory D. Koblenz, *Tracking Nuclear Proliferation: A Guide in Maps and Charts*, (Washington, DC: Carnegie Endowment for International Peace, 1998), 3–9.
6 See Senate Committee on Governmental Affairs, *Proliferation and Regional Security in the 1990s*, 101st Congress, 2nd Session, 9 October 1990, 49–54. Cited in Henry Sokolski, 'Fighting Proliferation with Intelligence', in Henry Sokolski (ed.), *Fighting Proliferation*, 282 and 298 n.8.
7 See, for example, Dennis M. Gormley, 'Hedging Against the Cruise Missile Threat', *Survival*, 40,1 (Spring 1998), 92–111. Modification of the venerable Silkworm missile constitutes a potential long-range threat as well. Other concerns include the French Apache, the UK Storm Shadow and the Russian air-launched AS-15, each of which poses a potential land-attack threat in addition to its primary anti-ship mission.
8 Countermeasures and defenses can substantially limit the effectiveness of even third-generation chemical agents. See Timothy D. Hoyt, 'Diffusion from the Periphery: The Impact of Technological and Conceptual Innovation', prepared for the annual meeting of the International Studies Association, Washington, DC, 18–19 February 1999, 14. Defenses and countermeasures against biological weapons are more difficult, but several of the most danger-ous agents have already been identified (anthrax and smallpox) and vaccines have been prepared.
9 Neither India nor Pakistan were signatories to the NPT or to the Compre-hensive Test Ban Treaty. India, however, has been one of the leading sup-porters of global nuclear disarmament in the international community.
10 Keith Krause, *Arms and the State: Patterns of Military Technology and Trade* (Cambridge: Cambridge University Press, 1992).
11 Timothy D. Hoyt, *Rising Regional Powers: New Perspectives on Indigenous Defense Industries and Military Capability in the Developing World* (PhD dissertation: Johns Hopkins University, 1996), 137–46.
12 Ibid.; and Timothy V. McCarthy, 'India: Emerging Missile Power' in William

C. Potter and Harlan W. Jencks (eds), *The International Missile Bazaar: The New Suppliers' Network* (Boulder, CO: Westview Press, 1994), 201–33.

13 '*Prithvi* Naval Version to be Test Fired on January 26', *The Hindu*, 1 December 1998.

14 See http://www.fas.org/irp/threat/missile/india.htm; http://www.bharat-rakshak.com/MISSILES/Prithvi.html

15 'India to Test New *Prithvi*', *Aviation Week and Space Technology*, 29 June 1998, 31; 'Fernandes will Seek Higher Defence Outlay: Decision on Nuclear Option after Strategic Security Review', *Times of India* news service, 15 April 1998.

16 R. J. Smith, 'India Moves Missiles Near Pakistani Border', *Washington Post*, 3 June 1997.

17 'German Defence Magazine Lauds *Prithvi* SRBM', *Indian Express*, 5 June 1999; 'Improved *Prithvi* Launched', *International Defense Review* (August, 1992), 784. The latter report, however, emphasizes the large number of support vehicles associated with the launch of the liquid-fueled *Prithvi*, which make the missile relatively vulnerable and tactically inflexible. This point is reinforced by Neil Joeck, *Maintaining Nuclear Stability in South Asia*, Adelphi Paper 312 (London: International Institute for Strategic Studies, 1997), 68. Development of a solid-fueled version will minimize this vulnerability and increase *Prithvi*'s military utility.

18 *The Military Balance 1995/1996* (London: International Institute for Strategic Studies, 1995), 133; R. Jeffrey Smith, 'UN Finds New Evidence of Iraqi Long-Range Missile Research', *Washington Post*, 5 February 1997; Hoyt, *Rising Regional Powers*, 373. Preventing transfers of the Scud is hard enough – banning SAM exports is a nearly impossible task.

19 Indian sources·claim an accuracy of .01 per cent at maximum range. See http://www.bharat-rakshak.com/MISSILES/Prithvi.html

20 Indramil Banerjie, 'The Integrated Guided Missile Development Project', *Indian Defence Review* (July 1990), 104.

21 The missiles Iraq used in the Gulf War were, of course, Scud derivatives.

22 W. Seth Carus, 'Ballistic Missiles in Iran and Iraq, 1988–1998' in *Report of the Commission to Assess the Ballistic Missile Threat to the United States – Appendix III*, Unclassified Working Papers, Pursuant to Public Law 201, 104th Congress, 15 July 1998, 83.

23 'U.S. clears software to Indian "missile developer"', *Rediff-on-line* (http://www.rediff.com), 16 May 1998; *Dawn on-line* (http://dawn.com/daily/today/top10.htm), Monday 8 June 1998.

24 Joint Staff, *Joint Vision 2010* (Washington, DC, 1996), 3.

25 See, for example, Thomas G. Mahnken, 'Deny U.S. Access?' *Proceedings of the US Naval Institute* (September 1998), 36–9.

26 Michael Eisenstadt, *Iranian Military Power: Capabilities and Intentions* (Washington, DC: Washington Institute for Near East Policy, 1996), 37. These reports included hundreds of MiG and Sukhoi third-generation fighters, a dozen Tu-22M Backfire bombers, and manufacturing facilities for the MiG-29 fighter.

27 Reports of multinational assistance to the Iranian missile program date back a number of years. See Jones, *Tracking Nuclear Proliferation*, 171, 176. See also David C. Isby, 'Barriers to Proliferation and Pathways to Transfer: Building Ballistic Missile Capabilities Under MTCR' in *Report of the Commission to Assess the Ballistic Missile Threat*, 167–76. Linkage between the North Korean *Nodong* or *rodong*, Pakistan's *Ghauri*, and the Iranian *Shahab-3* missile is revealed in 'U.S. Says North Korea Helped Develop Pakistani Missile', *New York Times*, 11 April 1998; and 'Iran Missile Test Shows Effort to Extend Range', *Washington Post*, 23 July 1998.

28 Eisenstadt, *Iranian Military Power: Capabilities and Intentions*, 51–4. Salt and seaweed clogged the submarines' intake filters; the batteries, designed for northern waters, had difficulty holding a full charge in the warmer waters of the Persian Gulf; and before the purchase of the *Kilos*, Iran's navy had no training or experience in operating submarines.

29 According to General Peay, then commander of US Central Command, Iran had purchased 20 *Huodongs* by January 1997, 15 of which were armed with the advanced C-802 anti-ship missile. Bill Gertz, 'U.S. Commander in Gulf Sees Increased Threat from Iran', *Washington Times*, 29 January 1997. Other sources report that Iran has ten *Huodongs* equipped with the C-802, and another ten French *Commandante*-class fast attack craft modified for the C-802. Institute for National Strategic Studies, *Strategic Assessment 1998* (Washington, DC: National Defense University, 1998), 60; and International Institute for Strategic Studies, *The Military Balance 1998/1999* (London: International Institute for Strategic Studies, 1998), 127.

30 Institute for National Strategic Studies, *Strategic Assessment 1998*, 60.

31 Jones, *Tracking Nuclear Proliferation*, 54. The United States agreed to approve the transfer of civilian nuclear reactor technology to China based primarily on China's commitment to stop supplying nuclear materials, C-802s and other defense technology to Iran. The agreement fell short, in the latter two categories, according to critics of the deal. 'China's Pledge to End Iran Nuclear Aid Yields U.S. Help', *Washington Post*, 30 October 1997.

32 Eisenstadt, *Iranian Military Power: Capabilities and Intentions*, 55.

33 Patrick Clawson, 'Dual Containment as an Effective Competitive Strategy', a paper prepared for the NPEC/USAF-INSS faculty mini-seminar on Strategic Proliferation, 20 June 1998, 3.

34 Office of Naval Intelligence, *Worldwide Maritime Challenges* (March 1997), 3.

35 A pledge by China to halt 'further sales' of the C-802 was instrumental in clearing the way for US nuclear technology exports. 'Limits on Iran Ties Open Way for China to Buy Nuclear Reactors', *Washington Post*, 25 October 1997. For a pessimistic perspective on this agreement, see Michael Eisenstadt, 'U.S. Policy and Chinese Proliferation to Iran: A Small Leap Forward', *Policy Watch*, 31 October 1997. According to government sources, there was still uncertainty about whether China would fulfill or cancel existing C-802 contracts to Iran in January 1998. 'Cohen Hails Achievements in Visit', *Washington Post*, 20 January 1998.

36 See Ashton B. Carter and L. Celeste Johnson, 'Beyond the Counter-proliferation Initiative to a "Revolution in Counterproliferation Affairs"', *National Security Studies Quarterly*, 5, 3 (Summer 1999), 83–90; and Thomas G. Mahnken, 'A Critical Appraisal of the Defense Counterproliferation Initiative', *National Security Studies Quarterly*, 5, 3 (Summer 1999), 91–102.

37 See, for example, Patrick J. Garrity, *Why the Gulf War Still Matters, Report No. 16* (Los Alamos National Laboratory: Center for National Security Studies, July 1993).

38 *The Proliferation Primer – A Majority Report of the Subcommittee on International Security, Proliferation, and Federal Services, Committee on Governmental Affairs, United States Senate* (Washington, DC: January 1998), 3–4. The first reports of transfers of the M-11 missile to Pakistan surfaced in 1991, and sanctions were imposed in June of that year and again in August of 1993. Pakistan recently tested the *Shaheen* missile, which bears a distinct physical resemblance to the M-series of solid-fueled missiles.

39 Testimony of Mr Michael C. Armstrong, Chairman and CEO, AT&T and Chairman, President's Export Council, to the Senate Subcommittee on

International Security, Proliferation and Federal Services, 29 July 1998.

40 Henry Sokolski, 'Space Technology Transfers and Missile Proliferation', in
    *Report of the Commission to Assess the Ballistic Missile Threat to the United States –
    Appendix III*, Unclassified Working Papers, Pursuant to Public Law 201, 104th
    Congress, 15 July 1998, 308.

41 See the Cox Commission Report overview, found at http://www.house.gov/
    coxreport/overbod.html, Accessed 26 May 1999. See also 'Chinese Said to
    Reap Gains in U.S. Policy Shift', *New York Times*, 19 October 1998.

42 Nonproliferation Policy Education Center, 'U.S. Satellite Transfers to China:
    An Increasingly Dangerous Business', September 1998.

43 'Report Outlines Damage to National Security in Companies' China Dealings',
    New York Times, 27 June 1998.

44 'Pentagon Inquiry Faults Missile Maker's China Aid', *New York Times*, 9
    December 1998.

45 'Satellite Transfers to China: An Increasingly Dangerous Business'. For a
    contrary perspective, see 'Export Controls Relating to Commercial Com-
    munications Satellites', prepared testimony of John Pike, Director, Space
    Policy Project, Federation of American Scientists before the House Rules
    Committee, *Hearing on the Creation of a Select Committee on US National Security
    and Military/Commercial Concerns with the People's Republic of China*, 16 June
    1998.

46 'Timeline: The Trail of Dealings With China's Rocket Gear', *New York Times*, 9
    December 1998.

47 Martin Van Creveld, *Technology and War*, 2nd ed (New York: Free Press, 1991),
    312.

48 This point is reinforced in *Report of the Commission to Assess the Ballistic Missile
    Threat to the United States – Executive Summary*, Pursuant to Public Law 201,
    104th Congress (Washington, DC, 15 July 1998), 17–19.

49 Raymond Vernon's product cycle, a frequently used model for international
    economics and the arms trade, suggests that the natural 'life-cycle' of any
    product will take it from the initial innovator/producer and eventually relocate
    it abroad, where labor costs are cheaper, leading the original customers to
    become, as the product matures, the primary producers. Raymond Vernon,
    Sovereignty at Bay (New York: Basic Books, 1971).

50 See the Cox Commission report, http://www.house.gov/coxreport/overbod.
    html

51 This can be observed most recently in the deafening silence surrounding
    Pakistan's '*Shaheen*' launch and the apparent Chinese technology link. A
    photograph of the *Shaheen* can be seen as part of the article 'Second Round
    Completed: Short-range Missile *Shaheen* tested', *Dawn (on-line)*, http://www.
    dawn.com/daily/19990416/top5.htm, 16 April 1999. After observing this
    photo, and a live video of the *Shaheen* launch, a colleague commented, 'If it
    looks like a duck, walks like a duck, quacks like a duck, then why isn't the
    Clinton Administration hopping mad over violation of the Duck Technology
    Control Regime?' The similarities between the solid-fueled *Shaheen* and the
    Chinese solid-fueled M-series are remarkable.

52 For suggestions on this theme, see Roger W. Robinson, Jr, 'Observations on
    Financial Sanctions', Nonproliferation Policy Education Center website
    (http://www.wizard.net/~npec), 21 March 1996.

53 This is particularly true after the decision to deploy a national missile defense
    system. The USA now stands officially committed to the development and
    acquisition of defensive technologies. 'Senate, 97–3, Endorses a Commitment
    to Deploy Anti-Missile System', *Washington Post*, 18 March 1999.

54 Bernard I. Finel, 'Strategic Planning and Competitive Strategy', paper given at the Seminar on Competitive Strategies and Nonproliferation, US Army War College, 22–25 June 1999; and David J. Andre, 'Competitive Strategies: An Approach against Proliferation' in Sokolski, *Fighting Proliferation*, 257–76.

Part II

Proliferation: How Appropriate Is Our Response?

4

What Strategic Weapons Proliferation Will Demand of Us

HENRY SOKOLSKI[1]

INTRODUCTION

By any standard, 1998 was an unprecedented year for strategic weapons proliferation, one that turned traditional nonproliferation on its ear. India and Pakistan acquired and tested medium-range ballistic missiles and a series of advanced nuclear devices, publicly declared they were nuclear weapons states, and faced only mild international reaction. Congress revealed intelligence that North Korea might be building covert nuclear weapons facilities in a set of tunnels near Yongbyong. North Korea tested a three-stage ballistic missile over Japanese air space, prompting Japan to announce a military space reconnaissance program, which strained Japan's stated prohibition against funding military space development. And Clinton administration officials threatened to terminate the Agreed Framework unless North Korea allowed international inspection of its suspect nuclear activities. Russia, China and North Korea, meanwhile, helped Iran develop two missiles: the *Shehab-3* (a largely North Korean missile that was successfully tested in Iran and Pakistan as the *Ghauri*), and the *Shehab-4*, a multi-stage ballistic missile (which incorporated Russian, Chinese and North Korean technology). Then, there was the US strike against a chemical facility in Sudan because it might be making chemical weapons agents that could find their way into terrorist hands. Finally, Iraq defied all previous pledges to allow UN inspections in such a fashion that the prospect of any meaningful monitoring or inspection in Iraq was eliminated.

Faced with these unprecedented developments, US officials have had difficulty. On the one hand, Congress passed legislation in 1994 requiring India and Pakistan to be sanctioned for their nuclear tests.[2] But when India and Pakistan tested and sanctions were invoked, Congress retreated and passed legislation that gave the White House authority to lift the sanctions. Then, in the summer and fall, Congress condemned the administration for hiding North Korea's covert nuclear activities and threatened to terminate funding for the Agreed Framework, though in the end it doubled the administration's appropriations request for this purpose in its Christmas omnibus spending bill. Finally, Congress reimposed tighter export controls over advanced computers and advanced US satellite technology going to Russia and China, but then, through inaction, allowed extensive nuclear and space cooperation or commerce with both countries in exchange for private pledges of improved nonproliferation behavior or results.

This is hardly a picture of consistency. In fact, looking at all this, most would conclude that the bank of US security policy was near insolvency and that something new was called for to rein in the chaos. Yet, if US hawks or doves were asked about these events, the response itself would be at least as exceptional as the events themselves. Rather than demanding anything new, both these camps, if asked, would have argued that 1998's record proves beyond a doubt that they were right all along. Doves would insist that we adopt all of the Cold War arms control not yet codified: the Comprehensive Test Ban Treaty (CTBT), Biological Weapons Convention (BWC) protocol, START III, a re-negotiated Anti-Ballistic Missile (ABM) Treaty, Military Nuclear Fissile Production Cut Off, and so forth. Hawks, meanwhile, would insist we redouble efforts to maintain our nuclear arsenal and deploy missile defenses. Finally, both would argue that each other's agenda was – as always – wrong.[3]

TWO DOMINANT VIEWS IMMUNE TO THE OUTSIDE WORLD

These opposing views, in fact, dominate US policy and are relatively immune to external events. Thus, following dovish guidance, the US government pretends to make progress in offensive strategic arms reductions by negotiating symbolic treaties (such as the BWC protocol) that will have little direct effect on the deployment of strategic weapons systems; slowing and limiting the development of missile defenses – even though missile defenses are not offensive strategic weapons; trumpeting reductions in the numbers of 'operational' strategic delivery systems START II will produce (50 per cent); downplaying how the number of operational and standby nuclear warheads will barely decline at all; and funding the recycling of military plutonium to produce electricity in Russia and the United States as a way to 'dispose' of weapons materials even though this will almost certainly encourage further recycling – a costly process that has already produced more weapons-usable material than is present in the arsenals of the United States and the former Soviet Union combined.

Meanwhile, none of this has satisfied hardcore doves. Indeed, they continue to complain that this is not enough and to argue creatively that, although great progress has been made, much more arms control (nuclear disarmament) is needed.[4] At the same time, following hawkish suggestions, the US government claims it is maintaining its nuclear stockpile and moving toward the deployment of missile defenses, spending billions of dollars annually for these purposes. Yet, as more is invested each year, US nuclear mobilization and development capabilities continue to decline while international access to weapons know-how and US weapons laboratories increases. Nor is there much to show in the way of deployed missile capabilities. Meanwhile, there is a growing realization that deterrence – what our nuclear and missile defense efforts are supposed to help maintain – may only work against peer competitors such as a resurgent Russia or a more developed and aggressive China.[5]

Again, despite the US government's efforts and spending, hardcore hawks are hardly happy. Doves, they complain, keep the United States from realizing the security that would be available if the country resumed nuclear testing, developed new nuclear warheads, and broke out of the ABM Treaty. Even if, somehow, they could get doves to relent, though, these hawks are clear that the United States needs to spend much more on nuclear stockpile stewardship and missile defenses. Finally, and perhaps in recognition of difficulties inherent to both the hawkish and dovish appeals, there is a growing willingness at the margins for members of each camp to seek comfort in each other's agendas. Thus, the growing mutual interest of arms controllers and the defense and weapons agencies of government to work together on issues ranging from the disposal of weapons-plutonium to arms control verification measures and programs to encourage Russia's nuclear and space industries to develop their strategic capital for 'peaceful' purposes.[6]

OUR FUTURE: LIKE THE 1930s BUT WITH STRATEGIC WEAPONS?

If, as is likely, the United States continues to pursue dovish and hawkish approaches in concert (or even separately), one thing is certain: it will do little to impede the kind of frightening strategic weapons developments presaged by 1998's events and may arguably help them along. What are some of these? Four of the most likely and important developments to the United States and its friends include:

- Russia, Japan, China and India with significantly larger strategic weapons mobilization bases (that is to say, with much greater breakout or ramp-up capabilities) than they now have and with a variety of motives for employing them, such as a response to continued NATO expansion, a desire to undermine US influence in the Pacific, or a desire to command the respect of the West;

- Iraq, Iran, India, Pakistan and North Korea with intercontinental range rockets armed with nuclear warheads;

- South Korea and Taiwan more able and interested to develop nuclear weapons or ballistic missiles at very short notice; nations such as Turkey, Saudi Arabia and Indonesia also interested and not all that far behind;

- a world awash with ever larger stockpiles of surplus weapons-usable plutonium moving throughout Europe and Asia (and to and from these locales) causing a major drain on international inspection resources and/or a major diversion source for sub-national or national weapons use.

Paralleling these technical developments is the increased likelihood of:

- a military competition between China and Japan that could be precipitated by Japanese reaction to further North or South Korean militarization or Chinese reactions to a militant, non-compliant Taiwan;

- greater reluctance to back US actions against proliferators from non-weapons states who do not want to acquire strategic weapons but who resent the dominance of nuclear nations, US double standards concerning Israel, Iran, Iraq and North Korea, and Washington's inclination only to be tough against weak proliferators it dislikes, such as Iraq, Sudan and Libya;

- the possibility of new strategic alignments between nuclear weapons states that reduce US influence, such as Russia with Iran, Iraq and India; China with Pakistan and Saudi Arabia (who has already gone ballistic and may want to go nuclear); and Israel with Turkey (who, if scorned by NATO or threatened by a nuclear Iran or Iraq, may seek new avenues for its own security);

- a set of strategically armed pariahs (North Korea, Iraq, Iran, Pakistan) willing and able to develop and market strategic weaponry of their own with and amongst one another and to Libya and Syria and perhaps others for cash, Western attention, and influence.

This is not a vision of a world as peaceful as the one we currently enjoy. Indeed, it might become as frightening a period as the 1930s were in Europe and Asia – an unstable period of military competition leading to war. This time, however, the nations jockeying for position will all be able to threaten the use of massively indiscriminate and destructive long-range weaponry.

This is hardly the way Presidents Clinton and Bush or Francis Fukuyama ever intended history to end. For them the idea of strategic combat between the world's major nations was to become a thing of the past. And perhaps it has. But the United States could hardly ignore an arms competition between Japan and China, or between Russia and NATO. More importantly, such an arms race would be worth some effort to avoid. This, however, would require that the United States and those other states with strategic arms take strategic arms proliferation much more seriously than they have to date. It certainly suggests that the Cold War agenda that still distinguishes doves from hawks in the United States, and that confines their debates and remedies, would have to give way to something new. What might such a new approach entail? At least one or more of the following.

True nuclear arms reductions

The United States and Russia must move away from merely separating more and more warheads from delivery systems and begin rendering more nuclear weapons and nuclear-weapons materials unusable. Making meaningful arms reductions 'priority one' would have a number of positive consequences. It would help secure the support of the world's non-weapons states to follow appeals for tough action against nations building up strategic arms. It would allow retention of critical long-range delivery systems for conventional force projection missions. Further arms reductions would decrease US requirements – now well into billions of dollars annually – to maintain such a large nuclear weapons mobilization base and hedge stockpile. Finally, true arms reductions would establish a precedent and perhaps the mechanisms for other weapons-usable materials producers, such as Japan, the United Kingdom, Israel and India, to join in the reductions as well.

The first imperative in such an effort would be to get a much more accurate tally of nuclear materials in the inventories of the former Soviet Union. Russia has so far refused to cooperate in this accounting and US arms control negotiators have tried to work around it by suggesting cooperative efforts that skirt or compound the issue. If the United States is serious, these skirting maneuvers – offering to build plutonium recycling factories in Russia and the United States, for example – must stop. If the United States cannot get a much better picture of what Russia has in the way of weapons and materials, it should cause a crisis worthy of overtly remobilizing our own strategic weapons base. We should make this accounting that much of a priority, and make it clear to Russia and the US public how critical Russian co-operation on this point is to US, Russian and world security. Depending on how accurate we believe the Russian inventory to be, we should be willing to jointly immobilize and, pending this, quickly remove (to a third, neutral location such as Greenland) as much surplus weapons-usable plutonium as is prudent. Factors that must be considered here include:

- the margin of error associated with the inventory, if any, that Russia finally offers or helps the US to calibrate;
- the relative number and operational capabilities of Russia's fissile production facilities and reactors (both civilian and military) as an indication of its ability to 'breakout'; and
- the relative size of other nations' civilian and military weapons-usable material stockpiles and production capabilities.

Certainly, the United States cannot reduce to levels so low that it might encourage other nations to exploit the situation by ramping up or breaking out themselves. But it ought to be willing to come down from its current level of over 9,000 operational and hedge warheads, assuming Russia shows its willingness to work toward this end by allowing an accurate inventory.

An appeal to weapons-usable material producers to reduce

As noted above, whatever procedures and mechanisms are devised to make US and Russian weapons-usable materials 'irreversibly' unusable in weapons should be made available to all other states with stockpiles of similar material, including China, India, Israel, Pakistan, North Korea, Brazil, Argentina, Japan and the multinational EURATOM. This would at least isolate the holdouts and give the more peaceful of these nations a serious, practical way to express their pacifism. Some experts have suggested that the world's major civilian fuel producers of lightly enriched uranium might offer this non-weapons-usable fuel in exchange for other nations' weapons-usable materials. The idea would be to give nations holding separated plutonium and highly enriched uranium an incentive to surrender these materials for immobilization.[7]

Discourage civilian use or production of weapons-usable fuels

Assuming the United States makes progress on the above points, it should push again actively to discourage production of separated plutonium or highly enriched uranium for civilian reactors worldwide.

Encourage new, private, non-nuclear and non-aerospace commerce for the nearly democratic weapons states: Pakistan, India and Russia

To help support friendly pacific elements in these nations, the United States, other peaceful democratic nations and the Organization for Economic Cooperation and Development should offer significant investment in development of non-nuclear energy – especially in Russia – and support commerce between Pakistan and India which, in time, could help transform politics in and between both nations.

Freer immigration of the world's scientists to the West

The United States and other friendly nations should actively try to attract strategic weapons engineers and scientists to leave their laboratories and countries to come to work in the West. Certainly, the United States and other Western nations should not cooperate in making such immigration as difficult as it currently is.[8]

Fundamental change to international inspections

Instead of establishing international organizations, such as the International Atomic Energy Agency (IAEA), to come up with a set of least common denominator inspection standards and institutions that do the inspecting, it would be useful to pocket existing inspection standards and encourage these organizations to suggest new, tougher inspection approaches that other nations might use to inspect rivals. Existing international inspection organizations, under this scheme, would be revitalized: not to do inspections themselves but to help negotiate, staff and facilitate bilateral inspections of the type done between Argentina and Brazil, for other rivals such as Pakistan and India, Israel and Iran and so forth.

The advantage of this approach is that such 'bilateral' inspectors would have a clear, national self interest in detecting possible violations (as opposed to the current situation where the IAEA and other organizations worry that violations might disrupt the harmony needed to secure continued support for the agency's promotion of nuclear activities). Also, this approach would actually help garner support for internationally facilitated inspections and the international norms behind them.[9]

Missile defenses, especially in space and at sea

As the ability to control missile proliferation through export controls and sanctions ramps down – along with the intelligence community's ability to identify who is proliferating what precisely – the importance of deploying missile defense as insurance increases. This is especially true of global, space-based missile defenses since these systems do not involve the possible transfer of missile technology (useful for offensive missile development) to 'cooperating' nations or the localization of missile–missile defense rivalries. This means the United States should work toward an ABM Treaty that eventually bans all ground-based systems beyond a certain range, but bans nothing else (that is to say, allows space-based and sea-based systems). Failing this, the United States should terminate the ABM Treaty.

Regime changes for Iran, Iraq, North Korea, China and stronger backing of Taiwan, South Korea and liberal democratic forces in the Persian Gulf

The US effort to support an Iraqi National Congress is a model of sorts for dealing with Iran, which has even more of a democratic opposition in place. The United States certainly should not accept the regimes in Iraq, Iran or North Korea merely to gain support for one or another form of inspection regime. Nor should the United States and its friends directly support the current governments in North Korea, Iran or hostile elements in China which are so tied to proliferation. Instead of backing such proliferating entities, the United States and its friends should make it clear that their ultimate goals include unification of Korea on terms acceptable to South Korea, unification of China on terms acceptable to Taiwan, and the creation of relatively pacific, liberal, democratic forms of rule for nations in the Middle East and Persian Gulf.

FALLOUT

This is an ambitious agenda. Yet, the alternatives – continued muddling or helping proliferators – seem far more foolish. Improving or increasing the number of weapons in the US arsenal is not much of an alternative. While small, crude arsenals are not as good as large advanced ones in fighting a war, the latter do not necessarily deter, much less neutralize the former. One final alternative is for the United States to continue to pursue nonproliferation policies à la carte – ones so tailored to specific cases that they are fundamentally at odds with one another. But this too is risky. As Victor Gilinsky has noted, in the end, there is no tenable position except one that applies the same rule to all countries. Failing that, the 'likely consequence is more states with nuclear weapons'.[10] And although a world with more nuclear states might be better in the minds of some academics,[11] no one in the real world, hawk or dove, (rightly) yet thinks so.

NOTES

1 Henry D. Sokolski is Executive Director of the Nonproliferation Policy Education Center.

2 See *The Nuclear Proliferation Prevention Act of 1994*, Pub. L 103–236, 30 April 1994.

3 For two excellent representative examples of such thinking, see the Board of Directors, 'Nine Minutes to Midnight', *Bulletin of the Atomic Scientists* (September/October 1998), 5; and Kathleen C. Bailey, 'The Comprehensive Test Ban Treaty: The Costs Outweigh the Benefits', *CATO Institute Policy Analysis*, 330 (15 January 1999).

4 See, for example, the Stimson Center, *Jump-START: Retaking the Initiative to Reduce Post-Cold War Nuclear Dangers* (Washington, DC: The Stimson Center, 25 February 1999).

5 On this point see, for example, William S. Cohen, 'Message of the Secretary of Defense', *Proliferation: Threat and Response* (Department of Defense, 1997), iii; and Victor A. Utgoff, *Nuclear Weapons and the Deterrence of Biological and Chemical Warfare*, Occasional Paper 36 (Washington, DC: The Stimson Center, October 1997).

6 See, for example, Proliferation Brief, 'U.S. Programs Face Growing Russian Threat' (Washington, DC: Carnegie Endowment for International Peace, 4 March 1999); and the Defense Department Website it references, http://www.ctr.osd.mil/

7 See, for example, Paul Leventhal and Steven Dolley, 'A Japanese Strategic Uranium Reserve: A Safe and Economic Alternative to Plutonium' (Washington, DC: The Nuclear Control Institute, 14 January 1994); and K. W. Budlong Sylvester, 'Global Plutonium Management: Security Option', presented at the American Political Science Association Annual Meeting, Boston, MA, 3–6 September 1998.

8 To avoid the appearance of plundering Russia's vast store of scientists, the United States has cooperated with Russia to restrict access to long-term multiple-visit visas to the United States. US access to Russian weapons institutes is restricted as well.

9 For a detailed account of how such bilateral inspections were encouraged between Argentina and Brazil, see John R. Redick, 'Latin America's Emerging Non-Proliferation Consensus', *Arms Control Today* (March 1994), 3–9.

10 See Victor Gilinsky, 'Nuclear Proliferation after the Indian and Pakistani Tests', *National Security Studies Quarterly*, 5, 3 (Summer 1999), 47.

11 See, for example, Kenneth N. Waltz, *The Spread of Nuclear Weapons: More May Be Better*, Adelphi Paper 171 (London: IISS, 1979); John Mearsheimer, 'The Case for a Ukrainian Nuclear Deterrent', *Foreign Affairs* (Summer 1993), 50–66; and Bruce Bueno de Mesquita and William H. Riker, 'Assessing the Merits of Selective Nuclear Proliferation', *Journal of Conflict Resolution*, 26 (June 1982), 283–306.

5

Beyond the Counterproliferation Initiative

ASHTON B. CARTER AND L. CELESTE JOHNSON[1]

INTRODUCTION

Most Americans take for granted current US conventional military superiority. But the ability of the United States to handily defend interests in the Persian Gulf and east Asia with conventional military power and without posing danger to the United States-proper is not an immutable fact of nature. Saddam Hussein's invasion of Kuwait in 1991 resembled a smaller version of the Warsaw Pact threat against which the United States and NATO had planned for decades. Facing the 'hammer' of such US and allied forces so soon after the peak of Cold War investments in them, Iraq configured its forces like the perfect 'nail'. The resulting rout in Desert Storm strongly reassured both defense planners and the US public.

But the Gulf War was a deeply misleading experience. US conventional superiority is only assured against challengers who choose the same playing field of symmetrical, conventional warfare. This was the mistake Saddam Hussein made in 1991, and a lesson that future challengers cannot have failed to learn. Beneath the surface was a sobering array of close calls and surprises involving every category of weapons of mass destruction. Iraq is now known to have produced and fielded an array of biological weapons in numbers and variety unknown to the United States before the conflict. Its nuclear weapons program was much larger and of a totally different technical character (involving the calutron method of enriching uranium) than US intelligence had suspected. Iraq was known before the war to have chemical weapons, and had used them in its war with Iran. But the US military understood little about which Iraqi units possessed the weapons or how they might use them against coalition troops. In the end, Iraq's Scud missiles defined the war for many television-watchers and might have changed the whole character of the war had they provoked Israel into entering the fray.

At the same time, US troops were under-prepared to deal with the battlefield threat of chemical and biological weapons. Units deployed with insufficient quantities and sizes of protective gear, expired detector paper and decontamination kits, and inadequate training. As the General Accounting Office (GAO) reported, 'While the six-month Operation Desert Shield buildup time allowed DOD [Department of Defense] to correct some of these problems, had chemical or biological weapons been used during this period, some units might have suffered significant, unnecessary casualties.'[2]

Despite the most vigorous efforts of US nonproliferation policy, nearly all military opponents whom US forces are likely to meet on the battlefield possess chemical and biological weapons and the means to deliver them, including ballistic missiles. A casual reliance on nuclear deterrence to deal with these threats is insufficient. These threats must be countered vigorously. The US Defense Department needs to take a new approach to proliferation – one commensurate with the energy DOD normally applies to a serious military threat – and not continue to treat proliferation as a diplomatic problem or an unorthodox, unlikely contingency.

The necessary approach has two prongs. The first prong would involve a 'Revolution in Counterproliferation Affairs' (RCA): an energetic pursuit of non-nuclear counters to the use of weapons of mass destruction (WMD) against US forces in regional conflicts through development of defense protections as well as specialized attack and intelligence capabilities. In the second prong, the Department of Defense would contribute its resources and technical expertise with higher priority to the US government's overall effort to prevent weapons of mass destruction from spreading in the first place. The Nunn–Lugar program is an example of this effort, as is the Defense Department's essential role in administering controls on the export of dangerous technology. But, despite the importance of these programs, they are insufficient given the magnitude of the security problems posed by increasingly dangerous proliferation threats.

A 'REVOLUTION IN COUNTERPROLIFERATION AFFAIRS'

Early in the Clinton administration, a strengthened approach to dealing with proliferation in DOD was given a new name: counterproliferation.[3] Much has been accomplished under the Counterproliferation Initiative, but much more remains to be done. The US military, like the population at large, still tends to view the 'major regional conflicts' that so dominate defense planning and budgeting as purely conventional contests. In such contests the United States continues to lead the information technology-based 'revolution in military affairs' (RMA). This revolution began in the 1970s with the development of satellite reconnaissance, smart weapons, cruise missiles, stealth aircraft and other breakthroughs made possible by the microchip.[4]

Superior US military technology first deterred the Warsaw Pact invasion of Europe and then handily defeated a Soviet-like conventional aggressor in Desert Storm. The RMA remains the main concept propelling modernization and innovation in the US military. It shows every sign of continuing to provide the US military with a decisive edge in symmetrical warfare. But an accompanying 'revolution in counter-proliferation affairs' is needed to deal with asymmetrical warfare, and that revolution is only beginning.

One reason for the delay is the lingering presence of a dangerous and casual reliance on non-strategic nuclear weapons to deter the use of WMD in a regional conflict. The United States cannot and should not depend on the reliability of such deterrence when dealing with desperate and 'rogue' states or with non-state, terrorist attackers. More importantly, the United States has not confronted the wisdom of supposing that it would – or should – ever be the first nation since 1945 to detonate nuclear weapons in anger. If non-nuclear counters to asymmetrical warfare can be devised, surely they are preferable to a nuclear response.

Non-nuclear counters to weapons of mass destruction, especially chemical and biological weapons, are feasible. A strengthened counter-proliferation effort, a revolution in counterproliferation affairs, would give counterproliferation weapons and techniques a priority equal to the RMA. This initiative should have five components:

First, US troops should be provided with better 'passive' defensive equipment to render ineffective the direct use of weapons of mass destruction on the battlefield. Such defensive equipment would include chemical suits, inhalation masks, detectors, decontamination equipment, air filtration systems and the detectors of chemical and biological agents needed to tell the troops when to apply their protection. In addition, training for operations in an environment in which weapons of mass destruction are used or in which there is a threat of use should be stepped-up and given greater priority by military commanders.

Second, key vulnerabilities should be eliminated from rear areas, especially the airfields and ports which US forces would depend upon to reach a given theater of operation. This would involve large-scale decontamination equipment and training, in addition to the provision of protective equipment to local and US civilian contractors working in these facilities as well as US military combat-support personnel.

Third, weapons and tactics should be devised to destroy weapons of mass destruction before they can be launched – much like the Cold War's notion of 'counterforce'.

Fourth, US troops should be provided with more effective defense systems that can intercept aircraft, cruise missiles and ballistic missiles that might carry WMD. Theater ballistic missiles defenses (TMDs) are being developed in a manner consistent with the Anti-Ballistic Missile (ABM) Treaty, and should be fielded as soon as development is complete. Since the performance of these systems will be less than perfect, however, they are a complement to, not a substitute for, protective suits and other passive defenses. A defense of US territory (including Hawaii and Alaska, which are closer to some potential launch areas) from ballistic missile attack may also become necessary as regional threats like Iraq and North Korea develop and deploy missiles capable of reaching US territory. The United States should be prepared to deploy such systems in a short time, first seeking amendment to the ABM Treaty. Once again, however, these defenses are unlikely to offer perfect protection.

Finally, friends and allies should be encouraged to acquire corresponding counterproliferation capabilities so that they could continue to carry out their own roles in collective defense and protect the lives and morale of their own people in the theater. Important progress has already been made on counterproliferation within NATO, under the US-inspired Defense Group on Proliferation (DGP), but much remains to be done to ensure that allies have the same level of protection and training as their US counterparts.

Enveloping these new counterproliferation capabilities must be a substantial augmentation of the intelligence and technology base that supports defense against asymmetric threats. Analyzing foreign WMD programs has long been a priority of US intelligence. However, mirroring the tendency to view proliferation as a diplomatic problem rather than a military threat, intelligence efforts still focus on detailing the facilities, scientists and technology transfers that contribute to a proliferator's WMD program. Instead, this effort should focus on the mindset, doctrine and specific military characteristics of the arsenals that have already crossed the line from proliferation to threat. Desert Storm demonstrated a lack of this kind of actionable military intelligence on proliferators. The United States does not have chemical or biological weapons of its own. As a consequence, the research laboratories and industries that support chemical and biological counterproliferation defensive measures are meager compared to the still-large nuclear weapons technology base. Yet a strong chemical and biological weapons technology base will be needed to devise new detectors, to develop protective suits, shelters and vaccines, and to analyze intelligence. Much of the relevant expertise resides in the commercial chemical and biotechnology industries – expertise that should be enlisted in counterproliferation efforts.

Counterproliferation programs of these types, if pursued vigorously, can reduce the vulnerability of US troops and citizens to WMD, and thereby reduce the utility and effectiveness of such weapons in the hands of regional aggressors. But they will not altogether nullify the military and psychological impact of weapons of mass destruction in aggressive hands.

DOD'S ROLE IN PREVENTING PROLIFERATION

To meet the challenges discussed above, the Department of Defense must enhance its contribution to the government's effort to prevent proliferation from occurring in the first place. The potential contribution is large. The international effort to prevent nuclear proliferation enjoyed substantial success in the 1990s. In 1995, US diplomacy was essential in securing the unconditional and indefinite extension of the global Nuclear Non-Proliferation Treaty. Without US interventions, most of them involving DOD directly, no fewer than six non-nuclear nations would have been likely to possess those weapons today. Iraq's program was stopped by war and the imposition of UN sanctions and inspections. North Korea's program was frozen by the Agreed Framework negotiated by the United States. South Africa's arsenal was voluntarily relinquished in the transition from apartheid to majority rule. And Ukraine, Kazakhstan and Belarus decided to forego nuclear weapons inherited from the Soviet Union when the United States supported their independence, assisted their new militaries, helped them negotiate fair compensation from Russia, and participated directly in the process of weapon dismantlement and cleanup through DOD's Nunn–Lugar program.

On the other side of the ledger, India and Pakistan acknowledged their long-standing nuclear capabilities and conducted underground tests of nuclear devices in 1998. Chemical, biological and ballistic missile programs have proliferated widely despite efforts to establish global regimes of restraint through the Chemical Weapons Convention, the Biological Weapons Convention and the Missile Technology Control Regime.

Global regimes are essential for establishing the norm against weapons of mass destruction and mobilizing international support behind counterproliferation. But the motives to proliferate are usually local, not global. The effort to prevent proliferation therefore requires tools that can be focused locally. US alliances, security relationships, military presence, regional security strategies and nuclear deterrent forces are not normally thought of as counterproliferation tools, but they are, and have been historically. Many nations have found it unnecessary to resort to nuclear weapons or other WMD to ensure their security because of the protection and stability provided by the United States. It is wise to keep in mind not only the 'rogue states' that seem bent on proliferation but also the nations that have elected not to develop WMD. The US goal should be to preserve the conditions that reduce the incentives for possession of weapons of mass destruction.

Attention to incentives is all the more important today because the technological capability to proliferate is widespread. At the end of the Second World War and for decades thereafter, it was sufficient for the United States to control the export of its advanced technology to foreign nations. Without such technology, proliferation was impossible. But today even backward economies like North Korea's can support an indigenous nuclear weapons program and a ballistic missile export business. The rising tide of advanced technology has lifted all boats, and reduced the efficacy of export controls.

Several other factors have contributed to the need to refocus export controls where they can still be effective. For one thing, much of the US export control system was designed to limit transfers to former Cold War adversaries. These controls need to be reoriented to the security challenges of the post-Cold War world, including counterproliferation. Other technologically advanced nations, including long-standing allies, do not always share US views on what items should be controlled or which countries should be denied them. Yet US controls will be ineffective if potentially threatening nations can get the technology they desire elsewhere. Thus it is crucial to secure the agreement of other nations to our export control standards. Unfortunately, this is not always possible. In addition, the volume of international commerce in high-technology products is so large that it is increasingly difficult for intelligence and law enforcement to sift through the haystack to find the dangerous needles. For these reasons, the export control system must focus on controlling what can actually be controlled in practical terms.

The US export control system therefore faces very real dilemmas. These dilemmas are obscured when they are characterized merely as a problem of weighing the economic objective of increasing US exports against the security objective of denying advanced military tools to potential adversaries. The security side of the balance is itself much more complex in the post-Cold War world, and the limits of controlling dangerous technology must be recognized in crafting effective measures. The Department of Defense plays a key role in the administration of export controls, contributing its military and technical expertise to decisions about which exports might augment foreign military capabilities. It therefore needs to adjust its policies and procedures to take account of new dilemmas.

Export controls on advanced computers are a good example of the need for adjustment. Computers are crucial to the design of nuclear weapons, ballistic missiles and a host of other threatening weapons. The very fastest supercomputers are made in small numbers by only a few companies in a few countries, all of them friendly to the United States. Denying such computers to proliferators is therefore practical if the United States and its allies can agree to control their export. If allies will not agree, of course, controls on US exporters alone are of little use. Laptop computers, on the other hand, are made in large numbers by many companies in many countries, and moreover are sold retail to millions of buyers whose use cannot possibly be monitored by law enforcement. Thus they can easily be diverted to proliferators, and controls on legal exports of such computers would be both cumbersome and ineffective. The march of technology and the globalization of markets renders useless any attempt to license the export of laptop computers. Since laptops have more computational power every year, the control level must be adjusted upward every year if the export controls system is to avoid being swamped with superfluous license applications. Progressive upward adjustment of computer export control levels is thus necessary to preserve the effectiveness of the remaining controls. Though sometimes criticized as 'relaxation of export controls', this process of progressive adjustment is an unavoidable consequence of technological advance and globalization. Thus, while export controls still play a role in reducing proliferation, it is increasingly a less decisive role.

CONCLUSION

The United States, in concert with the international community, has had some real success in limiting proliferation. The proliferation of nuclear weapons, for example, has been substantially less than many observers predicted at the dawn of the nuclear age. But the United States cannot completely control the proliferation of nuclear weapons, as 1998's nuclear tests in India and Pakistan demonstrated. Moreover, controls over the proliferation of chemical and biological weapons and ballistic missiles are far from complete. Therefore, the national strategy is correct. The United States must continue to do what it can to minimize the pressure to proliferate by protecting friends and allies, providing incentives to forego proliferation, promoting multilateral agreements such as the Chemical Weapons Convention, and enforcing vigorously those export controls that are still useful. But, because of the fundamental limitations of these actions, they cannot be the United States' complete strategy for dealing with dangerous proliferation threats. These actions, therefore, must be supplemented by counter-proliferation programs that include passive defenses such as defensive chemical suits, active defenses such as theater missile defenses, and counterforce programs. Given the urgency of the problem, these programs should be given higher priority and adequate funding.

NOTES

1 Ashton B. Carter is the Ford Foundation Professor of Science and International Affairs at Harvard's John F. Kennedy School of Government and Co-Director, with William J. Perry, of the Harvard-Stanford Preventive Defense Project. L. Celeste Johnson is an Associate in the Government Practice of DFI International, and a graduate of Stanford University and the John F. Kennedy School of Government at Harvard University.
2 'Chemical and Biological Defense: Observations on DOD's Plans to Protect US Forces', statement of Mark E. Gebicke, Director, Military Operations and Capabilities Issues, National Security and International Affairs Division, US General Accounting Office. Testimony before the Committee on Veterans' Affairs, US Senate, 17 March 1998.
3 Remarks prepared for Secretary of Defense Les Aspin, speech to the National Academy of Sciences, 7 December 1993.
4 See William J. Perry, 'Desert Storm and Deterrence', *Foreign Affairs*, 70, 4 (Fall 1991), 66–82.

6

Counterproliferation: A Critical Appraisal

THOMAS G. MAHNKEN[1]

INTRODUCTION

During the 1991 Gulf War, US troops for the first time fought an adversary that possessed weapons of mass destruction (WMD) and the means to deliver them. While the Iraqi army – for reasons that remain unclear – did not employ its chemical and biological munitions, it did launch ballistic missiles against both military and civilian targets. Even more ominously, Saddam Hussein's regime had begun to develop, but had yet to field, nuclear weapons. Iraq is not an anomaly. Despite the existence of treaties to ban the possession of nuclear, biological and chemical weapons and international agreements to limit the spread of sensitive technology, a growing number of states are acquiring such weapons.

Since assuming office in 1993, President Bill Clinton and his national security advisors have devoted considerable attention to the threat posed by nuclear, biological and chemical weapons and their means of delivery. The State Department repeatedly lists proliferation as one of the administration's top concerns, while the Defense Department portrays WMD as one of the key threats facing the United States. Indeed, on 14 November 1994, Clinton took the extraordinary step of issuing an Executive Order declaring a national emergency based upon the threat posed by these weapons.

On 7 December 1993, Secretary of Defense Les Aspin unveiled the administration's Defense Counterproliferation Initiative (CPI) in a speech before the National Academy of Sciences. The initiative represented a tacit acknowledgment of the limits of traditional policies aimed at preventing the spread of nuclear, biological and chemical weapons. Instead, it sought to augment preventive efforts with measures to protect US forces, friends and allies should they face such weapons. The CPI charged the department with preventing potential adversaries from acquiring WMD and rolling back proliferation where it occurred. Its responsibilities included deterring the use of WMD and adapting US forces and planning to such threats.

At the heart of the initiative lay an effort 'to develop new military capabilities' to counter nuclear, biological and chemical weapons and missiles.[2] Under Aspin, the Defense Department launched a review of the technology and weapon systems needed to counter WMD and began to explore how the United States and its friends might operate against an adversary armed with them. It also examined ways to improve the quality of information the intelligence community provided military and civilian customers regarding proliferation.

The Clinton administration trumpeted the CPI as a milestone in the battle against the spread of WMD. Early Defense Department statements argued that the initiative held 'the promise of reduced violence in armed conflicts, of reduced threats to civilians, and of increased international cooperation, and would enhance America's strengths'.[3] Many in the defense and scientific community welcomed the initiative as well. One journal heralded it as 'the major defense initiative of the 1990s', comparing it to Ronald Reagan's Strategic Defense Initiative.[4]

Not all in the administration shared the enthusiasm of CPI boosters. Indeed, reaction to the initiative in some parts of the government was cool. The State Department saw the CPI as a challenge to its traditional preeminence in nonproliferation policy. The Joint Staff and armed services resented what they saw as an attempt by civilians to foist a policy upon them. They feared that counterproliferation would become a drain on their increasingly scarce resources and resisted portraying it as a separate military mission. The arms control community recoiled, seeing in the initiative a renunciation of diplomatic efforts to stem the flow of nuclear, biological, chemical and missile technology. Still others dismissed the initiative as hype, yet another bumper-sticker slogan generated by a new administration eager to make its mark in history.

The results of the CPI have been decidedly mixed. While there is a clear need to protect US forces abroad from WMD, such efforts are not – and can never be – revolutionary. Moreover, the implementation of counterproliferation policy has left much to be desired. While the Pentagon has emphasized the acquisition of equipment to protect US forces, it has made considerably less progress in developing the doctrine and organizations needed to deal with the use of WMD. The CPI also ignores the threat a future adversary could pose to US forces by employing other weapons that could have a major impact upon a future war. These issues must be addressed if the initiative is to make an enduring contribution to US security.

COUNTERPROLIFERATION VERSUS NONPROLIFERATION

Although the Clinton administration portrayed the CPI as an innovative response to the threat of WMD, to a great extent it represents a continuation of efforts undertaken by the Bush administration to explore military responses to strategic weapons. Moreover, the quest for novelty has often obscured both the scope and limitations of counterproliferation policy and its relationship to traditional nonproliferation efforts.

Early statements by the administration described counterproliferation as a military response to the spread of WMD. According to this definition, counterproliferation efforts were separate from – though complementary to – nonproliferation policy, which sought to prevent states from acquiring these weapons in the first place. Left unstated was whether these options were confined to wartime measures to limit the damage an adversary armed with WMD could inflict upon the United States and its allies, or whether they also included the preemptive use of force.

Over time, the administration adopted a more expansive set of definitions, one that blurred the distinction between nonproliferation and counterproliferation. In February 1994, the National Security Council defined nonproliferation as 'the use of the full range of political, economic and military tools to prevent proliferation, reverse it diplomatically or protect our interests against an opponent armed with weapons of mass destruction or missiles, should that prove necessary'. It described counterproliferation as

> the activities of the Department of Defense across the full range of US efforts to combat proliferation, including diplomacy, arms control, export controls and intelligence collection and analysis, with particular responsibility for assuring that U.S. forces and interests can be protected should they confront an adversary armed with weapons of mass destruction or missiles.[5]

Whereas the administration had previously portrayed nonproliferation and counterproliferation as distinct activities, it now began to view counterproliferation as a subset of nonproliferation. Moreover, its criterion for determining which activities constituted counterproliferation became purely bureaucratic: all Defense Department programs aimed at preventing or responding to the spread of WMD became 'counterproliferation' activities.[6]

The current set of definitions obscures more than it clarifies. It lumps together traditional nonproliferation programs such as US support for the International Atomic Energy Agency (IAEA), export control regimes, and technology security with measures to mitigate the consequences of proliferation when it does occur. It has thus allowed the Defense Department to claim that over one hundred of its programs strongly support national efforts to counter nuclear, biological and chemical threats.[7]

It is the practice, rather than the theory, of counterproliferation that has separated the Clinton administration from its predecessors. Those charged with formulating and carrying out the administration's policy have taken a decidedly aggressive approach. Shortly before becoming Assistant Secretary of Defense for Nuclear Security and Counterproliferation, for example, Ashton B. Carter advocated the use of military force to prevent states from acquiring nuclear weapons.[8] More recently Carter, writing with L. Celeste Johnson, has called for the development of weapons and tactics to destroy missiles armed with WMD before they can be launched.[9]

Nor is the administration's commitment to using force to prevent other states from acquiring WMD purely rhetorical; since 1993, the United States has pursued a particularly muscular form of counterproliferation. During the 1994 showdown with North Korea over Pyongyang's nuclear program, the US Air Force briefed Secretary of Defense William Perry on a plan to bomb the North Korean nuclear reactor at Yongbyong.[10] The US cruise missile attack on Sudan in August 1998 and the Anglo-American strikes on Iraq in December 1998 were both aimed at destroying chemical, biological and missile production facilities. The results of this policy have, however, been at best modest. In Sudan the United States, relying on flawed intelligence, destroyed not a chemical weapons factory, as was originally claimed, but a pharmaceutical plant. Operation Desert Fox blunted neither Iraq's ability to manufacture chemical and biological munitions nor Saddam Hussein's willingness to stonewall the United Nations. Indeed, the Commander in Chief of US Central Command at the time, General Anthony Zinni, admitted that the ease of manufacturing chemical and biological weapons rendered the bombing futile.[11]

Recently, Carter and Johnson have called for a 'Revolution in Counterproliferation Affairs' to succeed the CPI.[12] While their proposal is a clear attempt to capitalize upon current interest in exploiting the information revolution to achieve a revolution in military affairs, the 'Revolution in Counterproliferation Affairs' is little more than the CPI clothed in new rhetoric. Four of the five elements that Carter and Johnson envision comprising the revolution – improved passive defense, counterforce, theater missile defense and coalition efforts – are areas of long-standing interest within the Defense Department. The fifth – increased protection of ports and airfields against chemical and biological attack – is clearly important, but hardly revolutionary.

Indeed, no counterproliferation policy, however well implemented, can ever yield revolutionary results. A revolution in military affairs occurs when new weapon systems combine with innovative doctrine and organizations in a way that fundamentally changes the character and conduct of war.[13] In the end, what defines a military revolution is not only its components – new systems, doctrine and organizations – but also its dramatic impact upon the conduct of war. While the US armed forces should develop innovative approaches to meet the threat of WMD, the prescriptions that Carter and Johnson offer hardly portend the sort of dramatic changes in the character and conduct of war that have accompanied past revolutions in warfare. If anything, nuclear weapons may trump elements of the emerging revolution in military affairs by, for example, offering adversaries the ability to disrupt US information networks through electromagnetic pulse. Neither the misnamed 'Revolution in Counterproliferation Affairs' nor the CPI holds the key to transcending the threat posed by WMD; at best, they offer a way to cope by limiting the damage US troops may sustain in a future conflict.

FUNDING COUNTERPROLIFERATION

Even here, however, recent efforts have fallen short. Although the administration has portrayed defense against WMD as a top priority, its record of funding research, development and acquisition programs to protect US forces against WMD threats is uneven. In May 1994, the then Under Secretary of Defense for Acquisition and Technology, John Deutch, estimated that the government needed an additional $400 million per year to pay for 14 'underfunded' programs to combat proliferation, including $230 million for those sponsored by the Defense Department. Despite this recommendation, the administration requested only $165 million to accelerate these programs. In 1996, not surprisingly, an internal Pentagon review concluded that the department had failed to allocate funds to field a number of high-priority programs, including biological agent detection systems. As a result, the Defense Department increased planned spending on counterproliferation programs by approximately $1 billion over the next five years.

While the vast majority of programs the CPI funds existed prior to the initiative, the administration has accelerated efforts to defend US and allied forces against nuclear, biological, chemical and missile threats. The Defense Department has, for example, devoted considerable attention to improving the ability of US forces to protect themselves against chemical and biological weapons. It has mandated vaccination against anthrax for all members of the US armed forces, and it has substantially increased funding for research, development and acquisition of chemical and biological detection and defense systems. The US Marine Corps, for its part, has founded a Chemical and Biological Incident Response Force to respond to terrorist attacks in the United States. Substantial shortfalls in biological agent detection and chemical and biological protection will nonetheless persist. In 2000, for example, collective protection zones designed into US Navy ships will be capable of shielding only 10 per cent of carrier battle group crews, 32 per cent of amphibious ready group crews and 23 per cent of embarked marines against WMD threats.[14]

The United States is also developing systems to protect US and allied forces against ballistic missiles. Despite generous funding, how-ever, active defense programs remain beset by a string of program delays brought on by poor management and serious technical chal-lenges. As a result, between now and 2007 – 16 years after the Gulf War – the nation's ability to protect its forces, friends and allies will at best rest upon two lower-tier systems: the Patriot Advanced Capability (PAC)-3 and the Navy's Standard missile.

While the Pentagon has devoted considerable attention to defense against ballistic missiles, two areas have received insufficient emphasis. The first is the need to improve the ability to identify, target and destroy mobile missiles. One of the Gulf War's most notable failures was the coalition air armada's inability to destroy a single Iraqi mobile missile launcher. Moreover, the United States has made only marginal gains in this area since the war. While joint doctrine views attack operations as the preferred method for countering enemy missiles, the Pentagon has not matched its rhetoric with resources: compared to this fiscal year's $3 billion spending on active missile defense, that on attack operations barely totals $150 million scattered across a spectrum of programs.

The second shortfall is the need to counter stealthy, low-flying cruise missiles. The Defense Department has conducted an Advanced Concept Technology Demonstration to examine the feasibility of intercepting cruise missiles, but a considerable amount of additional effort is needed. An investment of at least several billion dollars will be needed to acquire a mix of advanced airborne sensors, ground-based and air-launched interceptors, and greatly improved battle manage-ment systems. While the Air Force has begun to address this threat, the Army and Navy are years away from being able to make programmatic decisions on cruise missile defense systems.

ADAPTING TO BATTLEFIELD WMD USE

The Pentagon's current approach to counterproliferation emphasizes the acquisition of technology to protect US forces against WMD threats over the development of concepts and organizations to allow them to remain effective on a contaminated battlefield. This is understandable, given the fact that civilians in the Office of the Secretary of Defense formulated the CPI. For the initiative to enhance US national security over the long term, however, the military services must develop innovative concepts to protect their forces against attack.

The use of WMD would effect virtually every facet of military activity. An adversary could employ nuclear, chemical or biological weapons to degrade US command, control and communication systems, hinder the deployment and reinforcement of US forces, and isolate them within a region. Yet there has been remarkably little discussion, either within the Defense Department or in the defense community as a whole, of how an adversary's possession of nuclear, biological and chemical weapons would affect the ability of the services to carry out their missions. Nor have the armed forces achieved much progress toward reducing their vulnerability to WMD attack. For US forces to fight effectively against WMD-armed adversaries, the United States will have to address a range of deficiencies, including intelligence regarding foreign WMD capabilities; deterrence concepts; and the doctrine, organizations, and training necessary for US forces to maintain their effectiveness in the face of nuclear, biological or chemical use.

Intelligence

While the priority attached to collecting and analyzing information on the spread of WMD has increased in recent years, the intelligence community's efforts still emphasize the technology involved with proliferation rather than foreign operational concepts and employment doctrines. Military and civilian leaders need to recognize that there may be considerable limits to WMD intelligence, even after an attack has taken place. The US intelligence community may, for example, lack the clear-cut evidence of WMD use that the civilian leadership may demand before it authorizes retaliation. The controversy over whether US and allied soldiers were exposed to Iraqi chemical agents during the Gulf War shows that uncertainty may persist long after the war is over.

Deterrence

Current concepts of deterrence are the legacy of the Cold War competition between the United States and Soviet Union. Given the variety of threats the United States may face in coming years, there is a need to explore new approaches to deter adversaries from using WMD. A new deterrence concept should combine the threat of retaliation with the need to limit the effectiveness of WMD if they are used. To be credible, such an approach must take into account the strategic character of different potential opponents. Regional competitors may calculate costs and benefits in ways much different than we do. Moreover, it is unlikely that two adversaries will behave in exactly the same way. As a result, the United States will face a wide range of behavioral uncertainties among future regional adversaries, vastly complicating deterrence.

Doctrine and organization

Despite the CPI's efforts to accelerate the acquisition of systems to protect US forces, the US armed services are poorly configured to fight an adversary with nuclear, biological and chemical weapons. The United States plans to fight future regional wars by progressively building up US and allied combat power in theater before launching an attack upon an adversary. Current concepts of operations emphasize the concentration of forces to penetrate enemy defenses and minimize casualties. Threats from WMD pose a serious challenge to this approach.

The success of US power projection operations depends upon fixed infrastructure such as ports, air bases, depots and command and control facilities that are themselves vulnerable to attack. The logistical network upon which the United States would rely represents a particularly lucrative target set. Nuclear weapons could destroy and chemical and biological weapons contaminate the ports and airfields which the United States would use to project military power against an adversary. Most ports and airfields are manned by civilians who are more vulnerable to attack than US military personnel. Chemical weapons, for example, could not only inflict casualties upon US forces, but also contaminate aircraft bringing men and material into and out of the theater. Contaminated personnel, vehicles and equipment could, in turn, clog logistical channels, slowing the pace of deployment and reinforcement. They could also spread the effects of a WMD attack beyond the immediate theater of operations, potentially eroding allied support for US operations.

The US armed forces have yet to come to terms with the impact of WMD upon military operations. The lack of tactics and techniques for waging war on a WMD battlefield represents a major deficiency. Current joint and service doctrine lacks an appreciation both of how an adversary might employ WMD as well as concepts of operations for how to operate in a contaminated environment. Existing publications include broad statements about the threat of WMD and outline detailed technical procedures for personal protection and decontamination.

What is missing is doctrine and tactics for conducting operations in the face of WMD threats or use. While the Joint Staff has issued Joint Publication 3-11, *Joint Doctrine for Nuclear, Biological, and Chemical (NBC) Defense*, the threat of WMD is not well integrated into joint doctrine as a whole. The capstone document describing US joint operations contains a single page on WMD threats; that on command, control, communications, computers and intelligence has but a single sentence on the threat that nuclear electromagnetic pulse effects pose to communication networks; and that on logistics does not mention WMD threats to ports and airfields.

Current service doctrine reflects similar deficiencies. US Air Force publications, for example, emphasize procedures to protect individuals against WMD threats, such as donning Mission Oriented Protective Posture gear. They offer no guidance on how to shield aircraft, large groups of people, or supplies against contamination; decontaminate air base taxi ways and ramps; or handle contaminated cargo and casualties.[15]

Nor are the services well organized to meet WMD threats. They currently rely heavily upon reserve component units for WMD defense. Those units in the active force that are charged with WMD defense have other duties that may conflict with their ability to carry out the mission. The chemical companies assigned to Army divisions, for example, perform both smoke generation and WMD decontamination – activities that may be required simultaneously in a future conflict. Air Force civil engineer units have both base maintenance and base and aircraft decontamination missions.[16]

To remain credible, the US armed forces need to examine how best to operate in the face of WMD threats. The services should, for example, study how to reduce their dependence upon vulnerable fixed infrastructure such as ports and airfields. Rather than closing with an adversary, they should explore options to allow them to strike an adversary from a distance. Similarly, they should develop concepts to reduce their vulnerability to WMD through dispersion and mobility.

Training

Training for WMD contingencies represents another weakness. Although the CPI has raised awareness of the impact of WMD use upon military operations, service training has actually declined due to budget cuts and the reduction of the US nuclear inventory.[17] Moreover, command-level exercises only rarely include WMD threats because they interfere with other training objectives. Current simulations do not realistically portray the impact of WMD on land, sea and air operations. One reason is that they do not contain essential information regarding chemical, and especially biological, effects.[18]

EMERGING THREATS TO US FORCES

Of greatest concern over the long term is the fact that the CPI's exclusive focus upon nuclear, biological and chemical weapons and their means of delivery ignores other plausible threats to US forces that could have a strategic impact. Both the Quadrennial Defense Review and the congressionally mandated National Defense Panel recognized that adversaries may not only employ WMD and missiles, but also information warfare; attempt to deny US access to forward bases; and attack US space assets. Unless these threats receive the sort of focused study that WMD have received, the United States runs the risk of dealing with the threats of yesterday and today while ignoring the threats of tomorrow.

The administration's concentration upon WMD threats represents a break with the policy of the Bush administration, which focused not only upon reducing WMD threats, but also on developing strategies to counter high-leverage conventional technologies such as highly accurate ballistic and cruise missiles; unmanned air vehicles; improved command, control, communications and intelligence systems; and satellite imagery.[19]

In coming years, regional adversaries will possess a growing range of technologies that they could employ against US power projection forces. In addition to WMD and missiles, a number of states will have access to information from a wide variety of space systems that they can use for reconnaissance, surveillance, communications and precision location. These capabilities will enhance their ability to disrupt US efforts to project military power overseas and limit the effectiveness of forces once they have arrived in theater. An adversary could, for example, couple commercially available imagery and satellite communications with stealthy precision-guided munitions to threaten US power projection forces. Indeed, because the United States is reliant upon a small number of bases, we may be highly vulnerable to such an attack. As former Air Force Chief of Staff Ronald Fogelman put it:

> Saturation ballistic missile attacks against littoral forces, ports, airfields, storage facilities and staging areas could make it extremely costly to project U.S. forces into a disputed theater, much less carry out operations to defeat a well-armed aggressor. Simply the threat of such enemy missile attacks might deter the U.S. and coalition partners from responding to aggression in the first place.[20]

Unfortunately, the CPI – even if it spawns a 'Revolution in Counter-proliferation Affairs' – is poorly suited to address the new and very different threats the United States will face in coming years.

CONCLUSION

New slogans and initiatives are a regular feature of the Washington landscape. Yet words – however well intentioned – are no substitute for action. The most significant elements of the CPI predate the initiative. The focus upon developing military countermeasures to WMD proliferation, as well as the vast majority of chemical and biological protection and theater missile defense programs, existed long before the initiative. The novel portions of the initiative, such as its emphasis upon preemption, are potentially dangerous.

While the Clinton administration has accelerated the acquisition of systems to protect US forces against WMD threats, much remains to be done. First, the US intelligence community needs to expand its collection and analysis to encompass not only the transfer of nuclear, biological, chemical and missile technology, but also the doctrine, organization, command and control, and training of foreign WMD forces. Second, the defense community should explore new approaches to deterring adversaries from using WMD against US forces in future conflicts. Third, the US armed forces need to adapt their doctrine and organizational structure to allow them to operate effectively in the face of WMD threats. Fourth, US forces must regularly train under simulated WMD conditions. It is only through such exercises that the services will be able to develop tactics and techniques to operate effectively in the face of WMD threats. Finally, the United States should explore strategies to deal with emerging threats to US forces, such as accurate ballistic and cruise missiles coupled with air- and space-based reconnaissance and surveillance systems. Unless the United States addresses these issues, it is unlikely that the CPI will make an enduring contribution to US security. Instead, it will fade away, joining a host of other well-intentioned but poorly executed initiatives.

Counterproliferation offers nothing more than the ability to cope with WMD. While such efforts are unquestionably necessary, they are insufficient to deal with current and emerging threats. The United States should instead focus upon developing strategies to allow us to apply our considerable strengths to roll back proliferation. Such an effort would require the long-term, disciplined study of the relative strengths and weaknesses of the United States and a range of adversaries. It is clearly more difficult than throwing money at the problem, but it holds the greatest chance of achieving lasting results.

NOTES

1 Thomas G. Mahnken is Associate Professor of Strategy at the US Naval War College. The views expressed in this chapter are those of the author and do not reflect the official policy or position of the Department of Defense or the US Government.

2 Remarks by Honorable Les Aspin, Secretary of Defense, National Academy of Sciences, Committee on International Security and Arms Control, 7 December 1993, Defense Department press release, 4.

3 Les Aspin, *Annual Report to the President and Congress* (Washington, DC: Department of Defense, 1994), 34.

4 Gary Taubes, 'The Defense Initiative of the 1990s', *Science*, 267 (24 February 1995), 1096.

5 Office of the Undersecretary of Defense, Acquisition and Technology, *Report on Nonproliferation and Counterproliferation Activities and Programs* (Washington, DC: Department of Defense, 1994), 1.

6 'The DOD Counterproliferation Initiative encapsulates all DOD activities in support of overall U.S. nonproliferation policy, with particular emphasis on military countermeasures and intelligence programs.' Ibid., 7.

7 William S. Cohen, *Annual Report to the President and the Congress* (Washington, DC: Department of Defense, 1997), 52.

8 Robert D. Blackwill and Ashton B. Carter, 'The Role of Intelligence' in Robert D. Blackwill and Albert Carnesale (eds), *New Nuclear Nations: Consequences for U.S. Policy* (New York: Council on Foreign Relations, 1993), 234, 239–42.

9 Ashton B. Carter and L. Celeste Johnson, 'Beyond the Counterproliferation Initiative', Chapter 5 in this volume.

10 Don Oberdorfer, *The Two Koreas: A Contemporary History* (Reading, MA: Addison-Wesley, 1997), 323.

11 William M. Arkin, 'Desert Fox Delivery: Precision Undermined its Purpose', *Washington Post*, 17 January 1999, B1.

12 Carter and Johnson, 'Beyond the Counterproliferation Initiative'.

13 See, for example, Andrew F. Krepinevich, 'Cavalry to Computer: the Pattern of Military Revolutions', *National Interest*, 37 (Fall 1994), 30.

14 *The Impact of the Proliferation of Nuclear, Biological, and Chemical Weapons on the United States Navy* (Washington, DC: National Defense University, Center for Counterproliferation Research, 1996), 16.

15 *The Impact of the Proliferation of Nuclear, Biological, and Chemical Weapons on the United States Air Force* (Washington, DC: National Defense University, Center for Counterproliferation Research, 1996), 5.

16 Robert G. Joseph, 'The Impact of NBC Proliferation on Doctrine and Operations', *Joint Force Quarterly*, 13 (Autumn 1996), 77.

17 *The Impact of Nuclear, Biological, and Chemical Proliferation on U.S. Armed Forces* (Washington, DC: National Defense University, Center for Counterproliferation Research, 1996), 9.

18 Joseph, 'The Impact of NBC Proliferation', 78.

19 Henry D. Sokolski, 'Nonapocalyptic Proliferation: A New Strategic Threat?', *Washington Quarterly*, 17, 2 (Spring 1994).

20 Bill Gertz, 'The Air Force and Missile Defense', *Air Force* (February 1996), 72.

7

Getting Back to Basics:
Controlling Fissile Materials

FRANK VON HIPPEL[1]

INTRODUCTION

No nuclear weapon can be made without kilogram quantities of fissile material such as highly enriched uranium (HEU – uranium containing more than 20 per cent U^{235}) or plutonium.[2] Hopefully this situation will not change. Thus far it has been impossible to develop pure fusion weapons which would make it possible to bypass the choke point on nuclear weapons manufacture provided by controls on fissile materials.[3] Therefore, both arms control and nonproliferation policy must deal with the problems of safeguarding fissile materials, controlling additional production and securing disposition of materials made excess by nuclear disarmament or changes in nuclear energy policy.

These basic facts were understood at the beginning of the nuclear era. Indeed, had the 1946 Acheson–Lillienthal plan been accepted, there would be no fissile materials under private or national control. Only an international 'Atomic Development Authority' would be authorized to work with directly weapons-usable fissile materials.[4]

Following the rejection of the Acheson–Lillienthal plan, huge quantities of fissile material were produced for weapons and reactor fuel and the objectives of arms control became more modest, focusing on the limitation of numbers and characteristics of large missile launchers and bombers that could be counted from space. With the launching of major commercial plutonium recycle enterprises in France, Britain and Russia, the objectives of nonproliferation also became more modest: to assure that fissile materials in non-nuclear-weapons states were subject to international safeguards.

However, with the end of the Cold War, on-site inspection became permissible and it has therefore become possible in principle to have arms control agreements that limit stocks of unsafeguarded fissile materials. At the same time, plutonium recycling has proven to be both unneeded and uneconomic so that a phaseout of spent-fuel reprocessing appears feasible. This would make it possible to greatly reduce existing stocks of civilian fissile material. This chapter provides an overview of three major aspects of fissile material control:

1) the challenge of fissile material abundance;
2) the need to end production of fissile materials; and
3) the use of fissile material reductions as a tool for arms reductions.

Renewed efforts should be made in all of these areas. We have learned that such efforts will not yield significant progress, however, unless they are given priority at the presidential level.

FISSILE MATERIAL ABUNDANCE

The challenges to fissile material controls on nuclear weapons that are of greatest concern are:

- the spread of centrifuge uranium-enrichment technology;
- the huge quantities of civilian but weapons-usable plutonium being separated from spent power-reactor fuel; and
- the huge stockpiles of fissile materials extracted from nuclear weapons made excess by the end of the Cold War.

None of these problems is as yet beyond containment. However, they require more high-level policy attention than they have been getting.

Challenge number 1: The proliferation of uranium-centrifuge technology

Uranium-centrifuge technology has been commercialized in Russia, west Europe and Japan. It has also become a prime technology for proliferant countries interested in clandestine production of fissile material. The technology is simple conceptually and lends itself to the production of weapons quantities of HEU in a small facility. However, some countries have had difficulty mastering the technology.

Pakistan acquired uranium gas-centrifuge technology from west Europe through industrial espionage, and used it in an ordinary small factory-type building to produce enough weapons-grade uranium for a small nuclear arsenal. After the nuclear reactor it acquired from France with the intention of producing plutonium was destroyed by Israel, Iraq clandestinely obtained centrifuge technology from west Europe. However, even after its acquisition of the special materials and machine tools used in the production of gas centrifuges, Iraq had difficulty producing reliable machines. No production facility had been established by the time the effort was halted by the bombings during Desert Storm and the subsequent efforts of the UN Special Commission (UNSCOM). India has developed centrifuge technology for its naval-reactor program, but had so much trouble making it work reliably that India's nuclear establishment was openly skeptical that Pakistan could have done so before Pakistan's nuclear tests of May 1998. According to Mordechai Vanunu, Israel has obtained centrifuge technology. Brazil has deployed centrifuge technology. It has renounced its nuclear weapons ambitions but still continues the program to provide enriched uranium for its naval nuclear-reactor program. Iran has sought centrifuge enrichment technology from Russia. It would not be surprising if North Korea were seeking to acquire this technology, since it is more easily concealed than a plutonium-production reactor.

Historically, due to the great economies of scale of gaseous-diffusion enrichment plants, only the declared nuclear weapons states built them. Thus far, only a few additional countries have built centrifuge plants for civilian purposes (Germany, the Netherlands and Japan). It would be desirable to formalize an agreement that new individual countries will not be allowed into the enrichment club. Under such a regime, new enrichment plants could only be built by multinational consortia under international safeguards. Under the proposed Fissile Material Cutoff Treaty (see below), existing national enrichment plants would be brought under international safeguards at least to the extent required to verify that they are not producing HEU or, if they are, to assure that the HEU is not used for weapons.

Challenge number 2: Large-scale separation of civilian but weapons-usable plutonium

Plutonium is a directly weapons-usable material. Unfortunately, the United States ignored that fact for two decades, between President Eisenhower's 1953 'Atoms for Peace' speech and India's 1974 nuclear test. During those two decades, the US promoted plutonium as the fuel of a future world economy.

US policy turned around rather promptly after 1974, when India used, for a 'peaceful' nuclear explosion, plutonium extracted by US-trained reprocessing experts from the spent fuel of a reactor provided by Canada and filled with heavy water supplied by the United States. By then, however, most of the world's energy research and development funds were going into the development and demonstration of plutonium breeder reactors and plans were being laid for the separation of hundreds of tons of plutonium from the spent fuel of civilian power reactors. The dream of a 'plutonium economy' was also reinforced by a number of other interests:

- The plutonium production establishments of the weapon states saw it as an opportunity to stay in business after national demands for weapons plutonium had been satisfied.
- The security establishments in many non-nuclear-weapon states were interested in developing a nuclear weapons option without violating their commitments under the Non-Proliferation Treaty.
- The German and Japanese governments mandated reprocessing as the only acceptable method of spent-fuel disposal. The pre-paid spent-fuel reprocessing contracts signed by their nuclear utilities provided most of the capital for the construction of the multi-billion dollar commercial reprocessing plants operating today in Britain and France.

By the time the French and British reprocessing plants had been completed, demonstration breeder reactor projects were being cancelled and postponed worldwide. The anticipated demand for plutonium had been for the startup cores of hundreds of these reactors. But, because of the inertia of contracted commitments and because of the lack of political acceptance of the prolonged on-site or away-from-reactor storage of spent fuel ('radioactive waste'), large-scale reprocessing continued. In the absence of breeder reactors, it was decided to recycle the recovered plutonium back into fuel for the reactors from which it had come.

Today plutonium is being separated in France, Britain, Russia and India at a combined rate of about 25 tons per year and the world stockpile of separated civilian plutonium is approaching 250 tons, enough for tens of thousands of nuclear weapons.[5] Spent-fuel reprocessing is totally uneconomic. The price of natural uranium would have to increase about 20 times before the uranium savings from plutonium and uranium recycling would pay for reprocessing.[6] Therefore, as utilities are being deregulated worldwide, they are increasingly trying to shift to the much less costly alternative of interim storage of spent fuel. This shift is being delayed by the fact that, despite the safety of dry spent-fuel storage, no locality wants to host an interim storage facility. Germany has licensed two such facilities but each of the two shipments of spent fuel that have been made thus far to one of these sites had to be protected from demonstrators by 30,000 police. In the United States, major political battles have been raging over nuclear industry efforts to establish interim storage sites for spent fuel.

In an era of utility deregulation, the economic incentives are so great that it appears likely that solutions to the impasse over interim storage will be found and the era of large-scale reprocessing will come to an end within a decade. Unfortunately, as their customers find less expensive ways to manage their spent fuel, the British, French and Russian reprocessors are promoting their services to countries of ever greater proliferation concern – currently South Korea and Taiwan.

Although France's reprocessing company, Cogema, denies it, reactor-grade plutonium can be used to make bombs. Had reactor-grade plutonium been used in the Nagasaki bomb, its yield would probably have been reduced to about 1,000 tons of TNT because of premature initiation of the chain reaction. But 1,000 tons of TNT is 500 times the explosive power of the Oklahoma City bomb. With more advanced nuclear weapon designs, there is little yield penalty from using reactor-grade instead of weapons-grade plutonium.[7]

Civil plutonium is a significant part of the larger 'loose-nukes' problem in Russia. There is a large zero-power breeder reactor mock-up in Obninsk, for example, made up of tens of thousands of small disks containing tons of plutonium and weapons-grade uranium. It will be years more before all of these disks are bar-coded, assayed and entered into a database. In October 1994, I visited one of two adjoining warehouses in the closed Urals city of Chelyabinsk-65 where Russia stores its growing stockpile of civilian plutonium – then about 30,000 kilograms in about 12,000 very easily carried coffee-pot-sized containers.[8] Since then, the United States has put quite a bit of effort into upgrading the security of these containers. There may be little that the United States can do to accelerate the end of commercial reprocessing in Britain and France. However, Russia's reprocessing operation is truly marginal, grossing only a few tens of millions of dollars a year. The United States plans to spend in the order of $1 billion or more on plutonium storage and disposition in the same city. Should we not condition this assistance on Russia agreeing to a moratorium on further plutonium separation?

The interim storage alternative
The current alternative to both reprocessing and centralized spent-fuel storage is continued storage at the nuclear power plants. However, this alternative will not be accepted indefinitely. In the United States, 14 nuclear power reactors have been shut down and more will shut down during the next decade or so. Their owning utilities object strenuously to being put into the position of indefinitely safeguarding spent fuel at these sites – especially since the US government committed in the Nuclear Waste Policy Act of 1982 to have a federal repository available by 1998.

Recently there has been a flurry of interest in the possibility that Russia might be willing to provide final disposal for other countries' spent fuel. A group of US investors, the 'Nonproliferation Trust' (NPT), have, in fact, been exploring the possibilities of storing 10,000 tons of spent fuel in Russia for a price of $10–15 billion. But, even with Russia desperate for money for environmental cleanup and the other good things that are promised in the NPT deal, Russia's greens are battling against acceptance of foreign radioactive waste. More important, from a nonproliferation perspective, is the fact that Russia's Minister of Atomic Energy Adamov is interested in making much larger deals than that envisioned by NPT and insists, contrary to the NPT proposal, that any foreign spent fuel stored in Russia will eventually be reprocessed.

Disposing of already separated plutonium
It will take a long time to work off the 250 ton stockpile of civilian plutonium. Only France appears to be successfully recycling its separated plutonium within several years of separation. Britain does not even have plans for the plutonium that it is separating out of the spent fuel of its own power reactors. By 2010, it will have a stockpile of over 100 tons – comparable to the US and Russian stockpiles of weapons plutonium. Increasing unease is being expressed within the British establishment about the challenge of indefinite stewardship of this enormous stockpile of weapons-usable material. Britain may seem like the last country to worry about the possibility of civil instability and terrorism but, as its Irish problem illustrates, even it is not immune. And, compared with the 24,000-year half-life of plutonium-239, even British institutions seem ephemeral.

Russia's nuclear establishment plans to use its separated plutonium as startup fuel for a new generation of plutonium breeder reactors, but no one knows where the money to build these reactors could come from. And the foreign reprocessing customers of France and Britain are struggling. Germany and Japan have thus far between them contracted for the separation of about 100 tons of plutonium, of which more than 60 per cent has already been separated over the past decade. Very little of this plutonium has been recycled thus far because of the same nuclear allergy which forced Germany and Japan to export their spent fuel problem in the first place.

Challenge number 3: Excess stocks of weapons materials
We don't know how many nuclear warheads Russia intends to dismantle without replacement. My rough guess would be 20,000. This is the origin of the 500 tons of weapon-grade uranium that the United States has contracted to have blended down for approximately $12 billion for resale as nuclear fuel to Western nuclear utilities.

This 'HEU deal' is extraordinary in that it finances Russian nuclear disarmament through the market. The problem is that, because it is designed so as not to disrupt the uranium and enrichment markets, blending down the weapons is scheduled to take 20 years. Given the instability of Russia, that is a very long time. And, at the end of the 20 years, we may have another 500 tons to deal with. The blend-down stage should be accelerated, even if the marketing of the resulting low-enriched uranium is not. This might require some prepayment using US government funds, but the security benefit would be worth it. The US Department of Energy plans, in parallel, to convert into power-reactor fuel 174 tons of HEU which has been declared in excess of US requirements for weapons and naval-reactor fuel.

In 1998 Presidents Clinton and Yeltsin each also declared excess 50 tons of plutonium. Russia subsequently reduced its commitment to 34 tons when its nuclear weapons establishment learned that the United States had included in its parallel declaration large quantities of plutonium not coming from warheads, including plutonium in production waste and non-weapon-grade plutonium in unreprocessed production-reactor fuel.

The analysts who devised the HEU deal have thus far not been able to sell a scheme to get the market to finance the disposal of US and Russian weapons plutonium. The problem is that, unlike the case for weapons uranium, it costs more to fabricate plutonium into fuel than it would cost to buy an equivalent amount of prefabricated low-enriched uranium fuel. The United States therefore plans to spend billions of dollars to subsidize the disposition of its own excess plutonium and has been trying to persuade the other G7 countries to spend a similar amount to help Russia carry through its own preferred plutonium-disposition option of recycling into power-reactor fuel.

Once Russia's excess weapons plutonium is fabricated into fuel, it will have the same geometry and the same energy value per kilogram as fuel made with low-enriched uranium. However, it will be more demanding on reactor control systems. Western light-water reactors (LWRs) have enough margin in these control systems that they can use about 30 per cent 'mixed-oxide' plutonium-uranium fuel without modification. The control systems of Russia's LWRs, however, apparently have almost no margin. As a result, the United States has preliminary plans to pay at least $100 million each for significant modifications to Russia's four newest LWRs, and Japan plans to help modify Russia's demonstration breeder reactor so that it can accommodate plutonium fuel. Even with these modifications, however, Russia's capacity to irradiate plutonium will only be 1–2 tons a year – about the same as the current plutonium separation rate of the Chelyabinsk-65 commercial reprocessing plant.

More reactors – probably in other countries – will be required to burn Russia's excess plutonium at a higher rate. But few countries have expressed interest in even free plutonium fuel. Ukraine has more Soviet-style light-water reactor capacity than Russia. But those reactors too would have to be converted before they could take plutonium fuel. Utilities in other countries have expressed an interest in Russian mixed-oxide (MOX) fuel for reasons of their own. Canada's nuclear utility, Ontario Hydro, has expressed an interest *if* the associated G7 subsidy were large enough to make the operating costs of its reactors economically competitive with low-cost hydroelectric and natural-gas-fired power plants. Some German utilities would be willing to do so *if* there could be an alternative way to get rid of their own excess plutonium directly with spent fuel, *if* the German Greens would allow the continued operation of their nuclear plants, and *if* the spent MOX fuel could be exported back to Russia.

Alternatively, Russia might be persuaded to dispose of the plutonium directly with high-level waste as the United States plans to do with nine tons of impure plutonium. This would require much less processing and transport and would therefore reduce the risk of theft. Russia's nuclear establishment would probably insist on being paid for the 'energy value' of the plutonium, even though its economic value is negative. If Russia were paid as much per kilogram of plutonium as it is being paid per energy-equivalent kilogram of weapon uranium, the price would be about $800 million. Nevertheless, it might be worth it because the total disposal cost could still be less than subsidizing the fabrication of the plutonium into reactor fuel and paying for the conversion of reactors to use this fuel. The time scale for disposal could also be much shorter.

ENDING THE PRODUCTION OF FISSILE MATERIAL

The United States, Russia,[9] Great Britain and France have announced that they have ended their production of HEU and plutonium for weapons. China has stated privately that it has not been producing HEU or plutonium for weapons since 1987 and 1991 respectively, but it is keeping its options for the future open – especially given US plans for national missile defense. India, Israel and Pakistan are each producing plutonium for weapons on a scale of tens of kilograms per year and Pakistan may be producing more than 100 kilograms of weapon-grade uranium per year.

The overt production of more plutonium and HEU for weapons would end if we could negotiate a Fissile Material Cutoff Treaty. However, negotiations have not even begun in Geneva despite a 1983 UN General Assembly consensus vote to do so. A major problem has been the desire by many non-nuclear-weapon states to use US interest in putting a ceiling on the Indian and Pakistani stockpiles as a lever to force the United States and Russia to commit to the ultimate goal of total nuclear disarmament and, in the interim, to move more aggressively to reduce their nuclear weapons stockpiles.

By and large, the US and Russian nuclear establishments fundamentally oppose the goal of ultimate nuclear disarmament. However, there does seem to be widespread agreement that the huge stockpiles of nuclear weapons accumulated during the Cold War – more than 30,000 warheads at their peaks – are vastly in excess of any post-Cold War needs. In 1991, Presidents Bush and Gorbachev committed their countries to the elimination of most tactical nuclear warheads – about 10,000 in the case of the United States and perhaps twice as many in the case of the Soviet Union. If START II ever comes into force, the United States and Russia would reduce their *deployed* strategic warheads to fewer than 3,500 each; numbers as low as 1,500 have been discussed as the target for START III reductions. If each country kept 1,000 tactical nuclear warheads and bombs, the total stockpiles, including tactical and deployed strategic warheads, would be on the order of one-tenth of their peak Cold War levels.

FURTHER DOWNSIZING OF THE COLD WAR STOCKPILES

Thus far, however, less than half of the fissile material in the Cold War nuclear weapon stockpiles has been declared excess. In the case of the United States, this is owing to:

- stockpiling weapon-grade uranium for future use as fuel by nuclear submarines;
- the planned storage of warheads downloaded in the implementation of START II as an 'upload hedge' that would allow US forces to return to START I warhead deployment levels;
- the storage of additional downloaded modern warheads as back-up in case a reliability or safety problem should require taking an important warhead type out of deployment;
- the storage of thousands of reserve plutonium pits and HEU-containing 'secondaries' in case there should be a requirement to assemble additional or replacement warheads.[10]

In short, the US is wearing extra fissile material belts and suspenders 'just in case'. A similar logic may prevail in Russia's nuclear establishment.

Both nuclear establishments also keep their warhead stockpiles as large as they do because of their concerns about the size of the other's stockpile. Although either country could destroy the other with 100 warheads, nuclear war-fighting scenarios involve the use of thousands: there are concerns about losses due to first strikes and there is also the real concern about unequal stockpiles leading to a loss of bargaining leverage in reductions on the part of the country whose stockpile is smaller. This may already be a problem for the United States in the case of plutonium because Russia has thus far only been willing to make equal reductions, although its total stockpile of weapons plutonium is believed to be larger and it has, in addition, a large stockpile of civilian but weapons-usable plutonium. However, Russia has been willing to declare excess much larger quantities of weapons uranium than the United States, and Russia must take into account the stockpiles of fissile material held by US allies as well as China.

A major obstacle to further reductions is, however, uncertainties as to the sizes of the existing fissile material stockpiles. These uncertainties are larger than the quantities in the strategic warheads which would remain deployed under START III.

Dealing with the uncertainties

The United States and Russia might therefore be able to reduce their stockpiles of fissile material further and increase their credibility with the non-nuclear-weapon states if they declared their stockpiles of plutonium and HEU and started reducing them in proportion to their reductions of deployed strategic weapons.

In January 1994, the United States proposed to Russia comprehensive declarations of warhead and fissile material stockpiles. The exchange of such classified information would have required an Agreement of Cooperation on the protection of exchanged classified information. The Clinton administration was willing to sign such an Agreement of Cooperation but Russia was not able to overcome the paranoia of its security services and Duma.

It is not clear that information on total fissile material stocks needs to be classified, however. Indeed, also in 1994, the US Department of Energy declassified the total amounts of weapons-grade and non-weapons-grade plutonium in the US stockpile, including in weapons,[11] and promised to do the same for the US HEU stockpile. Unfortunately, Russia shows no sign of being able to follow suit.

Nuclear archeology

If we were able to get these declarations, we could start to negotiate on how to verify them. I call this 'nuclear archeology'. Steve Fetter of the University of Maryland has shown that the activation levels in the graphite core structures of the Russian and the US Hanford plutonium-production reactors could be used to determine quite accurately how much plutonium each reactor produced.[12]

If fairly complete paper records are still available, there would also be many consistency checks that a nuclear auditor could make – for example, between the records of electricity use at enrichment plants and records of their production of enriched uranium, or between the records of senders and receivers for shipments between facilities. This data could be correlated with the intelligence information that has been collected over the years, such as measurements of the residual contribution to the buildup of the fission-product gas Kr-85 in the atmosphere due to Russia's plutonium production[13] and satellite images showing the periods of operation at different nuclear sites. In the USA, tens of thousands of standard cylinders of depleted uranium hexafluoride have been stored outdoors at our uranium enrichment plants. The accumulation of these cylinders with time could be a useful supplement to our published record of enrichment work.

How good could this verification be? The one public data point we have is that, because of measurement errors and losses, the difference between US records of plutonium production and current stocks and disposition differ by about 3 per cent.[14] Another country carrying its own independent checks of our records would probably have additional questions. So I would guess uncertainties of 5–10 per cent. The longer we have to wait, the more physical artifacts and paper records that could help contain these uncertainties will be lost.

What do these uncertainties mean for how low a level the United States and Russia could reduce to? That depends upon how much difference you believe it would make if the US kept only enough fissile material for 5,000 warheads when, because of residual uncertainties, we could not be sure that Russia had not kept enough for 10,000. Would that uncertainty deter us from going down from a level where today we have kept enough fissile material for 15,000 warheads and Russia enough for, say, 30,000?

One strategy for dealing with this situation would be to give whistle-blowers time to surface with information about hidden stockpiles. In the meantime, the United States and Russia could put the fissile material that they do not currently need but are not quite ready to discard in bilaterally monitored storage on their home territories.

CONCLUSION

The collapse of the Soviet Union has created both problems and opportunities for nuclear arms control and nonproliferation. One opportunity created by Gorbachev's 'glasnost' is that Russia is willing, in principle, to accept on-site inspections. This means that the whole panoply of techniques that have been developed by the IAEA to verify that non-nuclear-weapon states are not diverting fissile material to weapons can now be applied to nuclear arms reductions. We can negotiate verifiable agreements to:

- exchange information on the stockpiles of nuclear warheads and the total quantities of fissile materials that they contain and negotiate reductions in these stockpiles;
- reduce the huge stockpiles of excess military and civilian fissile material; and
- end the production of further weapons-usable fissile material.

Such agreements will not be easy to achieve. Even if Russia had another Gorbachev, who embraced nuclear disarmament as an end in itself, his power to force Russia's nuclear bureaucracy to act in conformance with his vision would be much diminished. Multilateral negotiations would be complicated by the commercial interests in spent-fuel reprocessing in Britain and France and the volatile situations with regard to proliferation in the Middle East and south Asia. And, the further reductions proceeded, the greater the inevitable uncertainties in verification would loom. More buffers would be required in the forms of monitored excess but-not-yet-eliminated national stockpiles and stretched-out time scales to allow confidence in the process to grow.

US leadership will be required to move this process forward. The United States has thus far nibbled at this agenda but has been unable to mobilize the sustained high-level engagement required actually to achieve results. What is needed is an administration with both the understanding and the commitment at the presidential level to a comprehensive strategy to contain and shrink the world's huge stockpiles of fissile materials.

NOTES

1 Frank von Hippel is Professor of Public and International Affairs at Princeton University.
2 According to the IAEA, it would require about 8 kilograms of plutonium or 25 kilograms of weapons-grade uranium (90 per cent U^{235}), including processing losses, to make a first-generation (Nagasaki-type) nuclear weapon. Advanced designs would require somewhat less. Among possible alternative fissile materials are U^{233}, which is produced by neutron capture in natural thorium^{232} and neptunium^{237} which is produced by two successive neutron captures starting with uranium^{235}.
3 It should be international policy not to pursue the development of pure fusion explosives. In the near term, only the US has the technical and economic

wherewithal to do so. See also Suzanne Jones, Ray Kidder and Frank von Hippel, 'The Question of Pure Fusion Explosions Under the CTBT', *Physics Today* (September 1998), 57–9.

4 'Report on the International Control of Atomic Energy', prepared by the Secretary of State's Committee on Atomic Energy, US Government Printing Office, Washington, DC, 16 March 1946. On line at http://www.learnworld.com/ZNW/LWText.Acheson-Lillienthal.html

5 One metric ton is 1,000 kilograms.

6 The current price of natural uranium is about $25 per kilogram. It is unlikely to exceed $50 per kilogram for some decades. The price would have to exceed $500 per kilogram before the value of the recovered plutonium and uranium would make reprocessing economic. (This particular number for the break-even cost of reprocessing is obtained by assuming that the cost of disposal of the radioactive waste from reprocessing and plutonium recycling will not be less than that for direct disposal of spent fuel.) It is expected that uranium could be recovered from ocean water at less than half of this price.

7 *Nonproliferation and Arms Control Assessment of Weapons-Usable Fissile Material Storage and Excess Plutonium Disposition Alternatives* (US Department of Energy, 1997), 38–9. The classified reference for this conclusion is W. G. Sutcliffe and T. J. Trapp (eds), *Extraction and Utility of Reactor-Grade Plutonium for Weapons* (Lawrence Livermore National Laboratory, UCRL-LR-115542, 1995 (S/RD)). See also J. Carson Mark, 'Explosive Properties of Reactor-Grade Plutonium', *Science and Global Security*, 4 (1993), 111–28.

8 Virtually all the energy in the radiation from plutonium is carried by heavy alpha particles which are so short-range that they cannot even penetrate the dead outer layer of human skin. Plutonium can therefore be easily handled if in sealed containers which protect against its inhalation.

9 Russia is still producing and separating about 1.5 tons of weapons-grade plutonium per year using three out of its original 13 plutonium production reactors, which continue operating because they produce byproduct heat and electricity. The United States is working with Russia to convert these reactors to a fuel that does not require reprocessing. Russia has pledged that the plutonium that is produced in the interim will be subject to US monitoring to verify that it is not being used to make weapons.

10 According to unclassified estimates, in addition to its 3,500 START II deployed warheads and about 1,000 tactical warheads, the US plans to keep 500 spares, 2,500 'hedge' warheads that could be redeployed on strategic missiles and bombers, 3,000 'inactive-reserve' warheads and 5,000 reserve pits and secondaries which could be reassembled into warheads. Robert S. Norris and William M. Arkin, 'U.S. Nuclear Stockpile', *Bulletin of the Atomic Scientists* (July/August 1998), 69–71.

11 *Plutonium: The First 50 Years* (United States Department of Energy, DOE/DP-0137, February 1996).

12 Steve Fetter, 'Nuclear Archeology: Verifying Declarations of Fissile-material Production', *Science & Global Security*, 3 (1993), 237.

13 'Stopping the Production of Fissile Material for Weapons' (with D. A. Albright and B. G. Levi), *Scientific American* (September 1985), 40–7

14 *Plutonium: The First 50 Years* (US Department of Energy, DOE/DP-0137, 1996).

Part III

Is There Cause for Optimism?

8

Why a Rich, Democratic and (Perhaps) Peaceful Era Is Ahead

HENRY S. ROWEN[1]

PROLOGUE

My interest in the developing countries, and some consequences of their catching up with the advanced ones, has several origins. One is experiences in government, at the RAND Corporation and at Stanford's Graduate School of Business, experiences that brought me into contact with people from many developing countries – or at least data and analyses about them. One of these was the Soviet Union, although it was not then widely regarded as underdeveloped. In the mid-1980s, Charles Wolf and I edited two books on the economy of the Soviet Union whose principal thesis was the advanced state of decay of that system. It was, to be sure, a pathological case but pathologies can be instructive.

The immediate cause of my work on the developing countries was Professor Samuel Huntington's book *The Clash of Civilizations and the Remaking of World Order*. My immediate reaction was that most people in the future would be too rich to be engaged in 'clashing'. That was not an especially well informed opinion but it led to my investigating the current state of development economics and some of the known consequences of development. A profoundly important one of these is the connection, evidently a causal one, between economic and political development. If one accepts, as this chapter argues, that much of the world will become economically developed, then it seems to follow that it will become widely democratized as well. So I argued in 'The Tide Beneath the "Third Wave"' (Rowen, 1995). Of particular interest, because of its large and growing importance, is the political future of China; in 'The Short March' (Rowen, 1996) I proposed that it is on a path to become a democracy in the not terribly distant future.

The material that follows could be deficient in at least two ways:

one is that I undoubtedly have made errors both of omission and commission regarding the literature on development and only hope that they do not invalidate the central arguments. The other is that, despite an effort to anticipate events that could derail the path of progress, I might have missed something fundamental; but if this turns out to be true, so have many other people.

INTRODUCTION

It is easy to be confused about the world's prospects. On the one hand, since the collapse of the Soviet Union and its empire, many millions of people have been freed from economic and political shackles that had long kept them under authoritarian rule and in poverty – or at least far poorer than they should have been. On the other hand, several parts of the world are beset by political turmoil and conflicts, rapid population increases, and falling incomes.

This chapter makes three assertions.[2] The first is that much of the current turmoil is masking a process that promises to reduce greatly the incidence of poverty in the world over the next several decades. The second assertion is that the world will become more democratic. Not all democracies are rich, as India clearly demonstrates, but the correlation between income and freedom is high, not only worldwide but within almost all regions, and the main direction of causation runs from growing wealth to growing freedoms. The third claim is that, because democracies tend not to war with each other, the incidence of wars in time should recede as the proportion of democratic countries rises, assuming that other things are equal (admittedly a large assumption). A sobering qualification to this third proposition is that, inevitably, weapons capable of causing great destruction will become more widely accessible.

This (qualifiedly) bright prospect for the world might seem implausible after nearly a century of conflict and death on a staggering scale. Even now, several developing countries are suffering from the effects of financial crises (Russia, Indonesia); ethnic and religious conflicts abound (Balkans, Caucasus); populations are growing rapidly (Africa and the Arab world); economically destructive economic policies persist (Nigeria, among many others); and several states have recently acquired or are trying to get weapons of mass destruction (India, Pakistan, Iraq, North Korea). The decline of the old Cold War order, imperfect as it was, has exposed underlying hostilities, and it would be an error to believe that utopia will arrive any time soon. The only solution is development, but various social disabilities pose formidable obstacles to this end.

THE SHIFT IN THE IDEOLOGICAL WIND

Nonetheless, a change of monumental importance has occurred: the era in which the spirit of collectivism – the ideology in which the state dominates the individual – is over. A fitting analogy is the imagined fate of a fleet of sailing ships. Earlier, the prevailing ideological wind was blowing towards statism. On many ships a captain was in control and steered the ship downwind. So behaved Mao, Nasser, Tito and many others. In due course, some of these ships ran aground or were taken over by other skippers who changed their course. On others there were struggles over control of the tiller, the sails and the cargo (with much of it being looted). The course of these ships was naturally erratic, but the prevailing wind kept pushing them towards statism. Then the wind direction changed. Some skippers are now sailing downwind towards free markets while the struggle amongst the crews persists in other ships. The prevailing ideological wind now pushes them toward freedom.

1. THE PROSPECTS FOR CATCHING UP: THE UNPRECEDENTED INCREASE IN GROWTH RATES

With all the troubles in the developing world, it is easy to overlook that the condition of the average person in developing countries has improved at an unprecedented rate in this century, especially in the years since the Second World War (Maddison, 1994). Two hundred years ago, the modern economic growth that began in Britain was soon followed in parts of Europe and countries of British settlement. The fringes of Europe – Sweden, Russia, Ireland, Italy and Spain – lagged, however. Meiji Japan took off in the mid-nineteenth century and then, after a long lag, the Soviet Union began rapid industrialization in the early 1930s. There was another gap until after the Second World War, when the four Asian 'tigers' (South Korea, Taiwan, Hong Kong and Singapore) began to develop quickly, followed by Thailand, Malaysia, Indonesia and – most significantly – China. Chile is the first Latin American country to experience a rapid growth that promises to continue.

Before the Second World War, however, much of the world did not experience similar growth. From the early nineteenth to the mid-twentieth century, Latin America made the most progress, but it lagged well behind today's advanced countries. According to one estimate, per capita GDP from 1800 to 1913 grew 1.5 times in Mexico, not at all in Brazil, and sixfold in the United States (Haber, 1997).

Colonies did poorly in relation to their metropoles. India's income growth between 1820 and 1913 was 1 per cent less per year than the United Kingdom's, and Indonesia's was 0.6 per cent behind the Netherlands' (Maddison, 1992). Metropole-to-colonial growth disparities persisted in the first half of this century, with British India falling farther behind Britain, Japan growing markedly faster than its colonies in Korea and Taiwan, and the United States outperforming the Philippines. A similar pattern existed between France, Belgium and Portugal and their colonies.

There were also marked changes in the ranking of countries by income. It may be hard to believe today, but as late as 1950, the average income in Maddison's sample of African countries was higher than in his Asian sample. Even in 1989, only a few high-growth east Asian countries had incomes above the Latin American average. Indeed, countries' rankings shifted significantly over the years. For example, in 1890, Argentina was twelfth in the world in income, and its growth of real GDP from 1880 to 1914 was probably the highest in the world (Davis and Gallman, 1996); later, it plunged down the list (declining in absolute income between 1979 and 1989). As Vitorio Corbo puts it, Argentina went from the First World to the Third World without pausing in between.

THE REQUISITES OF DEVELOPMENT

One should not simply equate an increase in money income with development. For example, oil-rich sheikdoms provide many material things to their peoples, but they are deficient in creating wealth. And, while some countries that have expanded the flow of inputs into the economy with little growth in productivity achieved something substantial, they cannot maintain that process forever; the Soviet Union was such a case.

Countries can become developed only if three conditions are met:

- a high level of capital – physical and human – exists per worker;
- modern technologies – in a broad sense – are used; and
- competitive markets and other development-positive institutions are in place.

Physical capital

The advanced industrial countries save about 20 per cent of their national product – about the same share as mid-level developing countries. The highest savers have been the east Asians, who save and invest about 35 per cent. The much poorer and slow-growing south Asian and sub-Saharan African countries save only 10 per cent yet invest 17 per cent – an inflated rate made possible by foreign, largely government-to-government, capital inflows.

Why do savings and investments vary so widely?

- Savings behavior is not necessarily determined by autonomous decisions to save.
- Causation can in fact run the other way: anything that increases output – say, acquiring better technology – increases the incentive to invest and thus to save. There is evidence that 'growth induces subsequent capital formation more than capital formation induces subsequent growth' (Blomstrom *et al.*, 1993).
- Return on capital is affected by such government policies as taxes on capital, regulations, price controls, nationalization and unexpected inflation. A top-down allocation of capital by governments, versus the bottom-up process of the market, is predictably inefficient. In addition, a good prospect for peace, the protection of property rights, and stable economic rules encourage capital formation.
- Poorly performing countries often run large fiscal deficits, a form of national dissaving. For example, deficits have often been large in Latin America.
- The state of those financial organizations (banks, postal systems) that collect savings and distribute them to enterprises seems to affect savings rates. Governments can encourage private savings through tax-free postal savings accounts, funded social security systems, and limits on credit. Singapore's uniquely high savings rate of 39 per cent of its GDP, for example, is partly attributable to its forced savings system, the Provident Fund.
- Countries vary in the efficiency with which they use capital. Lau found that even high-performing east Asian countries use around three times as much capital per unit of output as the advanced industrial countries (Lau, 1995).

Human capital

Human capital is developed through formal schooling, learning at home, and work experience. In 1960, the average level of schooling among populations over 25 years of age in western Europe and its offshoots then averaged 6.5 years; in developing countries, the average ranged from 1 to 5 years. It now averages about 10 years in developed countries and is growing slowly. Schooling attainment in the developing world still varies widely: from about 3.5 years in the most backward region, Africa, to about 9 years in the most advanced, central and eastern Europe and the high-performing countries of northeast Asia. The Confucian (Chinese-cultural-influence-sphere) nations – including their most highly educated member, Japan – increased the most, by nearly 3 years; the eastern European group increased by 2.5 years, and the sub-Saharan African nations by the smallest amount, 1.5 years. With an increase of 2.2 years, the schooling level of Western nations had grown about as much as that of developing nations, but from a much higher level.

The high levels of school enrollment in east Asia in 1960 and low ones in sub-Saharan Africa (adjusted for their incomes then) help to explain their growth experiences later on (Baumol *et al.*, 1989, Barro and Lee, 1993, Lau *et al.*, 1993). Accordingly, as output increases, some part of it is spent on more schooling, and so on. Human capital can, so to speak, contribute to building itself. But, where there is a poor use of educated talent, there is also a drain of brains. Indian engineers thus find their way to Thailand and Malaysia, and graduates of the Indian institutes of technology come to Silicon Valley.

Technologies

The main task in applying technologies is acquiring them from the advanced countries where they are created and adapting them to local conditions. This task is more than a matter of simply reverse-engineering foreign products or buying licenses; it includes building a broad set of human and organizational capacities. (Indeed, the word 'technologies' in this context includes better ways of organizing work.) Trading with advanced countries and encouraging foreign investment are effective routes to this end. The east Asian Newly Industrialized Countries (NICs) built such competencies through education and involvement with the outside world; elsewhere, on the other hand, education was often neglected and policies autarkic which meant, among other adverse consequences, denying themselves use of modern technology.

Competition

Having institutions that encourage the mobilization of capital and its efficient use is the third requisite. Competition through markets is the *sine qua non*, and the failure to understand this fact was a cardinal sin of socialist dogma. There are other institutional obstacles: development laggards have unstable rules, weak legal systems and inefficient bureaucracies, and they are systems of privilege for elites.

Slowly, governments began to learn from their mistakes and the few developing world successes. As their consequences became more widely perceived, the major international financial organizations, the World Bank and the International Monetary Fund, began to promote an agenda for change during the 1970s. The resulting liberalizing program, whose principles were opposed to those of the policies listed above, came to be labeled the 'Washington Consensus' after the city where these organizations and the US Treasury are headquartered. Of the seven developing regions (where per capita incomes were less than $8,000 in 1995 international prices) – east Asia, south Asia, Latin America, central Europe, the former Soviet Union, the Middle East/north Africa and sub-Saharan Africa – major liberalizations have been made by the largest countries in all but the last two. The change that affected the most people was China's restoring property rights to farmers, a policy turnaround that directly affected the lives of about 500 million people.

Much attention has rightly been focused on those countries in transition from socialism. Within its four main parts – China, Russia and other Slavic parts of the former Soviet Union, the central European and Baltic states, and the Caucasus and central Asia – the differences are large. China and (north) central Europe/Baltics have achieved great success, Russia is a disaster, and the central Asians have hardly started to move. Russia's experience starkly illustrates the consequences of not getting right the order of liberalization in a country with weak or missing key institutions (although it would have been hard to get the order right given the rapid collapse of the old regime).

Although none of the east Asians get high marks for instituting liberal policies across the board (Hong Kong excepted), they were ahead of the rest of the world. In south Asia, India began to change fundamentally from self-sufficiency to openness after 1991, but it has privatized little and continues to retain rigid labor rules, impose huge subsidies for agriculture, and still maintains many distorting regulations.

Reforms in Latin America since the early 1980s have been substantial but far from complete. Chile pioneered and Argentina and Peru followed; Mexico has been engaged in economic and political liberalizing for over a decade; and Brazil is in the midst of a struggle between a reforming president (ironically, a former *dependentista*) and politicians supporting existing privileges.

In contrast, north Africa and the Middle East, the core of the Islamic world, have made only modest reforms and enjoyed only modest performance gains. After enjoying good growth from the 1950s to the early 1980s, Egypt, for example, then stagnated. Although its macro-economy has improved, the state's heavy hand is relaxing only very slowly through privatizations and deregulation, and there has been only modest opening to the world. Institutions are a large part of the problem; for instance it takes an average of seven years to resolve a commercial dispute (no doubt inspiring alternative dispute-resolution methods). Iran's performance has also been poor during the 1990s. Its two (related) primary economic accomplishments are improving education (including for females) and lowering the birth rate; it remains a highly statist system of privilege with few signs of reform.

Although conditions in sub-Saharan Africa remain dismal (worsened by the ravages of AIDS), there have been modest policy improvements. Most of the region's governments responded to the debt crisis of the early 1980s by placing controls on foreign exchange and imports, resulting in a vicious circle of declining trade balances and ever-increasing controls (World Bank, 1994); still, almost all of the region's nations are letting agricultural prices move closer to world levels, and some have abolished their notorious state marketing boards. About two-thirds have cut taxes on agriculture, a sector that accounts for 35 per cent of the region's output and 70 per cent of employment. Price controls and government monopolies – the sources of important rents for privileged elites – are being reduced. Labor controls on hiring, layoffs and wages, are being relaxed; state monopolies are being eliminated; and more goods can be freely imported. The World Bank found that whereas 25 of the region's countries were rated as imposing 'heavy' interventions in the market during the pre-reform period, only four were in that category by late 1992 – but with few having 'little' intervention. As a result, more than four percentage points in growth separate the countries with the best policies from those with the worst.

In some places, including Russia, Ukraine, Pakistan and Vietnam, reforms are advancing slowly or stalling, but few countries are regressing. Largely left out of the process are the communist remnants and countries ravaged by ethnic disputes, including Cuba, North Korea, Afghanistan, the Caucasus region and parts of central Asia, much of former Yugoslavia, and Sierra Leone, Zaire, Rwanda and Congo in Africa. But these unreformed and disrupted places contain a small minority of the developing world's peoples.

The financial crisis that hit Thailand in July 1997 and spread quickly has raised questions about the liberalizing program's benefits. At one extreme, countries not exposed to the global economy, like North Korea and Cuba, were little affected by the crisis, but they are hardly positive examples for autarky. A better case can be made for being cautious about opening financial sectors to short-term capital flows before institutions for coping with them are in place. Fortunately, the main reaction to the crisis among developing country elites is to blame not the liberal elements of their policies but the illiberal ones – the continued corporate statism in which banks, governments and firms are linked, coupled with poor government oversight of financial institutions. These connections are sometimes called CCN: corruption, cronyism and nepotism. However, norms are changing. According to one investment banker: 'Dealing in government bonds used to be fun because you knew governments would eventually screw up. But increasingly, governments around the world have realized they are the losing party, thus committing themselves to sound monetary and fiscal policies.'[3]

The effects of good policies (and good institutions, as discussed below) have been explored extensively in the 'correlates of growth' program of economics. Although findings differ among investigators, a broad consensus is that countries with macroeconomic stability, openness to the world economy, and investments in elementary and secondary schooling have grown markedly faster than those without them. These findings, which are of the highest importance, imply that although absolute convergence of incomes (catching up) has not generally occurred between advanced and developing countries, convergence conditioned on having adopted such policies did occur. In the past, large differences could be attributed to a category such as 'culture', one with virtually no explanatory power; or analysts would focus on some single variable as the key, grossly simplifying a complex topic. Although there is much more to be learned, the code for development has been partly broken.

LIFE IS UNFAIR

Not everyone has been dealt an equal hand. Physical and social factors that are unfavorable include living in the tropics (disease, plantation-type agriculture), lacking natural harbors (isolation, high transport costs), having high ethnic diversity (domestic conflicts) and having a great deal of oil or other natural resources (low incentives to learn how to make things and operate competently). Two of these factors are addressed here.

The curse of oil

The 1970s spending binge among oil-rich countries was a manifestation of a deeper problem: that abundant natural resources per person, especially oil, is associated with low productivity. Countries with this problem include the Middle East oil-rich countries, Libya, Algeria, Venezuela and Mexico. Such countries have little incentive to manufacture and export, activities that experience rapid increases in productivity. In addition, funds flow in large quantities to governments that need not collect taxes; welfare benefits are spread liberally; and corruption flourishes. This is a formula for creating rentiers, not workers.

The burden of ethnic diversity

Since the Second World War, ethnic conflicts have occurred in 37 developing countries (one-quarter of them). In 1995, about 5 per cent of the world's population lived in countries or regions afflicted by conflicts, mostly in Islamic and sub-Saharan African nations. (The obverse is that most people were spared such turmoil.) Although multi-ethnic countries obviously can succeed, high ethnic diversity seems to be a deterrent to growth (Easterly and Levine, 1997). Here, the record of democracies is better than those of authoritarian governments. India, although far from ideal, works better than one might have expected given its diversity, and one reason is its democratic politics.

Social dissension impedes timely and sound policy decision making, while bad policies can turn possibly manageable differences into refractory ones because resources with which to lubricate friction are scant. In Africa, ethnic fracturing and bad policies are correlated: because power is often insecure when diversity is high, the struggle for control takes precedence (Ake, 1996). Factions controlling different ministries each receive rents, and corruption tends to be unpredictable in a faction-ridden and unstable system. Damage can also be produced when opposing interests engage in a game of 'chicken', as each faction tries to displace onto others the costs of policies that would be beneficial overall (Alesina and Drazen, 1991). When ethnic divisions contribute to bad policies, the resulting poverty exacerbates the differences and leaves everyone in an ethnic-poverty trap.

Extreme Islamism supplies an example. This is not to assert that Islamic religiosity is destructive everywhere, but the violence that has accompanied it in Afghanistan, Algeria, Egypt, Lebanon, Sudan and Iran is certainly bad for business. Again, there is reinforcement: much of the trouble in the Islamic world is exacerbated by poverty that is increasingly perceived as a result of government incompetence and corruption. One Algerian ambassador explained the rise of dissension and terrorism in this light:

> The people have lost faith in their governments. There is a sense of failure, which has opened a gap between the rulers and the ruled.

It has led to a lack of self-confidence in Arab culture, and hostility to foreign influences (Field, 1994).

The most legitimate form of dissent is often extreme religiosity.

It is a mistake to believe that nothing can be done. The place for governments to start is the political equivalent of the Hippocratic oath: 'Above all, do no harm'. Those striving to deal with ethnic conflicts should try to depoliticize them by maintaining the rule of law, favor civil rights protection over minority rights, support secularism over official religions, and promote multilinguisticities. Regional decentralization and federal political structures can be an important part of such a strategy (Brown and Ganguly, 1997).

THE COMING SECOND GENERATION OF REFORMS

Mixed results from efforts to reform policies have revealed more clearly the need to reform institutions. This class of reforms is the 'second generation', focusing on the state: central banks, judiciaries, civil services, labor market institutions, and the delivery of social services (mainly education and health). They include political and administrative decentralization, and the creation of independent, professional and regulatory organizations. This class of reforms is aimed at providing impersonal and clear rules of the game (Edwards).

Such changes have occurred in east Asia. Political institutions (parties, bureaucracies, semi-open electoral procedures, and some rule of law) gradually changed in ways that improved property rights and bolstered stability. These political transitions paralleled or followed market-opening ones. (That still more changes were needed was revealed in the financial crisis of 1997–98, which exposed the dangers of overly close links between governments and banks.)

China has had many institutional changes (Stiglitz, 1998). After restoring some property rights to farmers, it went on to do much more, including adopting a central banking system modeled on that of the United States and Germany and gradually building a federal system with market-enhancing properties, including a two-layer tax plan that separates central government taxes from provincial ones (Montinola *et al.*, 1995). Rather than privatize inefficient state-owned industries, a change bound to be disruptive, it encouraged new enterprises, which resulted in the emergence of a new institution: town-and-village enterprises (TVEs). Being government-owned and successful seems an oxymoron, but the TVEs face competition and have hard budget constraints (no higher level of government rescues them when they lose money). Most important for the long run, the rule of law is slowly being introduced. This means that the writ of the Communist Party is gradually being replaced by rule-based decisions enforced by courts. China has a long way to go in this respect, but the course is set.

The combination of more education, the telecommunications revolution, and the presence of foreign firms is vastly expanding peoples' information and their ability to evaluate events within their homeland and throughout the world. These influences undermine systems of privilege and lead to more critical views of government. Such processes usually happen slowly, but with severe enough crises, like the Soviet Union's, abrupt changes can occur. As today's Russia amply demonstrates, the formidable task of building new institutions is still left.

Neighbors can be influential. Development in east Asia moved (more or less) from the northeast to the southwest. Japan's influence was extended first as a colonizer and later as an investor, ultimately becoming the model for South Korea. Ethnic Chinese from Taiwan and Hong Kong also transmitted ideas and practices throughout southeast Asia. In South America, Chile's success was followed by advances by neighboring Argentina and Peru. Mexico's policies and institutions are being greatly affected by its northern neighbor. And the central Europeans are rapidly adapting their institutions to make themselves eligible for membership in the European Union just as Spain and Portugal had done earlier.

Today (1999), the president of Brazil is trying to harden the budget constraints of states and municipalities by making it illegal for them to run fiscal deficits and to simplify its complex and inefficient tax structure. Meanwhile the Congress is investigating inefficiency and corruption in the judiciary and charges of insider dealings in the banking system. One proposed change would reduce the number of parties and another would introduce voting by districts. The full set of reforms needed will occupy many years, but it is significant that this effort is (finally) underway and is receiving more public support.

In many countries, well-trained professional people – technocrats – are playing larger roles (Williamson, 1994). South Korea, Indonesia, Chile, Mexico, Argentina, and India are among the countries in which economic technocrats have been prominent, including the 'Berkeley Mafia' in Indonesia, the 'Chicago Boys' in Chile, and much of the economic establishment of South Korea and Taiwan. Many of them have gone on to play the 'technopol' role of politician/expert.

A heightened attention to institutional failings is likely to produce a new institutional consensus that will be the core of a second round of reforms. Indeed, its outlines can be discerned from the list of failures above. As the set of what constitutes good institutions becomes better defined and publicized, political support for them will increase. More attention will be focused on tax systems, judiciaries, civil services, corporate governance and the like. And Transparency International annually publishes a ranking of corruption in countries, one which is generating much commentary (Transparency International).

FUTURE REFORMS: LIBERAL ECONOMICS AND BETTER GOVERNANCE

This century's great experiment with collectivism has gone a long way to clarify the proper role of government in development. Governments in almost all developing countries assumed a host of functions: running state-owned industries; owning banks; setting prices; regulating agriculture and industry; operating schools, hospitals, and transportation systems; providing jobs for university graduates; and much more. They were deficient in supplying fiscal stability, predictable legal outcomes, and honest and competent government services; collecting taxes; protecting property rights; and hardening budget constraints for lower government levels. They were also deficient in encouraging and supporting non-government institutions including: schools and universities, clinics, 'watchdog' agencies that monitor government performance, independent 'think tanks', and a free press.

Much of the debate about governments' role in promoting growth has focused on east Asia. Governments there, with the notable exception of Hong Kong, have actively intervened in the marketplace, favoring some industries and firms and disfavoring others. This practice did not distinguish them from governments elsewhere, almost all of which intervened similarly. The following is about all that can be firmly established:

1) almost all developing-country governments have favored some sectors over others with results that have been deemed poor, on average;
2) all successful countries perform their basic functions at least adequately and have adopted key elements of a liberal economy;
3) the high-performing east Asians have done a better job with the basics than others; and
4) the social capabilities of most of the east Asians are high, with improvements in education perhaps being the most notable.

Governments should be doing fewer things and doing them better. In addition to the now-familiar liberalizing program – which is good not only in and of itself but also enables governments to focus their efforts – more attention is needed on the reforms implied by the previous list of institutional failures. If one were to single out just one of many needed, competitive pay for government workers might be it. Singapore's government salaries are explicitly and periodically compared to those of the private sector, resulting in the most senior federal employees making close to US$1 million per year (which is not really comparable at that level, but there are limits even in Singapore). As Prime Minister Goh says, he may be the highest-paid person in government anywhere, but he isn't the most costly.

PROSPECTS TO 2025

Fortune telling is tricky. For example, two prominent forecasts made around 100 years ago were premised on the respective views that technological advances had made war 'suicidal' and that financial interdependence among nations had made war a ruinous proposition. These views were accurate enough on the consequences of war but bad predictions of what would actually happen (Bloch, 1899; Angell, 1914). Later on, almost all predictions from the end of the Second World War were influenced by the dreadful previous two decades and failed to forecast the golden age of growth that lay ahead in the already advanced countries.

Predicting what will happen to any given country is even more hazardous. For example, did any analyst in 1990 foresee that Japan, that paragon of growth, was about to enter a decade of stagnation? Positive surprises can also occur as the performances of Chile and China have illustrated. Any claim that projections are to be believed, then, might be met with understandable skepticism.

Two questions are of interest here. What will happen to absolute growth in incomes, and will the gap between rich and poor countries be narrowed? Two opposing points of view might be adopted. One view holds that the main candidates for development, those with adequate institutions, are already on a good trajectory and will join the club of advanced countries in due course. The other states that those countries not already making reforms and enjoying better results are unlikely to do so for a long time. The former view seems better justified. After all, it was not so long ago that China was caught up in the madness of the Cultural Revolution and India was described as the 'Permit Raj'. Of course, there will be exceptions, and some countries seem fated to remain in turmoil over the next several decades.

With respect to absolute growth, there are good reasons to expect many countries to do better than in the past, since the socialist model will not return soon. In short, countries will pursue the 'liberal economics and better governance' program widely, often in fits and starts and with reverses, because no other viable system exists. This program, contrary to the experience of the past 40 years, should lead to a general (but not universal) narrowing of the gap. What follows are several recent projections of world development for the next few decades. (Recall that average per capita growth from 1960 to 1995 was about 2 per cent per year.)

Angus Maddison

Angus Maddison has estimated world economic growth to 2015 and predicts substantial overall convergence, with per capita growth in the non-advanced capitalist countries averaging 3 per cent per year and the advanced ones averaging 1.4 per cent (Maddison, 1998). Many Asian countries, including China and India, will be relatively fast growers (with China's growth slowing to 4.5 per cent and India's speeding up to 3.5 per cent). Latin America (1.5 per cent), the Middle East (1 per cent) and Africa (1 per cent) continue to do poorly (but for Africa it would be no small accomplishment to have positive numbers).

The Inter-American Development Bank (IDB)

It estimates that reforms made during 1985–95 added about 2 per cent per year to Latin American output and that the region's potential growth with present policies is no better than 2.5 per cent per capita (IDB, 1997). The main obstacles are poor schooling, inadequate rule of law, poor judicial systems and a low quality of public institutions in general; with reforms in these areas, it sees a potential climb to 4 per cent per capita. According to the IDB, Latin America's prospect is 3.5 per cent per capita with more reforms, and 5.5 per cent if there is also a big increase in education. (For example, Brazil's 4 years' less schooling than Argentina and Chile implies a 2–3 per cent growth rate disadvantage.)

The Asian Development Bank (ADB)

For the ADB, Radelet *et al.* (1997) examined growth prospects to 2025 for a set of Asian countries. They assumed that each country would maintain its 1995 policy stance for the next 30 years. While average growth foreseen for these countries is 3.9 per cent per year per person, the four Asian NICs will grow at only 2.8 per cent per year per person (versus 6.6 per cent in 1965–95) because they have lost much of the advantage of backwardness, and demographics now work against them. Indonesia, Malaysia and Thailand do about as well as they have in the past (around 4 per cent) while China, the Philippines and the countries of south Asia improve their 1965–90 standings, largely from better policies. Despite a demographic drag, China (at 6 per cent) continues to do well because of its good policies and continued advantage of backwardness. South Asia, now home to a demographic boost, nearly doubles its per capita growth to 4.4 per cent.

Radelet *et al.* also examined two variations to the predictions: one with policies better than those of 1995 and one with worse. The better ones assumed are those of the four east Asian NICs in that year; their universal adoption would increase Asia's average performance through 2025 to 5 per cent per year, while poorer policies, defined as reduced openness and lower government savings, would produce growth of only 2.6 per cent per person.

Sachs (1998) sees the greatest potentials for change in overall openness and the implementation of a partnership between developing countries and developed ones over the global system of trade, finance and production.

Prospects for the largest developing countries

The Radelet *et al.* (1997) model was applied to 13 of the 15 most populous developing countries for which data were available (omitting Russia and Vietnam).[4] In these countries, live almost three-quarters of the population of all developing countries. Assuming that they maintain their policies of 1995 – and that there are no deep or long-lasting domestic or international shocks – average per capita growth to 2025 for the 13 nations is 3.9 per cent, although with significant variation in performance (see Table 1 and Appendix).

The projected future range is from 2.6 per cent annually in Iran to 5.7 per cent in Indonesia. Several countries' projections reveal a marked improvement over the 1965–95 period: India, Nigeria (from near zero), Pakistan, Bangladesh, Philippines, Turkey and Iran (also from near zero). Only Egypt shows a decline. Viewed in terms of people, China and India dominate. Home to nearly half of the people in the developing world, these two countries' successes would result in a large advance in human welfare. China's prospects for continued growth at over 5 per cent are good while India has not achieved as high a rate and might never do so. Still, its projected growth of 3.5 per cent per year is much better than its previous 1.5 per cent rate; if achieved, Indian incomes will nearly triple between 1995 and 2025.

If the better policies and institutions of the Asian NICs (the 'Improved Policies' in the Appendix) are adopted by these countries, their average growth would increase to 5.9 per cent, whereas if they

Table 1. Per Capita GDP Growth Rates (per cent)

	1965–90 Actual	1995–2025 Projected
China	5.5	5.1
India	1.9	3.3
Indonesia	4.5	5.7
Brazil	3.3	3.5
Russia	1.1	NA
Nigeria	0.1	2.6
Pakistan	2.5	4.6
Bangladesh	0.7	4.1
Mexico	2.8	3.0
Philippines	1.3	5.2
Turkey	2.6	4.3
Thailand	4.4	4.3
Iran	0.1	2.6
Egypt	4.1	3.2
Vietnam	NA	NA
Average	2.5	3.9

backslide on policies (the 'Inward Policies'), it would slow to 2.9 per cent. Of course, any such modeling exercise is simply an organized way of estimating the effects of seemingly significant parameters. Among them, the most certain is a demographic transition.

DEMOGRAPHICS, AGAIN

East Asians will continue to have few young dependents, but the number of older ones will increase greatly, and the support they require will be an increasing burden. According to Bloom and Williamson (1997), dependent care will mean a subtraction of 0.1 to 0.4 percentage points from annual growth, a swing of about 1.5 percentage points from the earlier period (Bloom and Williamson, 1997). They also see falling savings rates contributing to lower growth in east Asia, especially in the NICs, Thailand and Malaysia. In contrast, they forecast increases of 0.8 to 1.4 per cent in south Asia, 0.6 to 1.1 per cent in southeast Asia, and 0.5 to 1.1 per cent in Africa, and little change in South America.

The projections for some of the big 15 countries will be strongly influenced by demographics. Especially favored will be Iran, Bangladesh, Nigeria, Pakistan and Vietnam. Population dynamics will add 1.5 per cent a year to Iran's output and 1.4 per cent to the outputs of Bangladesh and Nigeria. It will contribute about half of estimated added output to 2025 for Iran and Nigeria.

LARGE CHANGES ARE COMING IN THE DISTRIBUTION OF WORLD INCOME

Today, the rich countries produce about 60 per cent of total world output. Their share will fall to about 40 per cent in 2025. The US contribution will fall from about 24 to 16 per cent, and a similar decline is likely for the European Union. Japan will recover from its stagnation of the 1990s, but it has now become a slow-growth country. It might catch up with the leader, but its share of the world output seems likely to decline from today's 10 per cent to around 7 per cent. China looms large in the future with a projected world output share of 15 per cent in 2025, about equal to that of the United States and the EU – compared with today's 8–9 per cent.

Even if some countries, or even some regions, do not participate in the great advance, the world scene will still change dramatically within a few decades if east and south Asia stay on course. That region's six most populous developing nations are home to half of the developing world's 4.5 billion people and produce nearly half of its output. These six nations will likely be producing about one-third of the world output by 2025.

In 1995, about one-third of the world's people lived in countries classified by the World Bank as 'low-income' (those with GDPs below $2,000 per capita in international dollars). This proportion will decline greatly and, to a lesser extent, so will the absolute number of poor people. By 2025, probably well under 10 per cent of the world's people will live in countries at that income level.

WHO MIGHT GET LEFT BEHIND?

There will be a significant overall narrowing of the gap between followers and leaders because leaders will probably grow at under 2 per cent per capita (not shown in the Appendix) and followers will probably grow at 3–4 per cent per capita. The main cause for the leaders' slow advance is that their additions to human capital through education, a major source of past growth, will henceforth be small (Jones, 1997).[5] They will also distribute a larger proportion of the national income from workers to retired people and will very likely spend increasing shares of output on environmental protection (which does not reduce welfare unless costs exceed benefits, as sometimes happens).

The countries most likely to get left behind are those that do not improve their institutions enough. Many of these countries will probably be those that are now lagging, especially in Africa (both parts), the Middle East, central Asia and perhaps the Slavic countries of the former Soviet Union (Russia, Ukraine, Belarus). Regarding this last group, it was expected through the 1990s that the Slavic economies would stop declining and begin to grow, but now there are serious questions about how long their turnaround will take. Their important assets include educated people and experience with manufacturing, but their many institutional deficiencies might take a long time to fix.

WHAT MIGHT GO WRONG?

The latter half of the nineteenth century was marked by a vast expansion of trade, economic convergence on the world's leader, Britain, and no large conflicts. But that golden age ended in 1914, and only after 1945 did the world get back on the track it had left 30 years earlier. In the period since, countries have gone awry after doing well for a decade or more. Brazil and Egypt have been mentioned and a more recent case is Indonesia. That few have been able to sustain good growth is a warning (Easterly *et al.*, 1994). Although one might expect a country's success to heighten interests in the policies that are pro-ducing it, politics are often unstable, rent-seeking forces do not disappear, and the temptation to redistribute gains rather than get more can become overwhelming.

Some recent literature has predicted mostly bad things in the future. One such view is Paul Kennedy's, who states that the 'poorer three-quarters of mankind' is in a 'growing Malthusian trap of popu-lation growth, malnutrition, starvation, resource depletion, unrest, enforced migration, and armed conflict' (Kennedy, 1993). Samuel Huntington also writes that the future will be marked by conflicts among 'civilizations' (Huntington, 1996). And William Greider warns that globalization will bring wrenching calamities (Greider, 1998).

Some of these concerns have been discussed above and dismissed (notably Kennedy's on population). Given the history of the twentieth century, however, one should not dismiss lightly the possibility of further catastrophes. One possibility is another large-scale war (dis-cussed below). Others include regression to trade protection by major countries, deep and long financial crises, widespread social upheavals, and a global environmental disaster. There is no guarantee that such things will not occur. Interests in protection are always present but, if a prolonged world economic slump can be avoided, most likely extreme protectionism can, too. There will be financial panics but, for them to become deep and lasting (unlike the panic of 1997–98), a degree of incompetence on the part of the major central banks is required that seems unlikely. There will be domestic, social, often ethnically based upheavals, but for them to affect the global economy, there would need to be a worldwide movement for which there is no current sign. And, although the accumulating evidence on global climate change is worrying, this phenomenon is unlikely to have a big economic impact by 2025.

In short, there is no good reason to expect that these troubles will prevent the movement of the vast majority of the world's people out of poverty – which, of course, leaves open the possibility of things unknown to us today.

2. SOME CONSEQUENCES FOR POLITICS: THE RISING TIDE OF DEMOCRACY

These economic changes will have enormous political consequences. Arguably the most important of them is the spread and consolidation of democratic forms of government. It has been recognized since Aristotle that well-being and popular governance are associated. In modern terms, when economic activities are largely independent of political control, the coercive power of government is limited. This effective decentralization of power creates checks to it. As peoples' livelihoods become independent of the state – with property, more education, and a level of living beyond that required for subsistence – they have more choices. Moreover, as people acquire such means, they want more influence over the rules with which they live. Such desire and range of action enlarge the domain of political freedoms.

In modern times, there is a close connection between wealth and democracy, defined in terms of both political and civil rights. Of the 43 countries with per capita GDPs over $8,000 in 1997 (omitting, for reasons given above, oil-rich ones), only three were rated less than wholly 'free' (Malaysia, Mexico and Singapore) and those were rated 'partly free' (Freedom House, 1998). There are, of course, poor democracies, including India, Costa Rica, Namibia and Malawi, but prosperity has been almost essential as the basis for stable democracy (Przeworski *et al.*, 1996).[6]

Because several successful east Asian countries began with authoritarian governments, it is often suggested that such systems have an advantage in producing growth. However, the worldwide record from 1960 on shows that these countries did no better economically than democratic ones. Moreover, several nations became politically more pluralistic as they became wealthier – most notably South Korea, Taiwan, Chile, Mexico, Thailand and Turkey. In Chile, a dictatorship allowed itself to be transformed into a democracy. Mexico's PRI presided over the end of its monopoly of power after 70 years of rule. And in Thailand the days of the military taking over the government whenever it sees fit may be over. Of course, it is not immediately clear that an authoritarian government's being succeeded by a democratic one is not just part of a cycle, but these evolutions have taken place over long periods of time and seem unlikely to be reversed.

East Asia experienced a clear pattern of moving away from weak democracies to authoritarian rule and then to pluralism (Pei, 1998). Initially, its institutions could not manage domestic conflicts, which led to the authoritarians taking over, but their rule gradually softened with the emergence of modern political institutions. This transition occurred under a dominant political party, but elections became increasingly open, and legal systems steadily acquired autonomy. This shift increased political stability and improved the security of property. Why this transition occurred more strongly in east Asia than elsewhere is an interesting question that is not pursued here (but see Rowen, 1998).

There is also the possibility that wealth and democracy have common causes. Northern Europe's joint evolution over several centuries of liberal politics and the institutions of capitalism suggests an organic relationship; the data also show that British colonial rule was good for democracy later. This suggests that democracy might be a largely European phenomenon. Nonetheless, a statistical analysis of incomes versus democracy worldwide that minimizes the European – and specifically British – influence still results in a significant correlation between income and democracy. This correlation holds (to various confidence levels) in every region or cultural area but one: the Arab and Iranian core region of Islam. In the non-Arab/Iranian Islamic countries, however, the pattern is similar to the rest of the world's (Rowen, 1995). This finding is relevant to the view advanced by some officials in east Asia that challenges the universality of Western democracy. In fact, east Asia closely corresponds to the worldwide pattern: the richer a region, the more (Western-type) democratic.

Democracies have a bright future. In 1998, only the Philippines among the Big 15 was rated wholly 'free' by Freedom House, while the others were rated 'partly free' (Bangladesh, Brazil, India, Mexico, Pakistan, Russia, Thailand, Turkey) or 'not free' (China, Egypt, Indonesia, Iran, Nigeria, Vietnam). This chapter's projection for 2025 shows that only four will have income levels that predict a 'not free' status (Bangladesh, India, Nigeria, Vietnam – and India is most unlikely to lose its long-standing 'free' status).[7] More broadly, countries with about 85 per cent of today's world population should be at income levels such that they would be rated 'free' or 'partly free' by current Freedom House criteria.

The projection suggests that several large Islamic countries will be at least 'partly free' by 2025, including Turkey, Egypt, Iran and Pakistan (Turkey and Pakistan were so rated in 1998 by Freedom

House). Several smaller ones will also probably be in this category, including Jordan, Tunisia and Morocco. Such development implies a profound change for the region. However, as elsewhere, there is a possibility that ethnic rivalries and institutional obstacles will prove this projection too optimistic. If the less optimistic 'Inward Policies' eventuates, incomes in 2025 will still be low enough that several countries will be at the margin of the stable democracy threshold or clearly below it.

THE SHORT MARCH TO A DEMOCRATIC CHINA

The growing economic weight of China makes its future politics particularly important. When will the Chinese people be at least 'partly free'? The probable answer is before 2020 (Rowen, 1996). If China continues on its trajectory, its per capita GDP will then be around $7,000 (in 1995 dollars), the income level at which 95 per cent of countries are rated at least 'partly free'.[8] Skeptics have to believe that either China is fundamentally different from all other societies (which it might be, but consider the evidence of Taiwan, rated as 'free', and Singapore, rated as 'partly free') or that it will not develop economically.

Institutions emerging within China are consistent with a projection of future political pluralism. One example is its grassroots democracy. In the early 1980s, communes were dissolved, leaving no local governments and leading to village elections; by the early 1990s, 90 per cent of village committees had been elected. Although there have been problems – namely, ragged progress, discrimination against non-Party candidates, and ballot fraud – the principle of competitive elections has been established. Those who oppose Party members are no longer 'enemies of the people'. And, in January 1999, Sichuan province conducted China's first free, albeit unauthorized, township mayoral election. Significantly, the authorities did not reverse its results. (Townships are the lowest level of the official government structure; the wide adoption of township elections would be a signal political event.)

A second and profoundly important development is the struggle for the rule of law. Under communism, law is an instrument of politics, but now many Chinese believe that the government should observe its own rules. Values consistent with Western ideals of equality, justice and legality, which are also ancient Chinese ideals, are expressed widely and some are now embedded in legislation. Officials also recognize that a market economy and foreign investment need stable and fair rules.

The demand for law is owed to several factors, including the weakness of a state with widespread corruption, illegal businesses run by government agencies, and theft of government assets. Most basic of these is the Party's being outside the jurisdiction of the ordinary courts. Other problems include enforcing decisions in civil proceedings, the immunity of military enterprises, and the bribery of judges. In response, the National People's Congress is rewriting criminal laws. Defendants will not be presumed guilty and will have their own lawyers, and the police no longer will be able to hold people without charge. There is a long way to go, and these new laws will often be violated, but their passage is significant. One recent anecdote illustrates this progress. The residents of a district brought a class-action suit against the local authorities in protest against arbitrary and brutal behavior in collecting taxes; for this case to be possible, something important has changed.

The third main development is the liberalization of mass media. This advance first happened in book publishing and then newspapers. Initially, the government had retained tighter control of electronic and film media, but falling demand led to the privatization of its unprofitable operations and the adoption by some government stations of live story coverage, talk shows, call-in programs, 24-hour broadcasting, and celebrity interviews of once-silenced liberal intellectuals. TVs, radios, cassette players, and VCRs became widely owned. By the early 1990s, 80,000 institutions had faxes, there were 16,000 satellite ground stations and, despite legal prohibition, 4.5 million home satellite dishes were operating. Computer ownership is increasing rapidly as is Internet use. Government censors try to control the Internet (and indeed prosecute some people), but it is an impossible task: once a totalitarian regime opts for market reforms, it loses control of information. Today, there is both self- and government-censorship, but, except for some journalists being accused of selling state secrets to Hong Kong newspapers, there have not been criminal proceedings against the press for several years.

Any inference that China's march to democracy will be smooth and peaceful is risky. But, if it is to be the economic success that the Chinese people so fervently desire, it will inevitably become politically pluralistic.

3. SOME INFERENCES FOR CONFLICT: SOME INFERENCES FOR PEACE

The spread of democracies might have one other major consequence: a decline in large-scale wars. There is a long record of claims that commerce promotes peace, yet over the centuries, as republican forms of government replaced monarchies and world trade burgeoned, terrible wars were waged. Those who assert today that military competition is now replaced by economic competition echo these earlier flawed predictions.

While the growth of commerce has been an inadequate indicator of peace, the growth of democracy has been a good one, albeit not in a simple way. Democracies are not inherently peaceable, but they have rarely waged war against each other. (Claims that there have been no such instances depend on debatable definitions both of democracy and of war.) Democracies have had many wars with non-democracies, and a world with both types of societies is not a safe place. Indeed, there is evidence that countries tend to get into conflict as they are democratizing (Mansfield and Snyder, 1996). (Mechanisms that might be responsible for the democratic peace are not addressed here, but see Buena de Mesquita *et al.*, 1999)

The two types of systems, democratic and non-democratic (or 'free' and 'not-so-free'), tend to be concentrated in distinct regions that can be regarded as zones of peace and zones of turmoil (Singer and Wildavsky, 1993).[9] A zone of peace is a region populated by relatively advanced and democratic countries within which international conflicts do not occur. Of these, there are four substantial ones: North America, western Europe, Australasia, and, provisionally, South America.

A zone of turmoil is one in which, with few exceptions, countries are poor (excluding wealth derived from oil), democracies are scarce, politics are unstable and sometimes violent, and international tensions are common. The largest zone of turmoil, one predominantly Islamic in culture, stretches from Morocco to central Asia and south Asia, with an extension into the Balkans. Others are sub-Saharan Africa, much of the former Soviet Union and one centered in China.

North-central Europe is a region currently in transition to becoming an extension of the west European peace zone, but with the caveat that troubles might come to it from Russia if democracy fails to take root there. More tenuous is the case of southeast Asia. It has been on a strong growth track, its politics have gradually become more pluralistic and there has been a decline in regional tensions. But the financial crisis of 1997–98 has destabilized Indonesia, a country comprising so much of the region that, if it stays unsettled, the outlook for peace throughout the area will be uncertain. Trouble might also come to this region from nearby China, and such intervention is more likely if the region is politically divided.

China's future will affect many countries. If it becomes more democratic, odds are it will become a peaceful zone, spreading beneficial effects throughout Asia and beyond; but, if this does not happen, it will be a continuing source of trouble for its neighbors.

Several qualifications surround this prospect of a more peaceful world. One is that the speed with which some nations are becoming rich raises a question about the development of their political institutions. The lag between the rise to economic – and potentially military – power and political evolution varies and might be significant. It would not be surprising if some countries become much richer while still behaving in an atavistic way (China? India?). It has happened before. Germany became a major industrial power and a democracy before Hitler's accession to power, and Japan, after 75 years of strong economic and political development, became highly militaristic (although the people in both Germany and Japan were much poorer and less educated than those in most of today's democracies).[10]

Another major caveat is that, as far as one can see ahead, there will still be many non-democracies that are unstable and prone to violence. Their activities will directly and less directly affect those who live in zones of internal peace. Direct effects of the activities within non-democracies on the zones of peace might be:

- military attacks;
- refugees, people seeking asylum, and other immigrants;
- terrorism of various kinds;
- uncontrolled epidemics;
- 'Chernobyls', and loss of control over nuclear weapons;
- environmental spillovers;
- denial of oil supplies; and
- denial of freedom of the seas.

Less direct effects from such activities might be:

- genocide, 'ethnic cleansing', and other extreme violations of human rights;
- disasters: famines, floods, epidemics;
- damage to the environmental heritage of humanity;
- incentives to help the destitute; and
- desire to support shaky democracies.

No nation is really an island.

Conflicts in the former Yugoslavia illustrate several of these spillovers, which are important given the destruction that has affected millions of people – many of them killed, wounded and raped. They have caused millions of people to flee to nearby countries. The case illustrates two points. The first is utilitarian: some troubles in zones of conflict can spill over and affect those in peace zones. The other point is moral: outrage in Europe and North America against Serbian 'ethnic cleansing' in Kosovo led them to attack Serbia (thereby supplying another illustration that democracies are not necessarily pacifist).

The Yugoslavia case also illustrates the problem that many countries in zones of peace have in being close to zones of turmoil. The Japanese see themselves as affected by what happens in Korea, Taiwan and China, and the Europeans are alert to developments in eastern Europe, the Balkans and north Africa. Even remoteness doesn't assure non-involvement as the list of direct and indirect effects above shows. The United States, which is geographically remote from zones of turmoil, has a legacy of commitments in such areas from the Cold War (for example, the Middle East and Korea) and, arguably, a continued interest in the fate of possibly endangered democracies.

Of the countries in zones of turmoil, China and Russia seem to have the greatest potential to cause serious trouble for those in zones of peace. China's power is rising and others will have to make room for it. By itself this power shift need not cause conflict, but such changes have sometimes inspired hostility (for example, Germany's challenge to Britain and Japan's to the United States led to conflict, while Britain's displacement by the United States was relatively smooth). China has territorial claims, most importantly over Taiwan, and its power to do something about them is growing. Much depends on China's behavior. If it is content within its borders (which, governments agree, includes Taiwan) much will go well in Asia. If it is not, then there will be a response from – and possible conflict with – some combination of Japan, India, Indonesia and Russia (to mention only its largest neighbors); the United States might also be involved as a supporter of Japan and others.

Someday, Russia might attempt to reincorporate at least the Slavic parts of the pre-First World War Russia, especially Ukraine. Any such effort by Moscow would probably not go smoothly and might engage the central and west Europeans in an effort to contain a potentially hostile (and, for this assumption, non-democratic) Russia.

Because the democracies in zones of peace share many values and interests, they tend to cooperate on a wide range of activities, both economic and military. But the overlap in these values and interests is far from complete. During the Cold War, a common threat helped to unite them on many issues, but it remains to be seen how much cooperation there will be in the future, especially in security matters. A simple prediction is that the demand for American support from those close to zones of turmoil will be determined by the scale of the perceived threat, while America's willingness to supply aid will depend not only on the threat, but who is threatened. Undoubtedly, the United

States will continue to be more forthcoming to places it cares most about: Europe, Japan and some other democracies (especially Israel).

There is also the large question of what will happen in the huge zone of turmoil that is Islamic in character. As we have seen, prospects for economic and political development in this region are less promising than those elsewhere. In addition, most of the countries known to be seeking nuclear weapons are in this area. There seem to be two main possibilities. One is that the potential dangers emanating from this region will cause the outside democracies to become more deeply involved out of self-defense; the other is that the area will come to be seen as too hazardous to be involved with. Depending on the case, both responses might eventuate.

POTENTIAL MILITARY POWER WILL BECOME MORE EVENLY DISTRIBUTED

As nations grow economically, their economic potential for war also increases:

1) greater wealth allows them to devote a higher proportion of output to the military sector while leaving at least as many resources for civil purposes; in other words, they can have both more guns and more butter;
2) they can make more weapons domestically, which renders them less susceptible to international controls; and
3) greater wealth is accompanied by higher levels of technology, which heightens their military competencies.

Of course, there is a big difference between an index of total economic output and actual military power. For one thing, the will to create such power must exist, and this can be weak, as illustrated by the strength of pacifist sentiments in Japan and Germany since the Second World War. In addition, if a nation is to compete militarily with advanced countries, it must have a strong scientific and technology base. Countries such as Indonesia, the Philippines and Thailand, whose aggregate output are projected to become substantial, might nonetheless not be strong in this respect.

Considering these conditions, the coming radical change in the distribution of world income implies a considerable shift in the distribution of potential military power. For example, in 1998, three of the top eight nations in total income were western European, while in 2025, five of the top eight are likely to be Asian, and only one – Germany – will be western European. (But if Europe has achieved political unity, it will rival the United States as a great power.) By 2025, Asia might contain four major military powers – China, Japan, India and Russia – and all are likely to be at least 'partly free'.

MASS DESTRUCTION WEAPONS ARE BECOMING EASIER TO GET

Perhaps the single most striking fact about the role of nuclear weapons since their introduction into the world is how apparently marginalized they have become (the recent Indian and Pakistani tests notwith-standing). The rate at which nuclear weapons have been initially tested by nations has declined nearly monotonically since the early 1950s, and only 10–20 per cent of the countries able to make them have done so.

There are several surprising facts about nuclear weapons development:

- any of the industrial countries could have acquired these weapons long ago, but only four have done so (the United States, Great Britain, France and Israel);
- a score or more of economically middle-level countries, including communist or formerly communist ones, have had the capacity to develop nuclear weapons, but only five have done so (Soviet Union, China, South Africa, India and Pakistan);
- nine nations developed these weapons; with South Africa giving them up and Russia inheriting those of the Soviet Union, eight apparently possess nuclear weapons today.[11]

The abstention of most industrial countries has come from their position in zones of peace and the existence of domestic opposition and supportive alliances. For these reasons (in addition to economic and technical inadequacies), all but a few of the middle-income and poorer nations, most of them in zones of turmoil, have not acquired these weapons.

Technical barriers that have been an obstacle to getting nuclear explosives and ballistic missiles (but not chemical or many biological ones, which are mostly low-technology weapons) remain difficult for poor, small countries but it is axiomatic that the ability to accomplish any given technological task becomes easier from the date of its introduction. Formerly exotic materials or processes become less exotic, cheaper and more widely used in commercial products. A nuclear weapons program is now a medium-cost, medium-technology program (May, 1990). The Manhattan Project cost the United States around $20 billion dollars in today's currency, but it has not cost India or Pakistan anywhere as much to achieve their current positions. North Korea's ability to make ballistic missiles and, presumably, nuclear explosives – despite its inability to feed its people – shows how far the barriers for making such weapons have fallen. Because supply constraints are weakening, the demand for such weapons is becoming relatively more important, so it is not surprising that all of the nations thought to be trying to get nuclear weapons in 1999 are in zones of turmoil.

One should not assume that nothing can be done. Supply constraints, even if diminishing, can still have effects, and other methods have been applied (with varying payoffs): economic sanctions (Pakistan and North Korea), economic rewards (Kazakhstan and North Korea) and force (Iraq). And it is worth repeating that some countries in zones of turmoil have voluntarily given up their mass destruction weapons. But the only real solution is for zones of peace to be extended, and many nations are not on paths that will lead to that desired end anytime soon. However, it is encouraging that most of the Big 15 countries are likely to have substantial democratic freedoms by 2025.

THE BEST ROUTE TO STABLE PEACE IS THROUGH DEVELOPMENT

The next several decades will see a competition between forces promoting development, democracy and peace, on the one hand, and retrograde forces of instability and conflict on the other – with practically everyone having a greater capacity, at least potentially, to inflict devastating damage. Therefore, nations in zones of internal peace will be safe only from each other, not from those in zones of instability and conflict. During what can be considered a period of transition, of at least several decades, the United States and other countries in zones of peace will be engaged, not always peacefully, with those in troubled areas. Perhaps, by the end of this period the troubled regions of the world will have greatly shrunk in scale.

Fortunately, many of the things that people in advanced countries should be doing to help themselves are also helpful to others, including maintaining stable, growing, open economies; creating new technologies and selling them widely (even though some inevitably will have military uses); educating talented students from around the world, some of whom will eventually go back bearing much human capital; creating cross-border linkages among firms; and adhering to the growing body of international rules such as those of the WTO.

They can do many other things as well: helping others to build better institutions, including conducting free elections; creating independent universities and judiciaries; and establishing competent and honest civil services.

Skeptics will view much of this argument as too speculative, too optimistic, or as neglectful of factors that don't fit. Nonetheless, the burden of proof should rest on those who maintain that no substantial catching up can occur, that the development–democracy connection will no longer hold in the future, and that democratic peace will not exist in the twenty-first century.

APPENDIX[12]

Annual Per Capita Growth Rates (per cent):
Growth Prospects for 13 Countries, 1995–2025

| | Projections | | |
| | *Per capita growth rate, 1995–2025* | | |
	Baseline Policies	*Improved Policies*	*Inward Policies*
China	5.1	7.9	4.4
India	3.3	6.7	2.7
Indonesia	5.7	6.3	4.1
Brazil	3.5	4.8	1.9
Russia	NA	NA	NA
Nigeria	2.6	5.6	2.0
Pakistan	4.6	8.1	4.0
Bangladesh	4.1	6.7	3.5
Mexico	3.0	3.6	1.4
Philippines	5.2	6.0	3.6
Turkey	4.3	5.5	2.7
Thailand	4.3	4.6	2.7
Iran	2.6	5.3	2.0
Egypt	3.2	6.0	2.6
Vietnam	NA	NA	NA
AVERAGE	3.9	5.9	2.9

The framework, based on Radelet *et al.*'s work for the Asian Development Bank (1997), is an extended version of the neoclassical growth technique as described by Barro (1991), Barro and Lee (1994) and Sachs and Warner (1995). The model estimates the convergence of income dependent on certain conditions. The farther an economy is located from its long run equilibrium level of income, the higher the growth rate of income at some point in time.

To estimate cross-country difference in growth rates, we used the same explanatory variables as Radelet *et al.* They fall into four categories:

1) *Initial conditions*: There are two initial conditions. First, real GDP per worker in 1965 is taken from World Table version 5.6. Second, the human capital stock comprises the average years of secondary schooling for the working-age population at the beginning (1965). These data are originally from Barro and Lee (1996).

2) *Natural resources and geography*: The first variable here is the ratio of primary-product exports to GDP in 1971 (the first year in which data are available for all countries.) The second is access to the sea, namely whether or not a country is landlocked. The third structural variable is a rough measure of the share of the population with relatively easy access to the seas; it is estimated by the ratio of a country's coastline distance to its total land area. The fourth structural variable is its location in the tropics.

3) *Policy variables*: The first policy variable is openness to international trade as constructed by Sachs and Warner (1995). Another is government saving (the difference between current government revenues and current government expenditures rates). The third is a measure of the quality of institution index, originally constructed by Knack and Keefer (1995).

4) *Demographic variables*: This variable incorporates the working-age population (aged 15–64) and the total population in the growth equation. We also include life expectancy at birth to estimate the health of the population.

We updated data for three policy variables: openness, quality of institution, and government saving rates. Unfortunately, we do not have the human capital stock for Egypt and Nigeria, so, for these two, we used the average secondary schooling years of the lowest three countries (India, Bangladesh and Indonesia). The 13 countries for which projection were made for the period 1995–2025 are Egypt, Nigeria, Mexico, Brazil, Bangladesh, China, India, Indonesia, Iran, Pakistan, Philippines, Thailand and Turkey. The 'Baseline' projection assumes that all countries maintain the policies recorded in 1995. The 'Improved' projection assumes that all countries adopt the same average policies as the NICs (Hong Kong, Korea, Singapore, Taiwan). The 'Inward' policies assumes openness changes from 1.0 to 0.5 and central government savings/GDP decline by 5 percentage points.

NOTES

The author would like to thank several former and current assistants for their help: Bruce Donald, George Wilson, Amy Searight, J. J. Lee, John Schafer and Sue Hayashi.

1 Henry S. Rowen is Director of the Asia/Pacific Research Center at Stanford University. He is a Senior Fellow at the Hoover Institution and a Professor of Public Policy and Management Emeritus at the university's Graduate School of Business. From 1989 to 1991, Rowen was the Assistant Secretary of Defense for International Security Affairs in the US Department of Defense. He was also Chairman of the National Intelligence Council from 1981 to 1983, served as President of the RAND Corporation from 1968 to 1972, and was Assistant Director of the US Bureau of the Budget from 1965 to 1966. He recently published an article in *The National Interest* (Fall, 1996) titled 'The Short March: China's Road to Democracy'. Most recently, he was the editor of *Behind East Asian Growth: The Political and Social Foundations of Prosperity*, published by Routledge Press, 1998.

2 The published argument that comes closest to this one is Francis Fukuyama's *The End of History and the Last Man* (Fukuyama). It has been much criticized, often by people who misunderstood him (some of whom seem to have been confused by the title), but its basic elements have not been convincingly refuted.

3 Jan Loeys, managing director at J. P. Morgan, London, quoted in *Financial Times*, 1 March 1999.

4 The results differ with Radelet *et al.* (1997) for some Asian countries. China's projected growth here is 5 per cent rather than 6, and India's is 3.3 per cent rather than 5.5.

5 The opinion is being voiced widely that advances in information technology are finally paying off in markedly high American productivity and growth. This might be so, but four years of data are too few to establish it firmly.

6 Przeworski *et al.* find that dictatorships die at a rate independent of their development level but that the survival of democracies increases strongly with development level. Above $6,000 (in 1985 dollars, equivalent to $8,000 in 1997 dollars) democracies can be expected to live forever.

7 Vietnam, whose future income was not projected, will clearly fall below the $8,000 threshold because it would have to grow annually at 10 per cent per capita from 1999 on to reach it by 2025. In contrast, Russia, whose future income level is also not estimated, would have to grow at no more than about 1.5 per cent per capita to reach $8,000, a rate modest enough to be achieved.

8 In the cited article, I wrote that China would become a democracy by 2015. That estimate was based on annual growth at 5.5 per cent from the World Bank's Purchasing Power Parity (PPP) estimate for 1995 of $2,900 per capita GDP. Lawrence Lau advises me that a better estimate for that year is $2,000. Using that number and the growth rate shown in the Appendix of 5.1 per cent yields $6,900 in 2020.

9 Singer and Wildavsky (1993) label them zones of 'Peace and Democracy' and 'Turmoil and Development'.

10 The income:democracy nexus is about absolute, not relative, incomes. At the end of the Weimar Republic, Germany was relatively well off for that era, but it had a GDP per capita of only $2,000–3,000 in 1995 dollars, a level well below that for which a stable democracy would be expected today.

11 When the Soviet Union disappeared, four states inherited its weapons (Russia, Ukraine, Kazakhstan, Belarus), but all except Russia discarded them.

12 Prepared by H. S. Rowen, J. J. Lee, and John Schafer. Thanks are due to Steven Radelet for help on data. He, of course, has no responsibility for our manipulation of it.

BIBLIOGRAPHY

Ake, Claude, *Democracy and Development in Africa* (Washington, DC: Brookings Institution, 1996).

Alesina, Alberto and Drazen, Allen, 'Why Are Stabilizations Delayed?', *American Economic Review*, LXXXI (1991).

Alesina, Alberto, Ozler, Sule, Roubini, Nouriel and Swagel, Phillip, 'Political Instability and Economic Growth', National Bureau of Economic Research Working Paper 4,173 (September 1992).

Angell, Norman, *The Great Illusion: A Study of the Relation of Military Power to National Advantage* (London: Heinemann, 1914).

Aoki, Masahiko, Murdock, Kevin and Okuno-Fujiwara, Masahiro, 'Beyond the East Asian Miracle: Introducing the Market-Enhancing View', CEPR Publication 442 (Stanford University, October 1995).

Asian Development Bank, *Emerging Asia: Changes and Challenges* (Manila, 1997).

Barro, Robert J., 'Economic Growth in a Cross Section of Countries', *Quarterly Journal of Economics*, 106 (May 1991).

Barro, Robert J. and Lee, Jong-Hwa, 'Losers and Winners in Economic Growth', National Bureau of Economic Research Working Paper 4,341 (April 1993).

Bates, Robert H. and Collier, Paul, 'The Politics and Economics of Policy Reform in Zambia', in Robert H. Bates and Anne Krueger (eds), *Political and Economic Interactions in Economic Policy Reform* (Oxford: Blackwell, 1993).

Baumol, William J., Batey Blackman, Sue Ann and Wolff, Edward N. (eds), *Productivity and American Leadership* (Cambridge, MA: MIT Press, 1989).

Baumol, William J., Nelson, Richard R. and Wolff, Edward N. (eds), *Convergence of Productivity: Cross-national Studies and Historical Evidence* (New York: Oxford University Press, 1994).

Bloch, Jean de, *The Future of War* (Boston, MA: Doubleday & McClure, 1899).

Blomstrom, Magnus, Lipsey, Robert E. and Zejan, Mario, 'Is Fixed Investment the Key to Economic Growth?', National Bureau of Economic Research Working Paper 4,436 (August 1993).

Bloom, David E. and Williamson, Jefferey G., 'Demographic Transitions and Economic Miracles in Emerging Asia', National Bureau of Economic Research Working Paper 6,268 (November 1997).

Brown, Michael E. and Ganguly, Sumit, *Government Policies and Ethnic Relations in Asia and the Pacific* (Cambridge, MA: MIT Press, 1997).

Buena de Mesquita, Bruce, Morrow, James, Siverson, James and Smith, Alastair, 'An Institutional Explanation of the Democratic Peace', Working Paper, Hoover Institution, Stanford University (1999).

Bulmer-Thomas, Victor, *The Economic History of Latin America Since Independence* (Cambridge: Cambridge University Press, 1994).

Davis, Lance E. and Gallman, Robert E., 'International Capital Flows and Economic Development: 1870 to 1914', cited in the *National Bureau of Economic Research Reporter* (Spring 1996).

Easterly, William, King, Robert, Levine, Ross and Rebelo, Sergio, 'Policy, Technology Adoption and Growth', National Bureau of Economic Research Working Paper 4,681 (March 1994).

Easterly, William, Kramer, Michael, Pritchett, Lant and Summers, Lawrence, 'Good Policy or Good Luck? Country Performance and Temporary Shocks', *Journal of Monetary Economics*, 32 (1994).

Easterly, William and Levine, Ross, 'Africa's Growth Tragedy: Policies and Ethnic Divisions', *Quarterly Journal of Economics*, 112, 4 (1997).

Edwards, Sebastian, 'Why Are Savings Rates So Different Across Countries? An International Comparative Analysis', National Bureau of Economic Research Working Paper 5,097 (April 1995).

Edwards, Sebastian, 'The Latin American Economies at the End of the Century', *Jobs and Capital*, The Milken Institute, VII, 1 (Winter 1998).

Engerman, Stanley L. and Sokoloff, Raymond L., 'Factor Endowments, Institutions, and Differential Paths of Growth Among New World Economies', in Stephen Haber (ed.), *How Latin America Fell Behind* (Stanford, CA: Stanford University Press, 1997).

Field, Michael, *Inside the Arab World* (Cambridge, MA: Harvard University Press, 1994).

Freedom House, *The Comparative Survey of Freedom*, 1998.

Fukuyama, Francis, *The End of History and the Last Man* (New York: Free Press, 1992).

Greider, William, *One World, Ready or Not* (New York: Touchstone, 1998).

Haber, Stephen, 'Introduction: Economic Growth and Latin American Economic Historiography', in Stephen Haber (ed.), *How Latin America Fell Behind* (Stanford, CA: Stanford University Press, 1997).

Hansen, Bent, *The Political Economy of Poverty, Equity and Growth* (Oxford: Oxford University Press, 1991).

Huntington, Samuel P., *The Clash of Civilizations and the Remaking of World Order* (New York: Simon & Shuster, 1996).

Inter-American Development Bank (IDB), *Latin America After a Decade of Reforms: Economic and Social Progress* (Washington, DC: Inter-American Development Bank, 1997).

Jones, Charles I., 'The Upcoming Slowdown in US Economic Growth', National Bureau of Economic Research Working Paper 6,284 (November 1997).

Karatnycky, Adrian, 'The 1998 Freedom House Survey', *Journal of Democracy*, 10, 1 (January 1999).

Kennedy, Paul M., *Preparing for the Twenty-First Century* (New York: Random House, 1993).

Knack, Stephen and Keefer, Philip, 'Why Don't Poor Countries Catch Up? A Cross National Test of an Institutional Explanation', University of Maryland Center for Institutional Reform and the Information Center Working Paper 60 (June 1993).

Lau, Lawrence J., 'How the East Grew Rich', prepared for the Salzburg Seminar project on 'The Rise of Industrial Asia and Its Implications for the Developing World' (February 1995).

Lau, Lawrence J., Jamison, Dean T., Liu, Shu-Cheng and Rivkin, Steven, 'Education and Economic Growth: Some Cross-Sectional Evidence from Brazil', *Journal of Development Economics*, 41 (June 1993).

Maddison, Angus, 'Monitoring the World Economy: 1820–1992', Organization for Economic Cooperation and Development (Paris, 1992).

Maddison, Angus, 'Monitoring the World Economy', Organization for Economic Cooperation and Development (Paris, 1994).

Maddison, Angus, 'Chinese Economic Performance in the Long Run', OECD Development Centre (Paris, 1998).

Mankiw, Gregory, Romer, David and Weil, David, 'A Contribution to the Empirics of Economic Growth', *Quarterly Journal of Economics*, 107 (May 1992).

Mansfield, Edward D. and Snyder, Jack, 'The Effect of Democratization on War', *International Security*, 20, 3 (1996).

May, Michael, 'Nuclear Weapons Supply and Demand', *American Scientist* (November–December 1990).

Montinola, G., Qian, Y. and Weingast, B. R., 'Federalism, Chinese-Style: The Political Basis for Economic Success in China', *World Politics*, 48, 1 (1995).

Pei, Minxin, 'Constructing the Political Foundations of an Economic Miracle', in Henry Rowen (ed.), *Behind East Asian Growth: The Political and Social Foundations of Prosperity* (London: Routledge, 1998).

Przeworski, Adam, Alvarez, Michael, Cheibub, Jose Antonio and Limongi, Fernando, 'What Makes Democracies Endure?', *Journal of Democracy*, 7, 1 (January 1996).

Radelet, Steven, Sachs, Jeffrey and Lee, Jong-Wha, 'Economic Growth in Asia', Development Discussion Paper 609 (Harvard University, November 1997).

Rodrik, Dani, *Has Globalization Gone Too Far?* (Washington, DC: Institute for International Economics, 1997).

Rowen, Henry S., 'The Tide Beneath the "Third Wave"', *Journal of Democracy*, 6, 1 (January 1995).

Rowen, Henry S., 'The Short March: China's Road to Democracy', *The National Interest* (Fall 1996).

Rowen, Henry S., *Behind East Asian Growth: The Political and Social Foundations of Prosperity* (London: Routledge, 1998).

Sachs, Jeffrey B., 'International Economics: Unlocking the Mysteries of Globalization', *Foreign Policy*, 110 (Spring 1998).

Sachs, Jeffrey B. and Warner, Andrew W., 'Economic Reform and the Process of Global Integration', Brookings Paper on Economic Activity, 1 (Washington, DC, 1995).

Schultz, T. Paul, 'Educational Investments and Returns', in Hollis Chenery and T. N. Srinivasan (eds), *Handbook of Development Economics*, Vol. 1 (Amsterdam: Elsevier Science, 1988).

Singer, Max and Wildavsky, Aaron, *The Real World Order: Zones of Peace, Zones of Turmoil* (Chatham, NJ: Chatham House, 1993).

Stiglitz, Joseph, Address given at Beijing University, July 20, 1998, http://www.worldbank.org/html/extdr/extme/jssp072098.htm

Summers, Robert and Heston, Alan, 'The Penn World Table (Mark 5): An Expanded Set of International Comparisons, 1950–88', *Quarterly Journal of Economics*, 106 (May 1991).

Summers, Lawrence H. and Thomas, Vinod, 'Recent Lessons of Development', *World Bank Research Observer*, 8 (July 1993).

Transparency International: http://www.transparency.de/

Vargas Llosa, Mario, in James Como, 'Hero Storyteller', *National Review*, 47 (April 1995).

Veliz, Claudio, *The New World of the Gothic Fox* (Berkeley, CA: University of California Press, 1994).

Weber, Max, *The Religion of China: Confucianism and Taoism* (New York: Free Press, 1962).

Williamson, John (ed.), *The Political Economy of Policy Reform* (Washington, DC: Institute for International Economics, 1994).

World Bank, *World Development Report 1991* (Washington, DC: World Bank, 1991).

World Bank, *World Development Report 1992* (Washington, DC: World Bank, 1992).

World Bank, *Adjustment in Africa* (Washington, DC: World Bank, 1994).

9

Muslim Exceptionalism: Why the End of History (and of Proliferation) Will Not Be Easy

DANIEL PIPES[1]

INTRODUCTION

Of the states commonly thought to be pursuing biological, chemical or nuclear weapons development, half or more can be found in the Muslim lands stretching from Morocco to Indonesia. Similarly, of those states thought to be developing ballistic missiles but who have yet to declare their possession of nuclear weapons, most are Muslim. In other words, if the proliferation of strategic weapons has a home, it is among Muslims, especially those living in the Middle East.

While there clearly is no direct connection between faith and the proliferation of weapons of mass destruction (WMD), this pattern is more than coincidental. What is it? To start, let us note that in his chapter in this volume, Henry S. Rowen assembles data from around the world to establish a connection between prosperity and freedom: the first usually leads to the second. But he notes one notable exception to this rule of thumb, an exception that consists of one distinct cultural region: the Arab core region of Islam. What causes this exception?[2]

The lack of correlation between wealth and freedom results mainly from the fact that Muslims in the Middle East show special reluctance in adopting Western models. To be sure, they do adopt Western ways, but hesitantly and with a more troubled spirit than other peoples. This reluctance results from many factors, of which two in particular stand out: the fact that, as Muslim peoples gain in income, they tend to move toward an Islamic ideology; and a legacy of troubled relations between Muslims and Christians that goes back to the dawn of Islam. In combination, these two characteristics help understand the Muslim tendency to build arsenals of WMD; they also point to a rather different Western approach to problems in the Middle East than is now the case.

POVERTY AS THE CAUSE OF FUNDAMENTALIST ISLAM?

The conventional view

It has become a virtual article of faith in the Middle East and the West
that poverty has caused the surge in fundamentalist Islam that has so
wracked the Muslim world; and only its relief will cause fundamentalism to subside.

Secularist Muslims routinely make this point. Former prime
minister Tansu Çiller of Turkey says that fundamentalists did so well
in Turkey's March 1994 elections because 'People reacted to the economy'.[3] Süleyman Demirel, the Turkish president, has asserted that 'As
long as there is poverty, inequality, injustice, and repressive political
systems, fundamentalist tendencies will grow in the world'.[4] The chief
of Jordanian Army Intelligence, Tahsin Shardum, ascribed fundamentalism's growth to socio-economic travails: 'Economic development may solve almost all of our problems [in the Middle East].'
Including fundamentalist Islam? 'Yes', he replied. 'The moment a
person is in a good economic position, has a job, and can support his
family, all other problems vanish. The economy is an important
element, an incentive, a sedative.'[5]

Social scientists also ascribe to this view. For example, Galal A. Amin,
an economist at the American University in Cairo, writes that 'There
may be a strong relationship between the growth of incomes that have
the nature of economic rent and the growth of religious fanaticism'.[6]
Hooshang Amirahmadi, an academic of Iranian origins, argues that
'the roots of Islamic radicalism must be looked for outside the religion,
in the real world of cultural despair, economic decline, political oppres-
sion, and spiritual turmoil in which most Muslims find themselves
today'.[7] Leftist Muslims also concur, seeing that the fundamentalist
'resurgence is a sign of pessimism. Because people are desperate, they
are resorting to the supernatural.'[8]

Even fundamentalists themselves accept the connection between
poverty and radical Islam. In the words of a fiery sheikh from Cairo,
'Islam is the religion of bad times'.[9] Mahmud az-Zahar, a *Hamas* leader
in Gaza, says that 'It is enough to see the poverty-stricken outskirts of
Algiers or the refugee camps in Gaza to understand the factors that
nurture the strength of the Islamic Resistance Movement'. 'Behind the
strength of radical Islam', he goes on, 'there lies the dissatisfaction of
millions of people who feel betrayed by the West and by the corrupt
regimes [of the Middle East].'[10]

The poverty argument has also won nearly universal support in
the West. A former Foreign Minister of Germany, Klaus Kinkel, says
that fundamentalist Islam reflects 'the economic, political, and cultural

disappointment' of Muslims.[11] Prime Minister Eddie Fenech of Malta finds that 'Fundamentalism grows at the same pace as economic problems'.[12] Israel's former prime minister Shimon Peres flatly asserts that 'Fundamentalism's basis is poverty'.[13] It is 'a way of protesting against poverty, corruption, ignorance, and discrimination'.[14] Former interior minister Charles Pasqua of France finds that in Algeria fundamentalism (or Islamism) 'has coincided with despair on the part of a large section of the masses, and young people in particular'.[15] Martin Indyk, a ranking American diplomat, says that those wishing to deal with fundamentalist Islam must first solve the economic, social and political problems that constitute its breeding grounds.[16]

Implications

If poverty does cause fundamentalist Islam, then economic growth is the solution. Indeed, in countries as varied as Egypt and Germany, officials argue for a focus on building prosperity and fostering job formation to combat fundamentalism. In Algeria, when the government pleads for Western economic aid, it implicitly threatens that without it, the violent fundamentalists will prevail.

This interpretation has practical results: for example, the government in Tunisia has taken many steps toward a free market but has not privatized, fearful that the swollen ranks of the unemployed would provide fodder for fundamentalist groups. For their part, fundamentalist organizations offer a wide range of welfare benefits to attract followers;[17] and they energetically promote an Islamic economy as the solution to economic ills.

This emphasis on jobs and wealth creation has prompted a basic shift in understanding the Arab–Israeli conflict. For decades, its resolution was thought to lie in finding mutually acceptable borders and winning acceptance of the Jewish state; these days, building Palestinian wealth is seen as the key. For example, the Israeli analyst Meron Benvenisti argues that Islam's 'militant character derived from its being an expression of the deep frustration of the underprivileged … *Hamas*'s rise was directly linked to the worsening economic situation and to the accumulated frustration and degradation of the ongoing occupation.'[18] Serge Schmemann of the *New York Times* wrote (without providing evidence) that Arafat 'knows that eradicating militancy will ultimately depend more on providing a decent living than on using force'.[19]

Accepting this line of thought, Western states have committed billions of dollars in aid to the Palestinian Authority (PA) to stop the spread of fundamentalist Islam. They hope that a jump-start to the Gazan and West Bank economies will give Palestinians a stake in the peace process, and thereby reduce the appeal of *Hamas* and Islamic *Jihad*. The Israelis have followed the same approach; Shimon Peres explains that 'Islamic terror cannot be fought militarily but by eradicating the hunger which spawns it'.[20] So eager is the Israeli government for Yasir Arafat to receive foreign aid, it actually contributes its own funds to the PA. Furthermore, it has vigorously fought efforts by pro-Israel activists in the United States to stop American aid to the PLO unless Arafat fulfills his promises to Israel.

ECONOMICS NOT THE KEY

But is poverty truly the motor force behind fundamentalist Islam? At least one outspoken secularist, Saïd Sadi of Algeria, flatly rejects the thesis that poverty spurs fundamentalism: 'I do not adhere to this view that it is widespread unemployment and poverty which produce terrorism. There are terrorists for the simple reason that fundamentalism has assumed responsibility for human misery. Nature abhors a vacuum.'[21] Indeed, a close review of the record shows little correlation between economic misery and radical Islam. Wealth and economic growth do not predict in which countries fundamentalist Islam will be strong, and in which it will not.

- Wealth does not inoculate against fundamentalist Islam. Although Kuwaitis enjoy a Western-style income, fundamentalists took 40 per cent of the seats in the October 1992 elections and hefty percentages in subsequent votes. The West Bank is far more prosperous than Gaza, yet fundamentalist groups enjoy more popularity there than in Gaza.

- Poverty does not necessarily beget fundamentalist Islam. Bangladesh, the international basket case, has not exactly been a hot bed of virulent fundamentalism, nor have Yemen or Niger. Also, as an American specialist rightly notes, 'economic despair, the oft-cited source of political Islam's power, is familiar to the Middle East'.[22] Why was it not an even stronger force in years past, when the region was poorer than it is today?

- A flourishing economy does not impede radical Islam. Today's fundamentalist movements got going in the 1970s, precisely when oil-exporting states enjoyed riches beyond avarice. That's when Mu'ammar al-Qadhdhafi developed his eccentric version of fundamentalism; when fanatical groups in Saudi Arabia violently seized the Great Mosque of Mecca; and when Ayatollah Khomeini took power in Iran (though, admittedly, growth had slacked off several years before he overthrew the shah in 1979).

In the 1980s, several countries that excelled economically experienced a fundamentalist boom. Turks under Turgut Özal enjoyed nearly a decade of impressive economic growth at the same time that they joined fundamentalist parties in larger numbers. Jordan, Tunisia and Morocco have all done well economically in the 1990s, as have their fundamentalist movements.

• A declining economy does contribute to radicalism in general but not necessarily to fundamentalism. Iranian incomes have gone down by half since the Islamic Republic came to power in 1979: far from increasing support for the regime's fundamentalist ideology, this impoverishment has caused a severe alienation from Islam. Iraqis have experienced an even more precipitous drop in living standards: Abbas Alnasrawi estimates that per capita income has gone down since 1980 by nearly 90 per cent, returning it to where it was in the 1940s.[23] While the country has witnessed an increase in personal piety, fundamentalism has not surged, nor is it the leading expression of anti-regime sentiments.

Similarly, economic factors do not explain on the individual level who will become a fundamentalist Muslim. Conventional wisdom suggests that fundamentalist Islam attracts losers; but all research into this subject shows precisely the opposite.

The Egyptian social scientist Saad Eddin Ibrahim interviewed radical fundamentalists in Egyptian jails and found in a 1980 study that the typical member is 'young (early twenties), of rural or small-town background, from the middle or lower middle class, with high achievement and motivation, upwardly mobile, with science or engineering education, and from a normally cohesive family'. In other words, Ibrahim concluded, these young men were 'significantly above the average in their generation'; they are 'ideal or model young Egyptians'.[24] In a subsequent study, Ibrahim found that out of 34 members of the violent group *At-Takfir w'al-Hijra*, fully 21 had fathers in the civil service, nearly all of them middle-ranking.[25] These are not the children of poverty or despair.

Other researchers confirm these findings. Galal Amin concludes a study on the country's economic troubles by observing 'how rare it is to find examples of religious fanaticism among either the higher or the very lowest social strata of the Egyptian population'.[26] The American journalist Geraldine Brooks tells of her realization when her assistant in Cairo turned fundamentalist: 'I'd assumed that the turn to Islam was the desperate choice of poor people searching for heavenly solace. But Sahar [her assistant] was neither desperate nor poor. She belonged somewhere near the stratosphere of Egypt's meticulously tiered society.'[27]

The same applies in other countries. Fully one-quarter – an astonishing number – of the members in Turkey's fundamentalist organization, called the Virtue Party, are engineers. Indeed, the typical cadre in an Islamist party is an engineer born in the 1950s in a city to parents who had moved from the countryside.[28] Khalid M. Amayreh, a Palestinian journalist, finds that fundamentalist Islam 'is not a product or by-product of poverty'. In fact, 'a substantial majority of Islamists and their supporters come from the middle and upper socio-economic strata'. In the Jordanian parliamentary elections of 1994, for example, the Muslim Brethren did as well in middle-class districts as in poor ones.[29]

Even those fundamentalists who make the ultimate sacrifice and give up their lives fit this pattern of financial ease and advanced education. Fat'hi ash-Shiqaqi, leader of the arch-murderous Islamic *Jihad* until he was assassinated in Malta, remarked that 'Some of the young people who have sacrificed themselves [in terrorist operations] came from well-off families and had successful university careers'.[30] This makes sense, for suicide bombers offer their lives not in protest at financial deprivation, but to change the world.

That fundamentalists come so much more from the richer city than the poorer countryside, Amayreh observes, 'refutes the widely-held assumption that Islamist popularity thrives on economic misery'.[31] Indeed, with his usual pungency, Khomeini explicitly denied that he was motivated by economic issues: 'We did not create a revolution to lower the price of melon.' To be sure, fundamentalists seek economic strength because it is important, for it strengthens Muslims in their battle against the West; but they see wealth as a means, not as an end. Money serves to train cadres and buy weapons, not to enjoy the good life.

If fundamentalists rarely mention prosperity, they talk incessantly about power. In a typical statement, 'Ali Akbar Mohtashemi, the leading Iranian hardliner, predicts that 'The world in the future will have several powerful blocs. The Islamic power will play a decisive role in this ... Ultimately Islam will become the supreme power.'[32] Similarly, Mustafa Mashhur, an Egyptian fundamentalist, declares that the slogan 'God is Great' will reverberate 'until Islam spreads throughout the world'.[33] Abdessalam Yassine, a Moroccan fundamentalist, asserts 'We demand power';[34] and the man standing in his way, the late King Hasan, rightly concluded that, for fundamentalists, Islam is 'the elevator to take power'.[35]

This drive for power reflects the fact that, like fascism and Marxism–Leninism in their heydays, fundamentalist Islam attracts highly competent, motivated and ambitious individuals. These are not the laggards of society, but its leaders. In the experience of Geraldine

Brooks, a much-traveled journalist in the Middle East, fundamentalists are 'the most gifted' of the youth she encountered. Those 'hearing the Islamic call included the students with the most options, not just the desperate cases ... They were the elites of the next decade: the people who would shape their nations' future.'[36] Indeed, they hope to shape those futures for more than a decade.

Observations

Fundamentalist Islam not only appears not to result from poverty, but it may in fact gain in appeal as Muslim societies become wealthier. In a sense, this fits a universal pattern, for the historical record shows that peoples become active politically only when they have reached a fairly decent level of economic welfare. Revolutions take place only when a substantial enough middle class exists.

But there is also a specifically Islamic angle here. Throughout its first millennium, from battles won by the Prophet Muhammad through Ottoman victories in eastern Europe, Islam had been associated with mundane success. Muslims had more wealth and more power than other peoples, and were more literate and healthy. Eventually, worldly welfare came to be associated with Islamic faith. This connection appears still to hold for the twentieth century. For example, the great oil boom of the 1970s appears to have helped fuel a great surge in Islamic sentiments across the Muslim world.

Conversely, Muslims who are poor tend to be more impressed by the West's riches than those who can already dispose of riches and power. Apostasy and alienation from the religion seem to take place more commonly when things are going badly. That was the case in centuries past when Tartars fell under Russian rule and when Sunni Lebanese lost power to the Maronites. It was also the case in 1995 in Iraqi Kurdistan, a region under double embargo and suffering from civil war:

> Trying to live their lives in the midst of fire and gunpowder, Kurdish villagers have reached the point where they are prepared to give up anything to save themselves from hunger and death. From their perspective, changing their religion to get a visa to the West is becoming an increasingly more important option.[37]

Muslims differ from most other peoples (though perhaps not the Chinese) in that a significant percentage of their number believe their civilization superior to that of the West. Fundamentalist Muslims forward this notion most vociferously and explicitly, seeing themselves as 'pioneers of a movement that is an alternative to Western civilization',[38] but this view has many non-fundamentalist supporters as well. As Muslims flourish, then, they are likely to see their own civilization vindicated and so are less likely to turn to the West.

In the end, we are defined by ideas far more than by possessions. By reducing the economic dimension to its proper proportions, and appreciating the cultural dimension for the depth of its importance, we may find that the patterns that render the Middle East so distinct are not all that mysterious.

A LEGACY OF TROUBLED RELATIONS

Mutual hostility has characterized Muslim–Christian relations through the centuries; today, it has a role in explaining the Muslim reluctance to adopt Western-style institutions and practices.

Western hostility

Three historical factors account for a strong European animus toward Muslims. First, Muslims militarily threatened the Christians of Europe for roughly a millennium, AD 700–1700. Through that long era, Muslims conquered much of Christendom, including large portions of Europe, and frightened the rest. Indeed, with just one exception (the Mongols), Muslims launched every serious military threat against Christendom after the tenth century.

Second, during this same period, not only did Islam alone presume to complete the Gospel and supersede it, but substantial numbers of Christians converted to Islam. Alone of the great traditions, Islam offered an alternate and very attractive way of life to Westerners. For many of them, as for the prominent British orientalist Sir William Muir, it was 'the only undisguised and formidable antagonist of Christianity'.[39]

Third, the West historically has worse relations with the Muslim world than with any other major civilization. This pattern began at the very dawn of Islam: in a sermon on Christmas Eve in 634, the patriarch of Jerusalem referred to the Muslims as 'the slime of the godless Saracens [which] threatens slaughter and destruction'.[40] These initial responses set the tone for much of the Christian response that was elaborated in subsequent centuries. The hostility persisted well into the modern era. It is hard nowadays to conjure up the outspoken hostility that intellectual and political leaders showed to Islam. Again, William Muir speaks for many: 'the sword of Mohammad, and the Kor'an, are the most stubborn enemies of Civilisation, Liberty, and Truth which the world has yet known'.[41]

While this animus faded somewhat during the colonial era – a time of unparalleled European confidence – Western fears of Islam resumed as Muslims increasingly reasserted their independence, and with it their ability to challenge the West. The violent rejection of Israel by the Arabs, the Algerian war of independence, Nasser's nationalization of the Suez Canal, the aggressive pricing policies of the Organization of Petroleum Exporting Countries (OPEC), the Arab oil embargo of 1973, and the vitriolic anti-Americanism in Iran's revolution all contributed to the sense that Muslims had resumed their historic role as peril to the West.

Today, such varied phenomena as terrorism, rogue states, unconventional weapons, and protracted warfare worry Westerners. When asked in March 1994, 'Which country today do you think poses the biggest threat to world peace?', 26 per cent of Americans fingered Middle Eastern states, 17 per cent pointed to the ex-Soviet bloc, 16 per cent to East Asia, 1 per cent to western Europe, and 3 per cent to other regions.[42] A December 1994 poll focused on foreign policy issues rather than foreign countries: it found 16 per cent of Americans most worried about Arab–Israeli relations, making this the third most serious after Bosnia (25 per cent) and instability in the former Soviet Union (17 per cent).[43]

Muslim hostility

Things are not much prettier on the other side. Muslims harbored negative feelings of their own toward the Christian West. Christianity has always been Islam's main spiritual rival. For centuries, Crusaders landed in Muslim lands, unpredictable except in their readiness to kill Muslims. Between 1757 and 1919, European imperialists conquered nearly the whole of the Muslim world; only those regions either contested among European powers (Turkey, Iran, Afghanistan) or very remote from them (Arabia, Yemen) escaped the humiliation of colonial rule. With their religious imperative for independence, Muslims found colonialism even more degrading than did other peoples. Faced with Europeans' might, military heroes emerged in all parts of the Muslim world to fend them off. Names such 'Abd al-Qadir in Algeria, 'Umar al Mukhtar in Libya, the Mahdi in Sudan, the 'Mad Mullah' in Somalia, Muhammad 'Urabi in Egypt, Sultan al-Atrash in Syria, Kemal Atatürk in Turkey, and Shamil in the Caucasus remain revered today.

The battles of old still live in on in the minds of many Muslims and translate into anti-Western vituperation. Muslim hostility remains very much alive. A generation ago, leftists led the charge; today fundamentalists do. Take the case of Iran. The leader of the Islamic revolution, 'Ali Hoseyni Khamene'i, considers the United States 'the mother of corruption of the century'.[44] Naturally, Iranian schoolchildren get indoctrinated with this outlook: a 14-year-old Iranian reports learning from her teacher that 'Everything in the West is bad; everyone in America is going to hell when they die'.[45]

This hatred leads some fundamentalist leaders to encourage violence. Muhammad Husayn Fadlallah, the spiritual leader of Lebanon's fundamentalist Muslims declares that 'Just as there is an open war between the Islamists and "Israel", there is also open war between the Islamists and U.S. policy worldwide'.[46] 'Umar 'Abd ar-Rahman, the Egyptian sheikh convicted in New York of seditious conspiracy against the government of the United States, encourages his disciples to 'Hit hard and kill the enemies of God in every spot to rid it of the descendants of apes and pigs fed at the tables of Zionism, communism, and imperialism'.[47] While only a minority in the Muslim world, fundamentalist Muslims have a powerful voice that very much affects the tenor of relations with the West.

Consequences

Mutual antipathy makes it hard for fundamentalist Muslims to accept the Western achievement. They see Europe's power and wealth deriving not from science and technology but from trickery. The West stole both its knowledge and resources from the Muslims. And, that being the case, Muslims clearly should not emulate it. Also, funda-mentalists sometimes raise doubts about Western achievements. For example, they do not fully accept the fact of Western economic success. 'Ali Akbar Mohtashemi, one of Iran's leading hardliners, denounces the Western economic system as one of 'fetid and ailing ... bacteria'.[48] Khamene'i of Iran holds that 'Western culture has, for a long time now, shown its inability to bring prosperity to mankind ... The movement of reawakening Islam is the reason for the dwindling hegemony of the West over the world.'[49]

Such fundamentalist attitudes have an impact on the wider society, inspiring efforts not to emulate the West but to find alternative paths. Accordingly, as Muslim countries become wealthy, they rarely follow a Western path.

US POLICY

This analysis has several implications for American policy. First, do not expect economic growth to lead to improved relations with Muslim states. If poverty is not the driving force behind fundamentalism, then it stands to reason that prosperity will not take care of this problem. In some cases (for example, Algeria), it might help; in others (Saudi

Arabia), it might hurt. Also, while prosperity may reduce mass support for fundamentalism, it will have no effect on the core activists – precisely those individuals most likely to engage in violence. Foreign aid clearly cannot be the outside world's main tool to combat fundamentalism.

Second, do not think Westernization will provide a solution. To the contrary, many of the outstanding fundamentalist leaders are not just familiar with Western ways but expert in them. In particular, a disproportionate number of them have advanced degrees in technology and the sciences.[50] It almost seems that Westernization is a route to hating the West.

Third, acknowledge that the main problem in the Muslim world is cultural and political. Political legitimacy, the torment of despotism, questions of identity, spiritual malaise and sexual frustration drive public life more than does the lack of wealth. If Americans are to understand this complex of problems, they must change their approach. At present, David Wurmser of the Washington Institute for Near East Policy notes that Westerners mostly attribute the Arab world's disillusionment

> to specific material issues (land and wealth). Western observers tend to belittle belief and strict adherence to principle as genuine and dismiss it as a cynical exploitation of the masses by politicians. As such, Western observers see material issues and leaders, not the spiritual state of the Arab world, as the heart of the problem.[51]

This materialistic approach has transformed efforts to end the Arab–Israeli conflict. Israelis used to insist that the solution required Arabs to recognize that the Jewish state is a permanent feature of Middle Eastern life; now they put more stress on increasing Arab prosperity, thinking that this will lead to liberal politics, a decrease in anti-Zionist militancy, and an end to proliferation. But wealth does not smother hatreds and a prosperous enemy may simply be a more capable one.

The same goes for Iran. The European states and Japan fancy that economic relations with the Islamic Republic entrap it and discourage military adventurism. But it is far more likely that Tehran (like Moscow in the era of *détente*) will sacrifice economic interests for political and military benefits. Indeed, the Europeans and Japanese end up being the ones entrapped, for they are the ones who prize trade relations over principle.

Finally, concerning the proliferation of strategic weapons, the US government should be wary of pledges from intensely Islamicized countries. What is it worth that Iraq and Iran have both ratified the

Nuclear Non-proliferation Treaty, that Iran and Pakistan have signed the Chemical Weapons Convention, and Algeria is a member of the International Atomic Energy Agency? All of these states have chemical, biological or nuclear weapons programs and it seems likely that the International Atomic Energy Agency's experience with Iraq, both before and after Desert Storm, is idiosyncratic. Indeed, until major changes take place in Muslim states, until they have come to terms with modernity and with the West, nonproliferation efforts that rely on diplomatic exchanges and promises with them is destined for disappointment.

NOTES

1 Daniel Pipes is director of the Philadelphia-based Middle East Forum.
2 I shall somewhat amend Rowen's category to 'the Muslim world'. While Rowen finds that non-Arabic speaking countries fit the universal pattern of wealth leading to freedom, it's probably more true that all Muslims are to some degree exceptional. In general, the more intensely Islamicized (that is, the more thoroughly immersed in the thinking and the customs of Islam), the less well Muslims fit the otherwise universal rule. Among Middle Eastern Muslims, who are steeped in Islamic ways, wealth leads to freedom less than their more lightly Islamicized coreligionists in Indonesia or Kazakhstan. On the other hand, the language a people speak – Arabic or not – matters far less. If Lebanon or Tunisia wears its Islam more lightly than Iran or Pakistan, it probably fits the pattern more closely.
3 *Wall Street Journal*, 14 April 1994.
4 *Novoye Vremya*, 29 September 1992. Demirel was at that time prime minister.
5 *Yedi'ot Ahronot*, 25 November 1994.
6 Galal A. Amin, *Egypt's Economic Predicament: A Study in the Interaction of External Pressure, Political Folly and Social Tension in Egypt, 1960–1990* (Leiden: E. J. Brill, 1995), 138.
7 Hooshang Amirahmadi, 'Terrorist Nation or Scapegoat?', *Middle East Insight* (September–October 1995), 26.
8 Quoted in Geraldine Brooks, *Nine Parts of Desire: The Hidden World of Islamic Women* (New York: Anchor Books, 1995), 163.
9 Muhammad 'Abd al-Maqsud, quoted in *New Yorker*, 12 April 1993.
10 *L'Unita* (Rome), 28 December 1994.
11 *Der Spiegel*, 2 January 1995.
12 *Il Sole-24 Ore* (Milan), 16 July 1995.
13 *El Mundo* (Madrid), 30 November 1994.
14 *Middle East Quarterly* (March 1995), 78.
15 Europe No. 1 Radio (Paris), 24 October 1994.
16 Comments at an American Enterprise Institute conference, 3 November 1993.
17 Hilal Khashan, 'The Developmental Programs of Islamic Fundamentalist Groups in Lebanon as a Source of Popular Legitimation', *Hamdard Islamicus*, 18 (1995), 51–71, demonstrates the success of these efforts.
18 Meron Benvenisti, *Intimate Enemies: Jews and Arabs in a Shared Land* (Berkeley, CA: University of California Press, 1995), 145–6.
19 Serge Schmemann, 'The Enemy of My Enemy', *New York Times*, 23 August 1995.

20 *Jerusalem Post*, 21 September 1994.
21 *Le Soir* (Brussels), 7 February 1995.
22 Edward G. Shirley, 'Is Iran's Present Algeria's Future?', *Foreign Affairs* (May/June 1995), 40.
23 Abbas Alnasrawi, *The Economy of Iraq: Oil, Wars, Destruction of Development and Prospects, 1950–2010* (Westport, CT: Greenwood Press, 1994), 151.
24 Saad Eddin Ibrahim, 'Anatomy of Egypt's Militant Islamic Groups', *International Journal of Middle East Studies* (December 1980), 440.
25 Saad Eddin Ibrahim, 'Egypt's Islamic Militants', in Nicholas Hopkins and Saad Eddin Ibrahim (eds), *Arab Society, Social Science Perspectives* (Cairo: American University of Beirut Press, 1987).
26 Amin, *Egypt's Economic Predicament*, 136.
27 Brooks, *Nine Parts of Desire*, 7–8.
28 Olivier Roy, *L'Echec de l'Islam Politique* (Paris: Seuil, 1992), 50, 72.
29 Khalid M. Amayreh, 'Reality Behind the Image', *Jerusalem Post*, 24 February 1995.
30 *Die Tageszeitung* (Berlin), 25 July 1995.
31 Amayreh, 'Reality Behind the Image'.
32 *Keyhan Hava'i*, 7 March 1990.
33 *Ash-Sha'b* (Cairo), 11 October 1994.
34 Quoted in François Burgat and William Dowell, *The Islamic Movement in North Africa* (Austin, TX: Center for Middle Eastern Studies, University of Texas, 1993), 21.
35 *New York Times*, 13 March 1995.
36 Brooks, *Nine Parts of Desire*, 164.
37 *Tempo*, 29 March 1995.
38 Oguzhan Asiltürk, secretary-general of the Refah Partisi in Turkey, *Turkish Daily News*, 23 November 1994.
39 William Muir writing in the *Calcutta Review* in 1845, quoted by Norman Daniel, *Islam, Europe and Empire* (Edinburgh: University Press, 1966), 32.
40 Sophronius, 'Weihnachtspredigt des Sophronos', ed. H. Usener, *Rheinisches Museum für Philologie* N. F. 41 (1886): 506–7; cited in Walter Emil Kaegi, Jr, 'Initial Byzantine Reactions to the Arab Conquest', *Church History*, 38 (1969), 2.
41 William Muir, *The Life of Mohammed from Original Sources*, revised edn by T. H. Weir (Edinburgh: John Grant, 1912), 522.
42 'Polls in Four Nations, 1994', unpublished survey conducted by the *New York Times* in the United States and dated 24 March 1994. The survey shows that Britons share American fears of the Middle East, while Germans and Japanese most fear the ex-Soviet bloc.
43 *National Journal*, 14 January 1995, 130.
44 Voice of the Islamic Republic of Iran, 7 June 1995.
45 *New York Times Magazine*, 30 April 1995.
46 Al-'Ahd (Beirut), 10 June 1994.
47 *New York Times*, 8 January 1995.
48 *Salam* (Tehran), 27 July 1994.
49 Voice of the Islamic Republic of Iran, 7 June 1995.
50 On this phenomenon, see Daniel Pipes, 'The Western Mind of Radical Islam', *First Things* (December 1995), 18–23.
51 David Wurmser, 'The Rise and Fall of the Arab World', *Strategic Review* (Summer 1993), 43.

10

Argentine and Brazilian Nonproliferation: A Democratic Peace?[1]

MICHAEL BARLETTA[2]

INTRODUCTION

Does the spread of democratic government favor international peace and security? Contemporary US foreign policy is grounded on a bipartisan consensus that it does. This view enjoys remarkable agreement in the otherwise contentious academic field of international relations, especially since it is difficult to explain given the realist assumptions dominating the literature.[3] An impressive body of research has demonstrated that although democratic states go to war as often as any other type of political regime, they do not wage war against other democracies.[4] This dyadic finding is the core of a research agenda in search of a theory; scholars have yet to explain *why* this is true. We do not understand the causal factors that enable democracies to maintain peace among themselves, yet allow them to remain war-prone in relations with non-democratic states.[5]

A pattern of increasingly cooperative Argentine–Brazilian nuclear relations during the 1985–88 period appears to reflect the auspicious influence of the democratic peace. Following transitions from autocratic military to democratic civilian rule in 1983 and 1985, respectively, Argentina and Brazil engaged in intimate nuclear confidence building measures and sought to integrate their national nuclear industries. Changes in nuclear policies manifested, and helped facilitate the new governments' commitment to attain very close political relations and promote economic integration. Many scholars as well as policy makers credit democratization with bringing about improved relations in nuclear and other policy areas in the 1980s.[6]

But closer examination reveals that this experience is puzzling; it conforms to none of the causal arguments offered to account for the democratic peace. This chapter evaluates the proposition that democratization favored nonproliferation in South America, and is based on extensive field research in both countries. By contrasting the Brazilian and Argentine experiences, and considering evidence bearing on the causal mechanisms by which democracy purportedly favors international peace, it demonstrates that conventional explanations cannot account for these states' behavior. It employs a constructivist approach – which focuses on civilian leaders' shared ideas of how regional tension reduction would aid in the consolidation of democratic governance – to explain change in nuclear affairs and bilateral relations. This chapter recounts the creation of a democratic peace by design: the deliberate evocation of shared expectations of non-violent conflict resolution. A key element in this design was the establishment of a bilateral regime to govern these states' nuclear relations.

WAR AND NUCLEAR COMPETITION

The regional security environment and historical circumstances confronting Argentine and Brazilian policy makers in the early 1980s were hardly auspicious for nuclear cooperation. The Malvinas/Falklands War of 1982 marked the sudden and unexpected rise in the salience of interstate war in the region, and of the military potential of nuclear energy. A nuclear weapons state, determined to retain control over its colonial possession, defeated territorially dissatisfied Argentina in war off the Argentine coast. Britain employed nuclear-powered submarines to inflict the worst blow of the war – the sinking of the *General Belgrano* with the loss of hundreds of sailors and officers of the Argentine Navy – and subsequently bottled up the entire Argentine fleet in port. Rumors circulated in Buenos Aires that Britain had made tacit nuclear threats against Argentina,[7] and it was widely seen as having violated the Treaty of Tlatelolco that seeks to make the Americas a nuclear-weapons-free zone.[8] South American policy makers viewed explicit US support for British re-conquest of the islands as abrogation of the inter-American defensive alliance, voiding US security guarantees to Latin American states against extra-regional incursions. These circumstances evidently presented a nearly inescapable scenario: Argentina was primed to turn its latent nuclear technological capability into military power and go for the bomb.[9]

Brazilian officials were acutely aware of this. Argentina's emerging nuclear capability had been an important motivation for the intensification of Brazilian efforts in nuclear development in the 1970s.[10] Eruption of the South Atlantic war came as a surprise in Brazil, and postwar military analyses of the conflict viewed Argentina's unpredictability, its conventional capabilities, and its immediate postwar rearmament program with concern.[11] Military uprisings in Argentina during the 1986–90 period underscored the uncertainty of civilian rule and the endurance of belligerent nationalist sentiment in Brazil's most powerful neighbor.

Military rule in Brazil through 1985, and continued military influence in national politics and nuclear development throughout the 1980s, ensured that the national security concerns of the Brazilian armed forces were heard at the highest levels of government and reflected in nuclear policy making. The stage was apparently set for the emergence of a nuclear weapons competition in South America.

NUCLEAR REGIME BUILDING: 1985–88

But it did not happen. On the contrary, following transitions to civilian democratic rule, Argentina and Brazil embarked upon a rapid process of nuclear confidence and regime building. This process of regime building was largely driven by Argentine initiatives that were accepted by Brazil. Before recounting this process, some historical perspective is necessary to understand the significance of changes in nuclear behavior in the 1985–88 period.

Brazil and Argentina competed for regional preeminence for two centuries, but their relations always included cooperative dimensions and involved much more emulation than enmity.[12] The phrase 'rivals, not enemies' aptly characterizes their bilateral history.[13] Nuclear development was one such policy area marked by emulation and competition. Brazilian and Argentine scientists and diplomats collaborated informally since the 1950s, and the military governments even reached commercial nuclear accords in 1980.[14] However, in the late 1970s, they also initiated clandestine uranium enrichment programs: the crucial technological step toward gaining the capacity to produce nuclear weapons.[15] Moreover, the development of nuclear energy and technology remained a leading manifestation of these states' competition for regional preeminence.[16] Following transitions to civilian democratic rule, however, Argentina and Brazil embarked upon a rapid process of nuclear regime building.

Indeed, the changes that took place during the period from 1985 to 1988 constituted a metamorphosis. Democratically elected officials transformed nuclear affairs from an expression of regional rivalry to a means to advance regional tension reduction, political solidarity, and economic integration. Within four years, the Alfonsín administration in Argentina and the Sarney administration in Brazil established a full-fledged regime to organize bilateral nuclear relations. Although building on longstanding cooperative practices and the precedent set by the 1980 accords, creation of this regime by the post-transition democratic governments entailed impressive change in the scope, sensitivity, institutionalization and importance of bilateral nuclear cooperation.

The scope of nuclear cooperation expanded from narrow commercial accords to incorporate over a dozen projects within an ambitious program of sectoral integration.[17] These projects included information sharing, research and collaboration on reactor fuel production, nuclear instrumentation, isotopic enrichment, nuclear physics, non-destructive tests of nuclear materials, fast breeder reactor development, safeguard techniques, reporting and mutual aid in the event of a nuclear accident, as well as reciprocal provision of equipment, materials and supplies.[18]

Brazilian and Argentine officials engaged in confidence building measures even in the highly sensitive area of their uranium enrichment facilities. These initiatives, as well as unequivocal pledges to develop only peaceful applications of nuclear energy, were granted center stage in biannual presidential summits during this period.[19]

While nuclear cooperation had been limited to narrowly circumscribed accords, Sarney and Alfonsín established an ongoing consultative mechanism to identify and explore new opportunities for collaborative endeavors. This joint working group was created in their first meeting in November 1985, and was made a permanent commission on the occasion of Alfonsín's visit to the Brazilian Navy's Aramar ultracentrifuge enrichment plant in April 1988. This high-level body was established under the direction of the respective foreign ministries, and its members included deputy ministers of foreign affairs as well as the presidents of the respective two national nuclear energy commissions.[20]

Through these initiatives, the democratic governments of the 1980s built confidence between their respective technical communities,[21] and fundamentally changed the boundaries of reasonable debate in both countries. By 1988, military as well as civilian sectors in both countries ceased viewing the other as a security threat.[22] As a direct result of nuclear transparency, military planners in both countries revised war plans in light of diminished reciprocal security threats.[23] The waning of nuclear anxieties also eliminated one rationale for the Brazilian military's 'parallel' nuclear program.[24] While nuclear cooperation did not guarantee the success of economic integration efforts, it was a necessary step that allowed integration to proceed.[25] At no time before or since have nuclear policies played such an important role in bilateral relations.

CONVENTIONAL EXPLANATIONS FOR THE DEMOCRATIC PEACE

In this historical experience, improved relations and nuclear confidence building followed transitions to democracy. But exactly *how* did democratization lead to the emergence of a nuclear regime? Scholars offer three causal explanations to account for the democratic peace:

economic interdependence between liberal trading states,[26] institutional constraints on executive war-making,[27] and domestic norms of non-violent dispute resolution.[28]

The causal arguments of the first and second explanations are contradicted by the Argentine–Brazilian experience. The temporal sequence is reversed with regard to the first; economic interdependence followed as a consequence of political rapprochement. Indeed, a central objective for many advocates of political rapprochement was precisely to establish preconditions that would permit economic integration, which was in turn seen as necessary to foster economic growth and competitiveness, and to aid in the consolidation of democratic rule. Politics drove economics during this initial phase of integration in the 1980s.[29]

With respect to the second, structural constraints had the opposite result predicted. In Brazil, constitutional and political limits on executive power restricted the improvement of relations. In Argentina, centralized policy making and electoral support permitted Alfonsín to seek dramatic progress.[30] The Argentine–Brazilian experience thus suggests that instead of consistently facilitating pacific relations, domestic structural constraints are more likely to systematically favor policy inertia. Such constraints may thus cut both ways, restraining escalation during crises, but also impeding the progressive transformation of relations.

The evidence regarding domestic political norms is mixed, but on balance unconvincing, in accounting for the change observed. Scholars argue that leaders and citizens of democratic states are socialized to expect and to value norms of democratic governance, including rule-bound competition for power, and especially the non-violent resolution of conflicts. By communicating these shared values through extensive transnational networks, and by observing their transparent political processes, democratic states learn over time to apply their domestic norms in resolving disputes with other democracies.[31]

Some elements of this argument are borne out by the Argentine–Brazilian experience. The change between pre- and post-transition Argentina is significant. A decade of guerilla and state terrorism came to an end, democratic rule itself enjoyed widespread public support, and elites recognized the need to refrain from exploiting social antagonisms and to accept rules to govern their competition for power.[32]

But the changes in foreign policy were almost immediate in Argentina and nearly as rapid in Brazil. Too little time passed to allow either the socialization of elites and polities, or communication and learning, to take place. More importantly, other evidence demonstrates that democratic norms were at best weakly inculcated in these states' domestic politics. In Brazil, the transition did not halt the use of violence by the military to quash labor and rural organizations.[33] In Argentina, the Alfonsín government made policy unilaterally and employed a 'Hobbesian' strategy in addressing economic conflicts, refusing to collaborate or even to negotiate with union and business sectors or other political parties.[34] The Alfonsín administration rejected *concertación* that might have enabled social pacts at home, even as it helped promote the most active and effective period of Latin American diplomatic collaboration in contemporary history.[35] Ironically, to forestall public debate or legislative criticism in reaching integration accords with Brazil, Alfonsín relied on secret negotiations and diplomatic protocols that did not require parliamentary approval.[36]

On balance, Brazilian and Argentine foreign behaviors were more compliant with democratic norms than were their domestic politics. Thus the domestic norms argument fails to account for changing nuclear behavior.

DEMOCRATIC SECURITY AND DIVERSIONARY PEACE[37]

The key to accounting for change in nuclear relations during the 1985–88 period is to explain why Argentina took the lead and why Brazil accepted its proposals for nuclear regime building. The October 1983 elections in Argentina brought into office a group of civilians with no previous foreign policy experience but strong convictions on international affairs, who enjoyed great latitude in formulating policy.

The Alfonsín administration framed its approach to nuclear and security affairs in terms of a Latin American variant of Kantian idealism. They presumed that democratic neighbors would foster Argentine security, while military regimes would inevitably threaten it. They presumed that both foreign and domestic armed forces were threats to peace and security, that foreign peoples were natural allies, and that foreign states were enemies or allies depending on whether they were ruled by military officials, or by democratizing civilian leaders. In the words of Argentine Foreign Minister Dante Caputo, 'Authoritarian regimes, because they are supported by either a dominant minority or through alignment with a foreign power, are oriented to consider international relations – just like those within their own societies – in terms of domination.'[38]

Oriented by this conceptual framework, the Alfonsín government understood nuclear and bilateral affairs as a question of democratic security. They saw nuclear confidence building and cooperation as a means to reduce regional tensions, and thereby undercut the threat scenarios of their armed forces. Such a 'diversionary peace' would eliminate one rationale for military autonomy and claims on state resources, and thereby contribute to democratic consolidation at home and abroad. Argentine foreign policy makers presumed their civilian counterparts in Brazil shared this understanding.[39]

Similarly, these Argentine decision makers rejected power politics in part as immoral, but also because they saw it as a threat to democratic consolidation and civilian control over the armed forces. Appeals to *realpolitik* principles in justifying foreign policy would only engender their perpetuation among military and civilian sectors long accustomed to the ruthless pursuit of power in Argentine domestic politics.[40] Hence the Alfonsín administration consistently expounded one standard of legitimate political behavior, which even extended to repeated calls for the 'democratization' of the international system.[41]

The Alfonsín government framed nuclear and bilateral affairs in this way for three reasons: their sense of identity, their ideology and the agenda they confronted on assuming office. First, Alfonsín and other *Unión Cívica Radical* (UCR) Party leaders were human rights activists and advocates of constitutional democratic rule. Second, UCR thinking on international relations had been strongly influenced by Kantian idealist thought for a century,[42] and party ideology was 'confirmed', in a negative sense, by the excruciating experience of military rule. Brutal repression at home and a futile diversionary war abroad corroborated UCR officials' ideological predisposition to reject realist principles. Third, on arrival in office UCR officials found themselves surrounded by non-democratic states, facing an economic crisis with high inflation and burgeoning foreign debt, and acutely aware that civilian governments did not endure in Argentina. Their overriding imperative was hence to consolidate democratic rule, and so they made foreign policy an instrument of domestic policy.[43]

Their democratic security framework shaped Argentine foreign policy in this period for two reasons. First, a very small and homogenous group (Alfonsín, Caputo and two – sometimes three – close advisors) dominated decision making.[44] With the opposition Peronist party in disarray, the armed forces preoccupied by human rights trials and internal revolts, and enjoying strong electoral support from a public generally inattentive to foreign affairs, this small group enjoyed great license in molding Argentine foreign policy.[45]

Second, their framework proved compelling because they used effective means to promote it. Through public discourse, private negotiations, symbolic actions and the creation of bilateral and regional institutions, the Alfonsín government diffused its understandings abroad. Argentine officials framed their proposals both in terms of democratic consolidation, and of regional autonomy. These appeals were attractive to diverse sectors within the Brazilian state, but for different reasons. While the pursuit of regional autonomy dovetailed with the Brazilian foreign ministry's efforts to stabilize states in the region,[46] democratic statesmanship offered President Sarney a foreign source to gain legitimacy he lacked at home. Moreover, like Alfonsín, Sarney came to see geopolitically oriented foreign policy as conducive to military interference in national politics.[47] Framing policy initiatives in terms of technological autonomy was also useful in gaining the acceptance of the Brazilian armed forces,[48] which enjoyed *de facto* veto power over national policy during this period.[49] As a leading authority on bilateral relations noted, these appeals helped to create 'on the part of both governments the vision that this rapprochement can constitute an instrument to reciprocally fortify their respective processes of democratic transition'.[50]

But it was not just discourse that 'spoke' so effectively to these actors. The reciprocal visits of Presidents Alfonsín and Sarney to the uranium enrichment facilities of Pilcaniyeu in 1987 and Aramar in 1988 were of unsurpassed symbolic consequence.[51] Sarney was the second foreigner to set foot in the secretive Pilcaniyeu facility accessible only to very senior Argentine policy makers and technical specialists,[52] whose revelation in 1983 reportedly stunned the US nonproliferation and intelligence communities.[53]

Yet even more striking was Alfonsín's co-inauguration with Sarney of Brazil's Aramar ultracentrifuge enrichment plant at Iperó in April 1988, where he was the first non-Brazilian to enter the plant.[54] In a previously unthinkable public act, the president of Argentina inaugurated the Brazilian Navy facility designed to permit the development of nuclear powered submarines. From a purely military-strategic perspective, the plant's production could provide Brazil with the type of maritime power that had checked the Argentine fleet in 1982, as well as potentially producing weapons-grade fissile material. Alfonsín's participation was an extraordinary act of trust in Brazilian commitments to employ the plant only for non-weapon purposes. Like other joint visits, it was an act of mutual legitimation of the pursuit of nuclear technological autonomy,[55] as well as a very effective confidence-building measure.

These potent symbolic actions undercut the plausibility of a power politics interpretation of nuclear development. Before these confidence-building measures were undertaken, the possibility that either country could acquire nuclear weapons had helped perpetuate suspicions and military threat scenarios that identified the other state as a threat to national security.[56] But bilateral nuclear cooperation served to exorcise these 'dangerous spirits'.[57] In particular, it helped to further isolate the small sectors in the Brazilian military – notably in the Air Force – that advocated development of nuclear arms under the guise of a 'peaceful

nuclear explosive' program.[58] Nuclear cooperation diminished traditional fears in both countries, and bilateral confidence-building and
joint efforts provided a legitimate basis to promote nonproliferation.[59]
Through audacious and imaginative confidence building measures,
the UCR government transformed nuclear affairs from a source of
tension to a vehicle for the transformation of bilateral relations.

NUCLEAR REGIME BUILDING: AN INSTRUMENT FOR DEMOCRATIC PEACE

Although the causal arguments offered to account for the democratic
peace did not hold in this case, the emergence of democratic rule in
Argentina and Brazil did matter. It led to positive and consequential
changes in nuclear relations – not because it altered the balance of
military power or the distribution of material resources, nor by
creating domestic structures that impeded conflict, nor in producing
economic interdependence; it mattered because it brought officials to
power in Argentina whose identity, ideology and experiences led them
to frame nuclear development and bilateral relations in a new way, as
a question of democratic security. Their expectation that other democratizing governments would share their values and would likewise
reject the use of force led these Kantian idealists to take risky initiatives
to build confidence. Their appeals resonated with the experiences of
civilian officials in Brazil, and their symbolic actions reshaped the
boundaries of reasonable debate in both countries. Thus they elicited
cooperative behavior from Brazil – creating a bilateral nuclear regime,
transforming regional security relations, and launching the economic
integration project that became MERCOSUR, the Southern (American)
Common Market.

It is important to recognize that positive change in Argentine–
Brazilian nuclear relations was not a *necessary* product of democratic
rule, of transitions to democracy, nor of the democratization process
itself.[60] The transitions and their consequences differed in Brazil and
Argentina, most notably in the degree of autonomy enjoyed by the
military in the former, and executive domination over foreign policy
in the latter. The idea of democratic security that oriented the group
that came to power in Argentina, and its ability to diffuse this understanding among its Brazilian counterparts, was the key to the transformation of bilateral nuclear relations in the late 1980s. Another
leadership oriented by a different understanding – or the same one
with less effective control over policy making – would have entailed
quite different behavior in Argentine foreign policy and Argentine–
Brazilian relations.[61]

The focus of this study on policy areas where the Alfonsín government successfully achieved its objectives may lead to the inaccurate impression that this administration was either uncommonly shrewd, or that the solutions to the problems it faced were obvious. But there is no evidence that the other major actors (such as the Peronists or a reconstituted military government) would have held similar views or made similar policy choices.[62] It is true that any government that won office in Argentina in 1983 would have sought to sustain its power and ensure its survival. But not all would have identified the consolidation of *democratic* rule as *the* overriding national imperative. And no Argentine government other than that of Alfonsín and the UCR would have been oriented by the same understanding of how regional relations could be used to promote democratization, nor would any other have selected the same instruments to promote the consolidation of democratic rule.[63]

The Argentine–Brazilian experience accords with the observation that 'the presumption that the other is predisposed toward peacefulness leads to a self-fulfilling prophecy if both sides act on this assumption'.[64] It demonstrates that, like war, peace may be the product of misperception. Or more precisely, of expectations about other states that may not have solid empirical foundations, but that if shared, are nonetheless self-confirming.[65] The key to explaining the democratic peace is to account for the origins of these expectations. The Argentine–Brazilian experience indicates that they can arise rapidly, when leaders and polities draw negative lessons from painful experiences that result from policies oriented by *realpolitik*.

So does democracy favor international peace and security? The Argentine–Brazilian experience indicates that it depends on the democrats. In this case it brought to office a coherent group with Kantian ideas and the opportunity to implement them. The 1980s transitions to democracy in South America mattered because they fortuitously brought to power a community of like-minded Kantians, who deliberately sought to transform their international relations. Despite facing a regional security environment apparently predisposed toward the emergence of a nuclear arms race, in their efforts to transform relations these pro-democratic statesmen created a bilateral regime that laid the political, security and institutional foundations for verified nuclear nonproliferation in the 1990s.

NOTES

1 This chapter is based on field research funded by the Program on Peace and International Security of the Social Science Research Council and the MacArthur Foundation, and the Institute for the Study of World Politics. My

research was carried out in affiliation with the Facultad Latinoamericano de Ciencias Sociales/Programa Argentina, the Núcleo de Estudos Estratégicos, Universidade Estadual de Campinas, and the Instituto de Relações Internacionais, Pontífica Universidade Católica, Rio de Janeiro. I would also like to thank the Center for International Security and Cooperation at Stanford University and the Global Studies Research Program of the University of Wisconsin-Madison for financial and intellectual support, and Emanuel Adler, Michael Barnett, Dominique Fournier, Mônica Hirst, Gaurav Kampani, Jeff Knopf and Roberto Russell for insightful criticism of earlier drafts of this chapter. I am indebted to Scott Sagan for suggesting the term 'diversionary peace'.

2 Michael Barletta is Senior Research Associate at the Monterey Institute of International Studies, and Lecturer in National Security Affairs at the Naval Postgraduate School in Monterey, California. His current research focuses on the proliferation of weapons of mass destruction in the Middle East and Africa, and on foreign and security affairs in Latin America.

3 As one prominent scholar noted, 'This absence of war between democratic states comes as close as anything we have to an empirical law in international relations': Jack S. Levy, 'Domestic Politics and War', in Robert I. Rotberg and Theodore K. Rabb (eds), *The Origin and Prevention of Major Wars* (New York: Cambridge University Press, 1989), 270. See also Bruce Russett, *Controlling the Sword: The Democratic Governance of National Security* (Cambridge, MA: Harvard University Press, 1990), 123; Thomas Risse-Kappen, 'Democratic Peace – Warlike Democracies? A Social Constructivist Interpretation of the Liberal Argument', *European Journal of International Relations*, 1 (1995), 494; Zeev Maoz, 'The Controversy over the Democratic Peace: Rearguard Action or Cracks in the Wall?', *International Security*, 22 (1997), 162.

4 Steve Chan, 'Mirror, Mirror on the Wall … Are the Freer Countries More Pacific?', *Journal of Conflict Resolution*, 28 (1984), 617–48; Michael W. Doyle, 'Kant, Liberal Legacies, and Foreign Affairs: Part 1', *Philosophy and Public Affairs*, 12 (1983), 205–35; Zeev Maoz and Nasrin Abdolali, 'Regime Types and International Conflict, 1816–1976', *Journal of Conflict Resolution*, 29 (1989), 3–35; Zeev Maoz and Bruce Russett, 'Alliance, Contiguity, Wealth, and Political Stability: Is the Lack of Conflict Among Democracies a Statistical Artifact?', *International Interactions*, 17 (1992), 245–67; Bruce Russett, 'And Yet it Moves', *International Security*, 19 (1995), 164–75; Bruce Russett, *Grasping the Democratic Peace* (Princeton, NJ: Princeton University Press, 1993); Erich Weede, 'Some Simple Calculations on Democracy and War Involvement', *Journal of Peace Research*, 29 (1992), 377–83; Erich Weede, 'Democracy and War Involvement', *Journal of Conflict Resolution*, 28 (1984), 649–64. One scholar has dissented from the dyadic claim, however, asserting that democracies are categorically less warlike than other types of states. R. J. Rummel, 'On Vincent's View of Freedom and International Conflict', *International Studies Quarterly*, 31 (1987), 113–17; R. J. Rummel, 'Libertarian Propositions on Violence within and between Nations', *Journal of Conflict Resolution*, 29 (1985), 419–55.

5 For research on alternative explanations, see Clifton T. Morgan, and Valerie L. Schwebach, 'Take Two Democracies and Call Me in the Morning: A Prescription for Peace?', *International Interactions,* 17 (1992), 305–20; John M. Owen, 'Liberalism and War Decisions: Great Britain and the U.S. Civil War' (Stanford, CA: MacArthur Consortium Working Paper in Peace and Cooperation, Center for International Security and Cooperation, Stanford University, 1996); John M. Owen, 'How Liberalism Produces Democratic Peace', *International Security*, 19 (1994), 87–125; Risse-Kappen, 'Democratic Peace –

Warlike Democracies? A Social Constructivist Interpretation of the Liberal Argument', 491–517; David L. Rousseau, Christopher Gelpi, Dan Reiter and Paul K. Huth, 'Assessing the Dyadic Nature of the Democratic Peace, 1918–88', *American Political Science Review*, 90 (1996), 512–33; Randolph M. Siverson, 'Democracies and War Participation: In Defense of the Institutional Constraints Argument', *European Journal of International Relations*, 1 (1995), 481–9; Michael D. Ward and Kristian S. Gleditsch, 'Democratizing for Peace', *American Political Science Review*, 92 (1998), 51–61.

6 Analysts include David R. Dávila-Villers, 'Competition and Co-operation in the River Plate: The Democratic Transition and Mercosur', *Bulletin of Latin American Research*, 11 (1992), 266, 275; Eduardo B. Gana, 'Tendencias en la Integración Latinoamericana: El Caso de Argentina y Brasil', *Cono Sur*, 7 (1988), 5–9; Mônica Hirst, 'La Dimensión Política del MERCOSUR: Especifidades Nacionales, Aspectos Institucionales y Actores Sociales' (Buenos Aires: Facultad Latino-americana de Ciencias Sociales, 1993), 31–2; Carlos J. Moneta, 'El Acer-camiento Argentina–Brasil: de la Tensión y el Conflicto a la Competencia Cooperativa', in *Anuario Estratégico de América Latina*, 1986 (Ciudad de México: CLEE/Instituto Venezolano de Estudios Sociales y Políticos, 1987), 3; Riordan Roett, *Brazil: Politics in a Patrimonial Society* (Westport, CT: Praeger, 1992), 194; Roberto Russell, 'Type of Regime, Changes of Governments and Foreign Policy: The Case of Argentina (1976–1991)', *Documentos e Informes de Investigación*, 127 (Buenos Aires: Facultad Latinoamericana de Ciencias Sociales, 1992), 43; Phillippe C. Schmitter, 'Change in Regime Type and Progress in International Relations' in Emanuel Adler and Beverly Crawford (eds), *Progress in International Relations* (New York: Columbia University Press, 1991), 118; Wayne A. Selcher, 'Brazilian–Argentine Relations in the 1980s: From Wary Rivalry to Friendly Competition', *Journal of Interamerican Studies and World Affairs*, 27 (1985), 33; Alberto Van Klaveren, 'Democratización y Política Exterior: El Acercamiento entre Argentina y Brasil', *Afers Internacionals*, 18 (1990), 43.

In personal interviews, many Brazilian and Argentine officials attributed responsibility for improved relations to concurrent democratization, among other factors. Author's interviews with Marcos Castrioto de Azambuja (Ambassador to Argentina, mid-1990s), Buenos Aires, 9 November 1995; Oscar Camilión (Ambassador to Brazil, 1976–81; Minister of Defense, 1992–96), Buenos Aires, 26 July 1994; Dante Caputo (Argentine Minister of Foreign Relations, 1983–88), Buenos Aires, 7 November 1995; Luiz Augusto de Castro Neves (Brazilian negotiator on integration accords with Argentina, 1986–87), Brasília, 4 October 1995; José Goldemberg (Brazilian Minister of Science and Technology, 1990–92), Princeton, NJ, 31 March 1994; Celso Lafer (Brazilian Minister of Foreign Relations, early 1990s), São Paulo (telephone interview), 18 August 1995; Félix Peña (Argentine Undersecretary for Mercosur and Interamerican Economic Relations), Buenos Aires, 22 June 1994; Enrique de la Torre (nuclear and security affairs division director, Argentine Foreign Ministry), Bariloche, 20 April 1994.

7 In August 1984, the British magazine *New Statesman* claimed to have evidence that Britain sent a Polaris submarine armed with nuclear-armed missiles to the South Atlantic to threaten Argentina 'if need be'. British Admiralty spokesmen strongly denied the allegation. Leonard S. Spector, *The New Nuclear Nations* (New York: Vintage Books, 1985), 187, citing 'All Out War', *New Statesman*, 24 August 1984, 8; '2 Britons Deny a Plan for A-Arms in '82 War', *New York Times*, 25 August 1984.

8 Carlos Castro Madero and Steban A. Takacs, *Política Argentina Nuclear: Avance*

o Retroceso? (Buenos Aires: El Ateneo, 1991), 216–19.

9 In the contemporary words of one US analyst of Argentine nuclear development, 'Under current conditions, Argentina is likely to develop a nuclear
   device, although it will certainly keep it secret as long as possible. Most certainly
   the Argentine leadership will allow no one to curtail the nuclear weapon
   option': Cynthia Ann Watson, 'Will Argentina go to the Bomb after the Falk-
   lands?', *Inter-American Economic Affairs*, 37 (1984), 77. Another wrote that we
   'should see a proliferation decision followed by a first Argentine nuclear
   weapon operational within several years of such a decision'. Stephen M. Meyer,
   The Dynamics of Nuclear Proliferation (Chicago, IL and London: University of
   Chicago Press, 1984), 132.

10 On Brazil's nuclear energy development program based on West German
   assistance in the 1970s, see Norman Gall, 'Atoms for Brazil, Dangers for All',
   Foreign Policy, 23 (1976), 155–201; David J. Myers, 'Brazil: Reluctant Pursuit
   of the Nuclear Option', *Orbis*, 27 (1984), 881–911; Etel Solingen, 'Brazil', in
   Raju G. C. Thomas and Bennett Ramberg (eds), *Energy and Security in the
   Developing World* (Lexington, MA: University of Kentucky Press, 1990);
   Eduardo da Silva, 'A Nova Política Nuclear Brasileira', *Revista da Escola Superior
   de Guerra*, 7 (1991), 7–35.
       On the Brazilian armed forces' sense of nuclear rivalry with Argentina and
   Brazil's 'parallel' nuclear technological development program, see Michael
   Barletta, 'The Military Nuclear Program in Brazil' (Stanford, CA: Center for
   International Security and Arms Control working paper, Stanford University,
   1997), www.stanford.edu/group/CISAC/test/pub/barletta.pdf, esp. 15–17.

11 Author's interviews with Roberto Godoy (defense correspondent, *Correio
   Popular*), Campinas, 24 March 1995; Maximiliano Eduardo da Silva Fonseca
   (Minister of the Navy, 1979–84), 25 September 1995; Stanley Hilton, 'The
   Brazilian Military: Changing Strategic Perceptions and the Question of
   Mission', *Armed Forces and Society*, 13 (1987), 337.

12 Julio C. Carasales, 'The Argentine–Brazilian Nuclear Rapprochement', *The
   Nonproliferation Review*, 2 (1995), 39.

13 Mitchell Reiss, 'Argentina and Brazil: Rivals, Not Enemies', in *Bridled Ambition:
   Why Countries Constrain their Nuclear Capabilities* (Washington, DC: Woodrow
   Wilson Center and Johns Hopkins University, 1995). See also John R. Redick,
   Julio C. Carasales and Paulo S. Wrobel, 'Nuclear Rapprochement: Argentina,
   Brazil, and the Nonproliferation Regime', *Washington Quarterly*, 18 (1994),
   107–22.

14 Brazilian and Argentine scientists and diplomats lent reciprocal support in
   multilateral negotiations regarding the Nuclear Non-Proliferation Treaty
   (NPT) and the Treaty of Tlatelolco, and as well in the Board of Governors of
   the International Atomic Energy Agency (IAEA). Argentine leaders and
   scientists also publicly supported Brazil when its 1975 nuclear agreement with
   West Germany came under sharp US and international criticism. Castro
   Madero and Takacs, *Política Argentina Nuclear: Avance o Retroceso?*, 155, 232;
   John R. Redick, 'Nuclear Illusions: Argentina and Brazil', Occasional Paper
   25 (Washington, DC: Henry L. Stimson Center, 1995), 17–20; John R. Redick,
   'Latin America's Emerging Non-Proliferation Consensus', *Arms Control Today*,
   24 (1994), 4–5; Jorge A. Sábato, 'El Plan Nuclear Brasileño y la Bomba
   Atómica', *Estudios Internacionales*, 11 (1978), 73–82.

15 The Argentine project reportedly aimed to ensure access to nuclear fuel after
   the 1978 Nonproliferation Act called into question future US supply of reactor
   fuel. Author's interview with Dr Conrado Varotto (Pilcaniyeu director, late
   1970s–early 1980s), Buenos Aires, 6 November 1995. See also Castro Madero

and Takacs, *Política Argentina Nuclear: Avance o Retroceso?*, 81–2, 154. On the Brazilian enrichment program, see Barletta, 'The Military Nuclear Program in Brazil', 6–13; Secretaria de Assuntos Estratégicos, 'Programa de Desenvolvimento de Tecnologia Nuclear: Histórico', 14 November 1997, www.sae.gov.br/spp/pdtn/historic.htm; Sílvia Giurlani, 'Brasil Enriquece Urânio que Enriquece o Brasil', *Brasil Nuclear* (March 1998), www.alternex.com.br/~aben/brn-a4n16-mar1998/capa.htm

16 Nuclear cooperation with other Latin American countries was a 'cornerstone' of Argentine nuclear policy, but, until 1980, cooperation with Brazil was never formalized due to these states' rivalry. Carlos Martínez-Vidal and Roberto Ornstein, 'La Cooperación Argentino-Brasileño en el Campo de los Usos Pacíficos de la Energía Nuclear', in Mônica Hirst (ed.), *Argentina–Brasil: Perspectivas Comparativas y Ejes de Integración* (Buenos Aires: Editorial Tesis/Facultad Latinoamericana de Ciencias Sociales, 1990), 340–1. These states' nuclear programs were arguably 'the maximum expression of the competition for regional primacy', and manifested an action–reaction pattern akin to an arms race in the 1970s. Héctor Eduardo Bocco, 'La Cooperación Nuclear Argentina–Brasil: Notas para una Evaluación Política, *Documentos e Informes de Investigación*, 82 (Buenos Aires: Facultad Latinoamericana de Ciencias Sociales, 1989), 5; Emanuel Adler, *The Power of Ideology: The Quest for Technological Autonomy in Argentina and Brazil* (Berkeley, CA: University of California Press, 1987), 280. Following resolution of their dispute over the hydroelectric resources of the Paraná River, in 1980 the Videla and Figueiredo governments signed nuclear commercial accords. See Magdalena Segre, 'La Questión Ítaipu-Corpus: El Punto de Inflexión en las Relaciones Argentino-Brazileñas', *Documentos e Informes de Investigación*, 97 (Buenos Aires: Facultad Latinoamericana de Ciencias Sociales, September 1990); Bocco, 'La Cooperación Nuclear Argentina–Brasil: Notas para una Evaluación Política', 21–3; Mário Eduardo Olmos, *La Cooperacion Argentina–Brazil: Nucleo Impulsor de la Integracion Latinoamericana* (Buenos Aires: Instituto de Publicaciones Navales, 1986), 205–19. However, although the two military governments concurred on the desirability of dampening international nonproliferation pressures and exploiting respective industrial assets, rivalry and suspicions continued to afflict bilateral nuclear relations. As a consequence, until 1985 nuclear cooperation was eclipsed by political competition with latent military implications.

17 Diplomatic and business initiatives to promote nuclear commerce and the integration of these states' nuclear industries during in the 1980s are detailed in *Revista Argentina Nuclear*, 1986, 1 (5), 8–10, 49; 1987, 2 (7), 32–5; 2 (8), 35–8; 2 (9), 34–9; 1988, 2 (13), 42–5; 2 (14/15), 34–9; 2 (16), 8–9, 58–66; 1989, 3 (19/20), 42–5; 3 (21), 39.

18 Enrique de la Torre, 'Argentina–Brazil: Bilateral Confidence-Building Measures' (Washington, DC: document presented at a meeting on confidence building and security mechanisms, Organization of American States, 17–19 November 1994), 3; 'Joint Declaration on Nuclear Policy', INFCIRC/351 (Vienna: International Atomic Energy Agency, 16 May 1988), Annex 2, 1–2.

19 Presidents Alfonsín and Sarney signed joint declarations on nuclear policy at Foz do Iguaçú, Brazil, on 30 November 1985; in Brasília on 10 December 1986; at Viedma, Argentina, on 17 July 1987; at the Aramar facility at Iperó, Brazil, on 8 April 1988; and at Ezeiza, Argentina, on 29 November 1988. They also signed a protocol to promote nuclear sector integration at their December 1986 summit in Brasília. They pledged in the accords to develop only peaceful applications of nuclear energy, and identified nuclear cooperation as an important means of building mutual confidence. Translations in 'Joint

Declaration on Nuclear Policy', INFCIRC/351, Annexes 1–5; 'Joint Declaration on Nuclear Policy, Addendum 1', INFCIRC/351 (Vienna: International Atomic Energy Agency, 27 January 1989).

20 The 1985 Foz do Iguaçú Declaration established this working group to promote cooperation in the development of nuclear energy and 'to create mechanisms which will safeguard the vital interests of peace, security and development in the region'. Translated in 'Joint Declaration on Nuclear Policy', INFCIRC/351, Annex 2, 2. It subsequently met on a quarterly basis, alternating between venues in Brazil and Argentina. Three subgroups addressed technical cooperation, legal and technical issues, and foreign policy coordination. Its meetings were often accompanied by parallel reunions of nuclear industry executives from the two countries. De la Torre, 'Argentina–Brazil: Bilateral Confidence-Building Measures', 2–3.

21 Author's interview with Marco Antonio Marzo (safeguards division director, Brazilian nuclear energy commission, 1983–92), Rio de Janeiro, 15 May 1995.

22 Oscar Camilión, 'La Evaluación Argentina', in Mônica Hirst (ed.), *Argentina–Brasil: El Largo Camino de la Integración* (Buenos Aires: Editoral Legasa, 1988), 157.

23 Author's interviews with Antonio Federico Moreno (Director of Planning, Argentine Joint Chiefs of Staff, 1980s–90s), Buenos Aires, 29 June 1994; Manoel Augusto Teixeira (Director of Planning, Brazilian Army Ministry, 1984–87), São Paulo, 13 November 1994.

24 Author's interviews with Mário César Flores, Brasília, 7 July 1995; Othon Luiz Pinheiro da Silva, São Paulo, 20 September 1995. The former admiral was the institutional patron of the Navy's enrichment program at its inception in 1978 and later as Navy Minister in the 1980s; the latter directed the program for 14 years.

25 Author's interview with Julio Carasales (Argentine Ambassador to the UN Conference on Disarmament, and authority on Argentine nuclear diplomacy), Bariloche, 20 April 1994.

26 Michael W. Doyle, 'Liberalism and World Politics', *American Political Science Review*, 80 (1986), 1161.

27 Bruce J. Bueno de Mesquita and David Lalman, 'Domestic Opposition and Foreign War', *American Political Science Review*, 84 (1990), 747–65; Doyle, 'Liberalism and World Politics', 1,153; Carol R. Ember, Melvin Ember and Bruce Russett, 'Peace between Participatory Polities: A Cross-Cultural Test of the "Democracies Rarely Fight Each Other" Hypothesis', *World Politics*, 44 (1992), 577; Rousseau *et al.*, 'Assessing the Dyadic Nature of the Democratic Peace, 1918–88', 512–33; Siverson, 'Democracies and War Participation: In Defense of the Institutional Constraints Argument', 481–9.

28 Risse-Kappen, 'Democratic Peace – Warlike Democracies? A Social Constructivist Interpretation of the Liberal Argument', 500; R. J. Rummel, 'Libertarianism and International Violence', *Journal of Conflict Resolution*, 27 (1983), 28; Maoz and Russett, 'Alliance, Contiguity, Wealth, and Political Stability: Is the Lack of Conflict Among Democracies a Statistical Artifact?', 246–7; Rousseau *et al.*, 'Assessing the Dyadic Nature of the Democratic Peace, 1918–88', 513.

29 Daniel Chudnovsky and Fernando Porta, 'On Argentine–Brazilian Economic Integration', CEPAL *Review*, 39 (1989), 127; Mario Rapoport and Andrés Musacchio (eds), *La Comunidad Europea y el Mercosur: Una Evaluación Comparada* (Buenos Aires: Fundación de Investigaciones Históricas, Económicas y Sociales/Fundación Konrad Adenauer, 1993), 136; Gerardo Orlando Noto, 'The MERCOSUR Countries' Foreign Policies toward the United States. Foreign Policy Coordination among Economic Partners: Cooperation for Joint

Gains or Competition for Individual Benefits?', paper prepared for the
XXXIV Annual Meeting of the International Studies Association, Acapulco,
Mexico, 1993, 12.

30 In Brazil the president and foreign minister shared power with a much
stronger foreign policy bureaucracy. Mônica Hirst and Roberto Russell,
'Democracia y Política Exterior: Los Casos de Argentina y Brasil', *Documentos
e Informes de Investigación*, 55 (Buenos Aires: Facultad Latinoamericana de
Ciencias Sociales, 1987), 60. Sarney was also politically weaker than his
Argentine counterpart, due to his lack of an electoral mandate, the hetero-
geneity of his electoral coalition, and his clientalistic approach to governance,
while the role of the armed forces in Brazilian national governance after 1985
was pervasive. Mônica Hirst and María Regina Soares de Lima, 'Crisis y Toma
de Decisión en la Política Exterior Brasileña: El Programa de Integración
Argentina–Brasil y las Negociaciones sobre la Informática con Estados
Unidos', in Roberto Russell (ed.), *Política Exterior y Toma de Decisiones en América
Latina* (Buenos Aires: Grupo Editor Latinoamericano, 1990), 65; Alfred
Stepan, *Rethinking Military Politics: Brazil and the Southern Cone* (Princeton, NJ:
Princeton University Press, 1988). By contrast, as described in more detail
below, foreign policy making remained highly centralized under Alfonsín and
a small circle of his advisors.

31 Risse-Kappen, 'Democratic Peace – Warlike Democracies? A Social Constructivist Interpretation of the Liberal Argument', 500; Rummell, 'Libertarianism
and International Violence', 28; Maoz and Russett, 'Normative and Structural
Causes of Democratic Peace, 1946–1986', 246–7; Rousseau *et al.*, 'Assessing the
Dyadic Nature of the Democratic Peace, 1918–88', 513. Likewise, scholars
hypothesize that leaders in democratic states expect coercive tactics and
violence from non-democratic states.

32 Hirst and Russell, 'Democracia y Política Exterior: Los Casos de Argentina y
Brasil', 3–4.

33 João Quartim de Morães, 'La Tutela Militar en Brasil: de la Transición
Controlada a la Democracia Bloqueada', in Mônica Hirst (ed.), *Argentina–
Brasil: Perspectivas Comparativas y Ejes de Integración* (Buenos Aires: Editorial
Tesis/Facultad Latinoamericana de Ciencias Sociales, 1990), 181–6.

34 Carlos H. Acuña, 'Politics and Economics in the Argentina of the Nineties (Or,
Why the Future No Longer is What It Used to Be)', in William C. Smith, Carlos
H. Acuña and Eduardo A. Gamarra, *Democracy, Markets, and Structural Reform
in Latin America* (New Brunswick, NJ, and London: Transaction Publishers,
1993), 32, 55; William C. Smith, 'Democracy, Distributional Conflicts, and
Macroeconomic Policymaking in Argentina', *Journal of Interamerican Studies and
World Affairs*, 32 (1990), 1–42.

35 Dominique Fournier, *Democratic Consolidation and Foreign Policy: The Cases of
Post-Authoritarian Argentina and Chile, 1983–1993*, PhD dissertation (Oxford: St
Antony's College, Oxford University, 1996); Mônica Hirst, 'Las Iniciativas
Latinoamericanas de Concertación: Su Influencia sobre las Condiciones de
Paz en la Región', in *Desarme y Desarrollo: Condiciones Internacionales y Perspectivas*
(Buenos Aires: Grupo Editor Latinoamericano/Fundación Arturo Illia, 1990).

36 Chudnovsky and Porta, 'On Argentine–Brazilian Economic Integration', 115.

37 I am indebted to Scott Sagan for this evocative phrase. For an analysis of the
1982 Malvinas/Falklands conflict as a paradigmatic example of diversionary
war, see Jack S. Levy and Lili Vakili, 'Diversionary Action by Authoritarian
Regimes: Argentina in the Falklands/Malvinas Case', in Manus I. Midlarsky
(ed.), *The Internationalization of Communal Strife* (New York: Harper Collins,
1992).

38 Dante Caputo, 'Línea Conceptual y Hechos Fundamentales de la Política Exterior del Radicalismo 1983–1989' (Buenos Aires: unpublished manuscript, 1990), 17, author's translation.

39 Author's interviews with Raúl Alconada Sempé (Vice-Chancellor, 1984–87), Buenos Aires, 20 July 1994; Dante Caputo (Minister of Foreign Relations, 1983–88), Buenos Aires, 19 July 1994; Carlos Chérniak (UCR advisor in House of Deputies, 1985–89), Buenos Aires, 13 July 1994; Jorge F. Sábato (Vice-Chancellor responsible for nuclear affairs, 1984–87), Buenos Aires, 10 March 1994; Mario Toer (member of 'Esmeralda' advisory group to President Alfonsín), Córdoba, 5 November 1993. See also Caputo, 'Línea Conceptual y Hechos Fundamentales de la Política Exterior del Radicalismo 1983–1989', 20; Dávila-Villers, 'Competition and Co-operation in the River Plate: The Democratic Transition and Mercosur', 266, 271–2; Virginia Gamba-Stonehouse, 'Argentina and Brazil', in Regina Cowen Karp (ed.), *Security with Nuclear Weapons: Different Perspectives on National Security* (New York: Oxford University Press/SIPRI, 1991), 248.

40 Roberto Russell, 'El Sistema de Creencias del Gobierno de Alfonsín' (Buenos Aires: unpublished manuscript, 1992), 45–8.

41 Ibid., 54–5.

42 Fournier, *Democratic Consolidation and Foreign Policy: The Cases of Post-Authoritarian Argentina and Chile, 1983–1993.*

43 As Foreign Minister Dante Caputo recalled 'the nearly-obsessive objective was the establishment of democratic processes'. Author's interview, Buenos Aires, 7 November 1995.

44 Their inexperience and propensity for exclusionary decision making led to their acerbic description as the 'gang of four' by career diplomats. Roberto Russell, 'The Decision-Making Process During the Alfonsín Administration' (Buenos Aires, unpublished manuscript, 1992), 181–4.

45 After 1983, the threat of trials of officers accused of human rights abuses and an internal generational schism within the services consumed the attention of the Argentine armed forces. Andrés Fontana, 'La Política Militar en un Contexto de Transición: Argentina, 1983–1989' (Buenos Aires: Centro de Estudios Institutionales, 1990), 13; Augusto Varas (ed.), *Democracy under Siege: New Military Power in Latin America* (New York: Greenwood, 1989), 55; David Pion-Berlin, 'Between Confrontation and Accommodation: Military and Government Policy in Democratic Argentina', *Journal of Latin American Studies*, 23 (1991), 570. The Argentine military was marginalized in foreign and military policy making throughout the Alfonsín government. Author's interview with Angel Tello (Undersecretary for Policy and Strategy, Argentine Ministry of Defense, 1986–89), Buenos Aires, 19 July 1994; Roberto Russell, 'Política Exterior y Toma de Decisiones en América Latina: Aspectos Comparativos y Consideraciones Teóricos', in Roberto Russell (ed.), *Política Exterior y Toma de Decisiones en América Latina* (Buenos Aires: Grupo Editor Latinoamericano, 1990), 26, 59. Foreign Minister Caputo declined to consult with military officials on anything except minor technical issues. Dante Caputo, interview in *América Latina/Internacional*, 6 (1989), 262. The military services had no organizational positions on economic integration and nuclear cooperation with Brazil, and the personal opinions of individual officers carried no weight. Even ranking military officials learned of foreign policy initiatives related to defense and regional security from the daily newspapers. Author's interview with General Heriberto Auel (Chief of Policy and Strategy, Argentine Joint Chiefs of Staff, 1983–85), Buenos Aires, 24 June 1994.

46 Author's interview with Dr Mônica Hirst (authority on Brazilian–Argentine

relations at FLACSO/Buenos Aires), Buenos Aires, 1 June 1994.

47 David J. Meyers, 'Brazil: The Quest for South American Leadership' in David J. Meyers (ed.), *Regional Hegemons: Threat Perceptions and Strategic Responses* (Boulder, CO: Westview Press, 1991), 239.

48 On the vision of technological autonomy that oriented nuclear development in Brazil and Argentina, see Adler, *The Power of Ideology: The Quest for Techno-logical Autonomy in Argentina and Brazil*. On technological autonomy as a motivation for military and civilian specialists in Brazilian nuclear development, see Barletta, 'The Military Nuclear Program in Brazil', 13–15, 29–31.

49 Lacking an electoral mandate and suffering from historical identification with the official military party in congress, Sarney had little choice but to rely on the armed forces for political support. Carlos H. Acuña and Catalina Smulovitz, 'Ajustando las FF.AA. a la Democracia: Éxitos, Fracasos y Ambigüedades de las Experiencias del Cono Sur' (Buenos Aires: Centro de Estudios del Estado y la Sociedad, 1993), 13; Eliézer Rizzo de Oliveira, *De Geisel a Collor: Forças Armadas, Transição, e Democracia* (Campinas: Papirus Editora, 1994), 97–115.

50 Hirst, in Hirst and Russell, 'Democracia y Política Exterior: Los Casos de Argentina y Brasil', 44; see also Camilión, 'La Evaluación Argentina', 160; and Hirst, 'Las Perspectativas del Diálogo Bilateral', in *Argentina–Brasil: El Largo Camino de la Integración*, 191–6.

51 This visit was aptly characterized in the presidents' joint declaration as a 'fundamental landmark … within the process of mutual confidence-building and the unshakable commitment of both Nations to use nuclear energy for exclusively peaceful purposes'. Translated in 'Joint Declaration on Nuclear Policy', INFCIRC/351, Annex 4. However, its efficacy in verifying nonproliferation was of course quite limited. As the 1987–89 president of the Argentine national nuclear energy commission wryly noted, the presidents had no technical understanding of what they observed in these facilities; 'they saw large machines that made noise'. Author's interview with Emma Perez Ferreira, Buenos Aires, 4 July 1994.

52 International Atomic Energy Agency Director-General Hans Blix was reportedly the first foreigner to enter Pilcaniyeu, in the course of Argentine efforts to ally international concerns about the unsafeguarded enrichment plant. Castro Madero and Takacs, *Política Argentina Nuclear: Avance o Retroceso?*, 87.

53 Author's interview with Richard P. Kennedy (US Ambassador at Large on Non-Proliferation, 1980–92), Washington, DC, 29 March 1994.

54 Author's interview with Othon Luiz Pinheiro da Silva (director of Brazilian Navy's nuclear development program, 1979–94), São Paulo, 20 September 1995.

55 The presidents' joint declaration proclaimed that the Brazilian Aramar and Argentine Pilcaniyeu installations were 'clear testimony of the capacity of both nations to develop, through their own resources, advanced technologies for peaceful purposes'. They underscored their nations' 'inalienable right to develop, without restrictions, their nuclear programs for peaceful purposes'. Translated in 'Joint Declaration on Nuclear Policy', INFCIRC/351, Annex 5, 1–2.

56 Cavagnari Filho, 'Brasil–Argentina: Autonomia Estratégica y Cooperación Militar', in *Argentina–Brasil: Perspectivas Comparativas y Ejes de Integración*, 329–31.

57 Camilión, 'La Evaluación Argentina', 162.

58 General Danilo Venturini (chief of the Brazilian National Security Council,

1979–85) confirmed that in the mid-1980s at least two ranking officials in the Brazilian air force promoted development of 'peaceful nuclear explosives' (PNES). Author's interview, Brasília, 4 October 1995. Air Force interest in PNEs was also evident in a secret memo written by Venturini and approved by President João Figueiredo on 21 February 1985, *Exposição de Motivos 011/85*. This document is described in part by *Folha de São Paulo*, 16 May 1995, 14, and provided to the author in a context that left no doubt as to its content or authenticity. According to Fernando Collor de Mello (President of Brazil, 1990–92), Air Force officials expressed interest in developing nuclear explosives as late as 1990. Author's interview, Miami, 24 November 1997. It is a mistake, however, to view military nuclear development efforts in Brazil as a dedicated nuclear bomb program; there was governmental and military consensus only on developing the technological capacity to create the *option* to build atomic weapons. Moreover, programmatic efforts were driven as much or more strongly, even within the armed forces, by non-weapons objectives. See Barletta, 'The Military Nuclear Program in Brazil', esp. 15–19, 29.

59 Hirst, 'Las Iniciativas Latinoamericanas de Concertación: Su Influencia sobre las Condiciones de Paz en la Región', 103, 105.

60 This is not surprising. Acquisition of nuclear weapons may be incompatible with democratic decision making, but the United States, Britain, France, Israel and India have all produced nuclear weapons under democratic regimes. In each case, secretive and largely unaccountable decision making coexisted with formal democratic institutions.

61 It is worth recalling that virtually no one anticipated UCR electoral victory in the presidential elections of October 1983. Russell, 'El Sistema de Creencias del Gobierno de Alfonsín', 49. Likewise, as Michael McFaul has noted, the Russian experience with democratization could have turned out very differently. Russia's surprisingly pacific foreign policy behavior in the 1990s was the *contingent* result of domestic political victories by liberal reformists, who identified their political interests and Russian national interests as requiring that they avoid belligerence in foreign affairs, to win acceptance into the international community. Their initial approach to foreign affairs was oriented by ideas formulated while in opposition, which had little to do with Russia's national interests abroad. Economic actors with tangible interests in peaceful foreign relations eventually bolstered the reformists' ideological orientation. Michael McFaul, 'A Precarious Peace: Domestic Politics in the Making of Russian Foreign Policy', *International Security*, 22 (1997), 5–35. The Brazilian–Argentine experience differs, however, not only because neither state was a great power. More importantly, the content of the conceptual frameworks shaping their behavior and that of Russia in the 1990s differ markedly, thus the respective actors identified their interests in nuclear affairs, as in other areas, quite differently.

62 Thus this is not a conventional 'interests story', in which any reasonably rational actor would have understood its incentives and selected its policy instruments in roughly the same way. Nor can this experience be captured adequately by a two-level game approach, which presumes actors' interests and anticipates their strategies based on domestic and international structural constraints.

63 My examination of UCR officials' behavior and discourse across a broad range of foreign policy questions indicates a consistent pattern of interest identification. The interests they identified in nuclear and bilateral affairs were appropriate, and the measures employed to realize them were efficacious. But they were unrealistic and ultimately disastrous in other areas. The UCR government misunderstood the nature of the *carapintada* military uprisings

and the international consequences of the Condor II ballistic missile program, and overestimated western European social democratic solidarity and creditor responsiveness to the Cartagena debt-relief initiatives, as well as the prospects for import substitution industrialization in the 1980s. In the end, Alfonsín left office months before his term was to conclude, in political disgrace, due to economic instability and UCR electoral defeat by the Peronists.

64 Risse-Kappen, 'Democratic Peace – Warlike Democracies? A Social Constructivist Interpretation of the Liberal Argument', 504–5.

65 Some studies of the democratic peace argue that shared liberal democratic culture is but one side of a perceptual 'coin'. Democratic commonalities imply differences with non-democratic societies. Thus, 'fellow liberals benefit from a presumption of amity; nonliberals suffer from a presumption of enmity. Both presumptions may be accurate; each, however, may also be self-confirming.' Doyle, 'Liberalism and World Politics', 1,160–1. Even if such expectations are grounded in myth, they may still shape behavior. Ember, Ember, and Russett, 'Peace Between Participatory Polities: A Cross-Cultural Test of the "Democracies Rarely Fight Each Other" Hypothesis', 576.

11

Proliferation Theory and Nonproliferation Practice

PETER D. FEAVER[1]

INTRODUCTION

Do theoretically oriented political scientists have anything to offer policy makers in the area of nuclear proliferation? If this question is asked of policy makers themselves, the answer would probably be in the negative. Ironically, if this question is asked of many academics, the answer may well be negative, too. Policy makers generally see little value in theory, at least as it is understood by academic political science. Sadly, many academic political scientists see little value in policy orientation. These views are understandable but triply unfortunate: understandable, because they reflect the reasonable institutional incentives and predictable prejudices that influence both scholars and practitioners. But they are triply unfortunate because what Alexander George has called the 'gap between theory and practice' is neither true, nor necessary, nor conducive to good policy and good scholarship.

The gap between theory and practice is more rhetorical than real, since all policy depends on theory and most good theory has implications for policy. Although conventional wisdom holds that the gulf between theory and policy is quite large, in fact, the gap is not as large as most academics and policy makers think, a claim which can be supported by assessing the policy significance of two key academic debates regarding proliferation. In fact, proliferation, as a policy issue, can make contributions to academic political science, especially at the level of pedagogy. In truth, policy and theory are inextricably linked. Although the argument in these cases applies to political science generally, the issue of nuclear proliferation provides a particularly illustrative case.

WHY DO PERCEPTIONS OF THE GAP PERSIST?

The conventional wisdom is that most theoretical debates in political science are irrelevant for policy and that most policy debates are irrelevant for theory.[2] The conventional wisdom can marshal an impressive bill of particulars supporting this view.

First, policy makers rarely make explicitly theoretical claims. Usually, the closest a policy maker comes is to invoke some 'lesson of history', such as the claim that 'appeasement of dictators leads to further challenges', or that 'democracies do not fight each other.' Part of this may be due to the fact that public policy is interdisciplinary, drawing on economics, political science, history, sociology, law, business and other disciplines. Thus, public policy discourse hunts for language common to all these disciplines, and seeks to avoid the jargon that usually attends the theoretical discussion of a single discipline. Nevertheless, policy discourse is still heavily theory-laden, but just not explicitly so. Institutional incentives reinforce this tendency. Because many senior policy makers are not students of theory, they tend to view theoretical discussions with a jaundiced, if not a mocking, eye. An advancement-minded junior actor quickly learns in his presentations to principals to mask even that theory of which he is aware.

Second, many political scientists ignore policy. This is less true in the security and international relations subfield, where norms dictate that every scholar at least attempt to close out published work with a ritualistic addendum on 'policy implications'. Likewise, certain specialty topics in comparative politics, such as democratization and transition to market economies, lend themselves rather naturally to a policy focus. Scholars working in such areas do make explicit efforts to tease out policy implications from the theoretical debates. These laudable subfield norms, however, cut directly against the several institutional and disciplinary prejudices in political science writ large that create disincentives for policy-oriented work. Junior faculty at research institutions know that policy interest counts against them at tenure time. Indeed, most departments distinguish between 'serious' work and 'policy' work when making promotion and raise decisions. The flagship journal for academic political science, the *American Political Science Review*, is notorious for the extent to which it is inaccessible to a policy audience. Scholars who are oriented to policy debates boast of not reading the journal, let alone trying to publish in it. The three other principal subfields in most research political science departments – political philosophy, comparative politics, and American politics-all keep more than an arm's length away from the policy world. The most celebrated work in the American subfield, for example, is not accessible to practitioners of American politics. Indeed, accessibility may even count against such scholarship. Accessibility often is taken to imply an unsophisticated methodology, because the subfield defines sophistication in terms of the complexity of the game theoretic or statistical methods employed.[3]

Third, on the rare occasions when one side does explicitly consider the other, it is often a caricature (of theory or policy) that is considered. Consider, for example, how reviewers from the policy community responded to Robert Pape's book, *Bombing to Win*. This book makes a theoretically informed evaluation of the policy of strategic bombing.[4] It argues that strategic bombing rarely coerces opponents. Barry Watts, a retired military officer and current head of the Northrop Grumman Analysis Center (and so on the policy side of the fence but arguably with corporate interests to represent on the efficacy of air power), takes issue with Pape's argument. The bulk of Watts' critique is a detailed dissection of Pape's argument, showing logical problems and challenging the interpretation of the evidence Pape presents. Unfortunately, Watts' otherwise compelling analysis is undermined by his gratuitous assertion that Pape mistakenly assumes that war has the 'regularity and predictability that Newton's laws of motion and gravitation uncovered'. Watts argues that this leads Pape to try in vain to construct a 'pure, abstract theory of military coercion'.[5] Watts goes on to draw an implicit (and unflattering) comparison to Simon Pierre de Laplace, Newton's successor who infamously claimed that all future events were, in theory, predictable. The caricature he draws is rhetorically effective but egregious and unfair. Few if any political scientists, and certainly not Pape, claim that political phenomena are as regular and predictable as Newton found celestial movements to be. None would venture a theoretical model that could be considered even remotely Laplacian. Good political scientists (and Pape is a good political scientist) deal in probabilistic claims. Good theory gets at tendencies and patterns of behavior, not certainties.

The point here is neither to defend Pape's theory nor to rebut Watts' general critique. Rather, the point is that Watts deliberately frames his objections in terms of the gap between policy reality and political science theory. This alleged gap (at least in this instance) is frequently the result of a flawed understanding of what social science theory really is. If theorists acted as Watts thinks they act, then policy makers would be wise to ignore them. Of course, theorists do not act this way, or at least should not and need not, and so Watts' rhetoric is wasted on a strawman.[6]

IS THERE REALLY A GAP?

The gap is not as large as it appears, however. Indeed, the gap between rhetoric about theory–policy mismatches is much larger than the actual gap between political science theory and public policy.

Policy makers concern themselves with making policy, that is with deciding what should be done and then doing it. Deciding what should be done necessarily involves a prediction about the future.[7] Should the United States continue to bomb Iraq because of its continued obstinacy in blocking inspections of its weapons of mass destruction (WMD) arsenal? The answer depends on what one thinks will happen if the United States bombs Iraq versus what one thinks will happen if it does not bomb Iraq. In other words, the decision depends on a prediction about alternative courses of events. Logically, there are only four ways one can make such a prediction:

1. Refuse to make a prediction and randomly (or at least, capriciously) select a policy.
2. Make a conjecture or wild-guess.
3. Prophesy, invoking a transcendental source of knowledge.[8]
4. Pursue a cause–effect syllogism laying out antecedents and consequents in some fashion.

While all four are used by policy makers, only the last would pass muster as the method of choice. In other words, when policy makers are doing well what they set out to do, they are necessarily making propositions about cause and effect that can be presented as logical syllogisms. This is indistinguishable from what political scientists call theory.

Social science theory basically seeks to articulate and test statements that posit correlative or causative relationships between events, actors or variables. The social science understanding of theory hews closest to Webster's fourth definition of theory: 'a formulation of apparent relationships or underlying principles of certain observed phenomena which has been verified to some degree'.[9] Theory can be distinguished from a paradigm, which is a framework or way of looking at the world and so is somewhat grander than a theory. Multiple theories tend to cluster into one paradigm, as in the collection of theories known as the Realist paradigm. Theory can also be distinguished from a hypothesis, which usually refers to a single propositional statement that is derived from and expected by a theory. Put another way, paradigms generate theories, theories generate hypotheses, hypotheses generate predictions, and predictions generate policy.

Theories can be strong or weak. Theories are considered strong if they explain a lot of important phenomena with relatively few input requirements, or if they make quite confident and precise predictions, or if the empirical record closely tracks the expectations of the theory.[10] Strength is desirable, but if the theory is too strong it skirts on the edge of a tautology. Lenin's theory of imperialism is the classic example of a strong theory whose strength derives from a tautology: his theory that capitalism leads to imperialism rests on his definition of imperialism as the highest stage of capitalism. Weak theories require a lot of inputs before they make a predictive output, or make very vague and hard to falsify claims, or only loosely fit the empirical record. Weakness is less desirable, but most social science theories are weak, at least relative to the theories available to natural and physical scientists.

The subjects of political science are volitional actors and aggregated collectives of volitional actors. The subjects, in other words, have the ability to choose to behave contrary to how they 'ought' to behave. Explaining and predicting the course of an atom is hard enough simply taking into consideration the multitude of forces that operate on that atom. When one imputes to the atom a will, not to mention whimsy, the atom becomes much harder to predict. The subjects of political science theory even have the ability to learn the theory, anticipate its implications, and then change their behavior so as to achieve an outcome more favorable than the one implied by the theory. Good theory takes this into account through *ceteris paribus* caveats, scoping conditions, and, above all, by limiting the claims to tendencies, probabilistic patterns, and so on.

Theories can be distinguished in still one more way – and this is where the true policy-theory gap emerges – whether they are implicit or explicit. Implicit theory is a set of propositional statements where the assumptions, grounds or evidence, implications and limitations are all left unstated and probably under-scrutinized. Explicit theory makes clear all of those elements and exposes them to the harsh light of day. Analysts using implicit theory are more prone to logically incoherent statements or even tautological assertions. Analysts using explicit theory may be prone to bore their audience with jargon about independent variables, dependent variables, causal mechanisms and the like, but the payoff is greater rigor, precision and clarity.

The policy–theory gap, then, is quite simply this: good policy makers use theory implicitly while good political scientists use theory explicitly. Policy makers use theory because in selecting a policy from a menu of options, they must make predictions, hypotheses if you will, about what will happen. To make predictions, policy makers must understand cause and effect (the causal mechanism): how Policy Tool A (the independent variable) contributes to Outcome B (the dependent variable). Otherwise policy makers are making wild-guesses, reading entrails, or whimsically acting on a lark. Policy makers, policy-oriented analysts, historians, and other fellow travelers who dismiss theory are like Moliere's *bourgeois gentilhomme*, who used prose all his life without realizing it.

Policies may fail because policy makers are unlucky or because the implicit theory which informs the policy is flawed.[11] Improving the policy process, then, requires either selecting luckier policy makers or, better yet, examining and improving the theories underlying different policy options. This last task reads like a mission statement for political science. Like all mission statements, it corresponds only imperfectly to what the institution actually does on a day-to-day basis, but the prospects are much rosier than the conventional wisdom holds.

To be sure, policies based on accurate predictions may 'fail' because of difficult value tradeoffs. To return to the Iraqi example, even if one knew the effects of alternative policies, there would still be room for differences of valuation. Is a nuclear-armed Iraq worse than the 10,000 civilian casualties that might result from a military strike that destroyed Iraqi WMD once and for all? That is a judgment call. Political science theory can facilitate that call by giving ever more precise estimates of the consequences of alternative policies, but in the end the judgment turns on questions outside the scope of political science theory.[12]

In any case, theory is a necessary component of good policy making and, *ceteris paribus*, the richer the theoretical debate the richer the contribution to policy.[13]

POLICY IMPLICATIONS OF PROLIFERATION DEBATES

To make the case that political science theory is policy relevant, consider two ongoing academic debates on proliferation: the 'optimist–pessimist' debate, and the closely related 'managing proliferation' debate. The optimist–pessimist debate concerns whether the spread of nuclear weapons leads to greater geopolitical stability because nuclear weapons are conducive to mutual deterrence (optimism) or whether the spread of nuclear weapons leads to greater instability because the new nuclear arsenals might be more prone to accidental, unauthorized or even intentional use than were the superpower arsenals (pessimism).[14] The debate has been conducted in academic circles for decades, and each new wave earns a new moniker. Paleo-pessimists (Dunn, Spector) worried that new nuclear nations might be undeterrable.[15] Paleo-optimists (Waltz, Bueno de Mesquita and Riker, and Brito and Intriligator) applied the logic of rational deterrence theory to proliferation and argued that minimal arsenals would suffice to deter wars.[16] Neo-pessimists (Sagan, Blight and Welch, myself) argued that the elements that made deterrence work (sometimes only barely) during the Cold War – specifically, robust command and control – were unlikely to be replicated in proliferating states.[17] Finally, neo-optimists (Seng and Karl) claimed that the problems neo-pessimists worried about – command and control, safety, incentives for preemption and so on – would be *less* likely to arise in new proliferators because their arsenals would be comparatively small, simple, and therefore easier to manage.[18]

This academic debate has largely gone unnoticed in the policy world. Policy makers are bemused when they learn of it, since the first tenet of US proliferation policy is that the spread of nuclear weapons is unambiguously wrong. This belief is ritually repeated in every policy pronouncement on the subject. Indeed, the cachet of proliferation optimists is precisely the idea that they are advancing such a heretical idea. As I have argued elsewhere, this particular proliferation debate may be a case where there is a difference between the great policy significance of the debate on the one hand and the not-so-great significance of the debate for US policy on the other.[19] If pessimists are right, then the spread of nuclear weapons will increase the risks of nuclear war. The policy implications are that proliferation is bad and should be inhibited, as much as possible. The implication for the United States is that its policy – which seeks to inhibit the spread of nuclear weapons – is correct. If optimists are right, on the other hand, then the spread of nuclear weapons will not increase the risk of nuclear war. Thus a different set of policy implications becomes clear: concerns about multiplying nuclear wars are unwarranted and so extraordinary measures to deter or prevent them are not needed. But still another set of policy implications flows logically from the optimists argument: new nuclear states will be able to deter the United States and thereby greatly complicate regional military operations. A nuclear-armed Iraq may not be more likely to wage a nuclear war (intentionally or other-wise) but, based on the optimists own causal mechanisms, it will be better able to grab and hold Kuwait. In other words, even if optimists are right, the outcome is bad from a parochial US policy point of view. This latter policy implication trumps the others, insofar as US policy makers are concerned. This does not mean that the theoretical debate between optimists and pessimists is policy irrelevant.[20] Rather, it means that the policy implications, though profound, do not lead to different policy prescriptions for the policy maker.

The second debate, how to manage proliferation, grows out of the first and has more interesting implications for policy makers.[21] The logic of both optimist and pessimist theory suggests that some forms of proliferation are better than others. Safer proliferation is preferable to less safe proliferation. Safer proliferation occurs when the new nuclear arsenals more closely fit the command and control requirements for deterrence to hold. In contrast, less safe proliferation occurs when the command and control and other operational features of the arsenal run counter to the prescriptions of deterrence theory. This implication is counter to US declaratory policy, which purports to treat every new nuclear nation alike, as the undesirable n-th nuclear nation.[22]

This issue is so interesting, however, because US proliferation policy makes the problem worse. Efforts to prevent the spread of nuclear weapons increase the likelihood that those states who successfully proliferate will have arsenals that are less safe than they otherwise might be. The nonproliferation regime denies would-be proliferators access to information and technology and forces them to develop their weapons in great secrecy with minimal testing. Although the *existence* of this problem is implied by both optimist and pessimist theory, the *extent* of the problem depends on which theory is correct: if neo-optimists are correct, this is a very small problem because new proliferators have countervailing advantages in the area of command and control, but, if neo-pessimists are correct, this is a very serious problem indeed.

The general policy implications are profound. It may make sense to help new nuclear states solve the command and control problems inherent in possession of an arsenal so as to bring their capability in line with the requirements for adequate deterrence, especially if the prospects for getting them to give up their arsenals are bleak. The specific implications for US policy are harder to nail down and depend on the value tradeoff between a higher risk of nuclear accidents and a higher risk of future proliferation.

In any case, this theoretical debate handles rather well the most dramatic proliferation development of 1998: the rapid escalation of the nuclear arms race in south Asia. Neo-pessimist theory specifically predicted that the arms race in south Asia would escalate.[23] Events since then correspond rather closely to the logic of the proliferation management theory. The US initially hewed to traditional anti-proliferation rhetoric and even imposed sanctions on Pakistan and India. This tough policy quickly gave way to a more nuanced policy, and it is not implausible that the United States might consider sharing some command and control information with both sides as part of a carrots-and-sticks policy designed to bring both arsenals under a robust confidence building and arms control regime.

PROLIFERATION'S CONTRIBUTION TO POLITICAL SCIENCE

If academic political science has something to offer proliferation, so too does proliferation have something to offer political science. The proliferation topic is particularly useful for teaching the basics of political science methods because it is intrinsically interesting and holds obvious *prima facie* importance to students. It is something of a challenge (though certainly not impossible) to convince students that they should care about the causes of the First World War or the relative stability of bipolar versus multipolar international systems. It takes little work to convince them that a Russian black market in nuclear materials should occupy their attention. Consequently, when the task is to instruct students in the tools of social science, the appeal of proliferation issues is especially helpful.

Consider how the proliferation topic can enliven the study of the following basic issues in political science.

Rudiments of social science argumentation

The optimist/pessimist debate is easily grasped by undergraduates and is particularly well-suited to teaching students how to argue according to the dictates of social science: how to marshal evidence, how to address counter-arguments, how to examine critically the assumptions of contending views, and so on.

Counterfactual analysis

Counterfactual analysis, which is an important method in social science, involves thought experiments in which the analyst makes specific changes to history and then considers the impact.[24] Nuclear proliferation problems lend themselves to counterfactual analysis. For instance, what happens if you rerun Desert Storm but with an Iraqi nuclear weapon? Would the Cold War have remained cold if there had not been nuclear weapons?

Equifinality

Equifinality is the problem that arises when different theories make the same core prediction, thus making it difficult to determine which theory is correct.[25] This is a common problem in political science, and one of the more famous examples comes directly from the proliferation issue area: how does one adjudicate the competing claims of one theory that the Cold War remained cold because of nuclear weapons and another theory that the Cold War remained cold because fear of another conventional conflict on the scale of the Second World War?[26] The appropriate method is to look for other secondary but observable implications of the theories and evaluate those: did nuclear weapons play a role in crises, did arms races follow the patterns implied by the theories, and so on?

Small-n methods

Since there are relatively few cases of proliferation, the topic area is well-suited to showing students how to use non-statistical social science methods, including game theory and comparative case studies.

Levels of analysis

One of the core analytical concepts in political science, at least central for the international relations subfield, is how different sets of factors that cluster together at distinguishable levels can work to shape the same basic event. One can explain the origins of the First World War by looking primarily at individual-level factors (the weakness of Kaiser Wilhelm, the effects of stress during the crisis, and so forth), at societal-level factors (the problems of civilian control and the Iron–Rye coalition) or at system-level factors (changes in the European balance of power and the incentives this created for preventive war). Debates over the causes of proliferation – is it organizational interest or balance of power security considerations? – and debates over the consequences of proliferation – will organizational pathologies lead to bad operational measures or will the system logic of deterrence theory discipline nuclear operations? – are essentially debates over which level of analysis is more important.

Perhaps the most important way that proliferation studies can contribute to political science, however, is simply to reinforce the theme of this chapter: the interrelationship of policy, prediction and theory. Proliferation, which is at once a salient policy issue and also a rich area for political science theorizing, is ideally positioned to bridge unnecessary gaps.

CONCLUSION: RESOLVING A NEEDLESS AND DETRIMENTAL DEBATE

Political scientists and policy makers alike need to understand just how essential theory is to policy. The view that theory and policy are unrelated is not simply wrong. It is also detrimental to goals of crafting better policy and building better theory.

Policy making necessarily involves theorizing so better theorizing should lead to better policy making. The policy maker or policy analyst who thinks that he or she need not bother with abstract theory is simply unaware of how dependent on theory the policy really is. Policy involves predictions and predictions involve statements of cause and effect, that is to say, theory. The best policy makers and analysts may have sufficient intuitive feel for the associated theory that they can afford to ignore these foundational issues. But it is far more likely that ignoring theory leads to ignorance about the assumptions and scope conditions underlying the policy and that ignorance leads to avoidable errors.

At the same time, virtually all good theory has implications for policy. Indeed, if no conceivable extension of the theory leads to insights that would aid those working in the 'real world', what can be 'good' about good theory? Ignoring the policy implications of theory is often a sign of intellectual laziness on the part of the theorist. It is hard work to learn about the policy world and to make the connections from theory to policy. Often, the skill sets do not transfer easily from one domain to another, so a formidable theorist can show embarrassing naivete when it comes to the policy domain he or she putatively studies. Often, when the policy implications are considered, flaws in the theory (or at least in the presentation of the theory) are uncovered.[27] Thus, focusing attention on policy implications should lead to better theorizing.

The gap between theory and policy is more rhetoric than reality. But rhetoric can create a reality – or at least create an undesirable kind of reality – where policy makers make policy though ignorant of the problems that good theory would expose, while theorists spin arcana without a view to producing something that matters. It is therefore incumbent on those of us who study proliferation – a topic that raises interesting and important questions for both policy and theory – to bring the communities together. Happily, the best work in the proliferation field already does so.

NOTES

1 Peter Feaver is Associate Professor of Political Science at Duke University. He has written extensively on nuclear proliferation and command and control issues. In 1993–94, he served on the National Security Council Staff as director for defense policy and arms control where his responsibilities included counter-proliferation policy, regional arms control, and other defense policy issues.

2 Laurence E. Lynn, Jr (ed.), *Knowledge and Policy: The Uncertain Connection* (Washington, DC: National Academy of Sciences, 1978); Alexander George, *Bridging the Gap: Theory and Practice in Foreign Policy* (Washington, DC: US Institute of Peace, 1993); Alexander George, 'Bridging the Gap: Introduction', *Mershon International Studies Review*, 38, Supplement 1 (April 1994), 171–2; General John C. Galvin, 'Breaking Through and Being Heard', *Mershon International Studies Review*, 38, Supplement 1 (April 1994), 173–4; Edward A. Kolodziej, 'What is the Challenge and Will We Accept It?', *Mershon International Studies Review*, 38, Supplement 1 (April 1994), 175–8; Joseph Kruzel, 'More a Chasm than a Gap, But Do Scholars Want to Bridge It?', *Mershon International*

Studies Review, 38, Supplement 1 (April 1994), 179–81; Philip Zelikow, 'Foreign Policy Engineering: From Theory to Practice and Back Again', *International Security*, 18, 4 (Spring 1994), 143–71; 'Bridging Theory to Practice', *IGCC Newsletter XVIII*, 1 (Spring 1997); Joseph Lepgold, 'Is Anyone Listening? International Relations Theory and the Problem of Policy Relevance', *Political Science Quarterly*, 113, 1 (Spring 1998), 43–62; Barry D. Watts, 'Problems of Theory and Evidence in Security Studies', *Security Studies*, 7, 2 (Winter 1997/98), 115–23.

3 As I will argue below, even inaccessible theory may be relevant for policy. Such scholarship, however, is manifestly *not* trying to speak to a policy audience, even if it has something of value to say.

4 The original book is Robert A. Pape, *Bombing to Win: Air Power and Coercion in War* (Ithaca, NY: Cornell University Press, 1996). The debate over the book is found in a symposium in the Winter 1997/98 (Volume 7, Number 2) issue of the journal *Security Studies*: Robert A. Pape, 'The Limits of Precision-Guided Air Power', 93–114; Barry D. Watts, 'Ignoring Reality: Problems of Theory and Evidence in Security Studies', 115–71; John A. Warden III, 'Success in Modern War', 172–90; and Robert A. Pape, 'The Air Force Strikes Back: A Reply to Barry Watts and John Warden', 191–214.

5 Watts, 'Ignoring Reality', 118.

6 The wasted effort is unfortunate, as it turns out, because the rest of Watts critique is on point and shows him to have the analytical skills one would expect from the director of a prestigious analytical unit – and from a good social scientist, for that matter.

7 The choice also depends on an evaluation of the value tradeoffs involved, an issue which will be treated further later in the text.

8 History is replete with examples of policy makers relying on such sources and some would consider the professional intelligence community to be latter-day soothsayers. In point of fact, however, most intelligence work falls into one of the other three categories, albeit glorified with a mysterious veil of classified 'sources and methods'.

9 *Webster's Third College Edition*.

10 For example, feminist theories are 'strong' by the first measure because they purport to explain a whole range of political phenomena based entirely on one factor (the gender of the actors), and are strong by the second measure because the theories are rarely presented with extensive caveats, but are weak by the third measure because, at least to date, the data do not support the more confident predictions.

11 It is important to stress that good theory does not guarantee policy success any more than it guarantees predictive success. Every political science theory is probabilistic and bounded by the *ceteris paribus* condition. Even a theory that works 95 per cent of the time (and I know of no social science theory this strong) will falsely predict 5 per cent of the time. And theories may 'fail' in ways that lend even greater support for the theory. For instance, a theory that the checks and balances contained in a democracy will inhibit it from going to war against another democracy is not disproved by a war between two democracies – if closer examination reveals that the normal checks and balances inherent in a democracy were uncharacteristically weak in that instance for idiosyncratic reasons (such as because opposition parties were extraordinarily weak or because the leader enjoyed demagogic popularity).

12 That is, outside the scope of positive political theory, which seeks to explain what is happening and why. Normative political theory, which seeks to understand what ought to happen and why, does contribute directly to

judgment calls like this.

13 There is yet another way that theory can inform policy. Social scientists must explain the world even (or especially) in those instances when outcomes are beyond the control of policy makers. Social scientists, then, can tell us when policy debates are irrelevant to the real world. One important enterprise for social science is to distinguish situations in which policy debates are and are not irrelevant. I am indebted to Christopher Gelpi for suggesting this point to me.

14 The literature is too large to cite here. Although I would catalogue the literature differently, the best introduction is Peter R. Lavoy, 'The Strategic Consequences of Nuclear Proliferation: A Review Essay', *Security Studies*, 4, 4 (Summer 1995), 695–753. See also, Bradley Thayer, 'The Risk of Nuclear Inadvertence: A Review Essay', *Security Studies*, 3, 3 (Spring 1994), 428–93. My stylized review gives the literature a bit more coherence than it in fact enjoys. For instance, while it is customary to begin the discussion with Waltz's optimistic response to traditional pessimists, in fact Waltz's argument was largely derivative of the work of an earlier generation of strategic analysts, especially Pierre Gallois. And Gallois' work was a reaction to Albert Wohlstetter who was reacting to Bernard Brodie. Pierre Gallois, *The Balance of Terror* (Boston, MA: Houghton Mifflin, 1961); Albert Wohlstetter, 'The Delicate Balance of Terror', *Foreign Affairs*, 37 (1957), 211–34; and Bernard Brodie (ed.), *The Absolute Weapon: Atomic Power and World Order* (New York: Harcourt Brace, 1946).

15 Lewis Dunn, *Controlling the Bomb: Nuclear Proliferation in the 1980s* (New Haven, CT: Yale University Press, 1982); and Leonard Spector, *Nuclear Proliferation Today* (New York: Vintage Books, 1984).

16 Kenneth N. Waltz, *The Spread of Nuclear Weapons: More May be Better*, Adelphi Paper 171 (London: IISS, 1981); and Kenneth N. Waltz, 'Nuclear Myths and Political Realities', *American Political Science Review*, 84, 3 (September 1990), 731–45; Michael D. Intriligator and Dagobert L. Brito, 'Nuclear Proliferation and the Probability of Nuclear War', *Public Choice*, 37, 2 (1981), 247–59; and Bruce Bueno de Mesquita and William Riker, 'An Assessment of the Merits of Selective Nuclear Proliferation', *Journal of Conflict Resolution*, 26, 2 (1982), 283–306.

17 Scott D. Sagan, 'The Perils of Proliferation: Organizational Theory, Deterrence Theory, and the Spread of Nuclear Weapons', *International Security*, 18, 4 (Spring 1994), 66–107; Scott D. Sagan and Kenneth N. Waltz, *The Spread of Nuclear Weapons: A Debate* (New York: Norton, 1995); James G. Blight and David A. Welch, 'The Cuban Missile Crisis and New Nuclear States', *Security Studies*, 4, 4 (Summer 1995), 833–45. Peter D. Feaver, 'Command and Control in Emerging Nuclear Nations', *International Security*, 17, 3 (Winter 1992/93), 160–87; Peter D. Feaver, 'Proliferation Optimism and Theories of Nuclear Operations', *Security Studies*, 2, 3/4 (Spring/Summer 1993), 160–5; Peter D. Feaver, 'Optimists, Pessimists, and Theories of Nuclear Proliferation Management', *Security Studies*, 4, 4 (Summer 1995), 754–72; Peter D. Feaver, 'Neo-optimists and Proliferation's Enduring Problems', *Security Studies*, 6, 4 (Summer 1997), 93–125; Stephen R. David, 'Risky Business: Let Us Not Take a Chance on Proliferation', *Security Studies*, 4, 4 (Summer 1995), 773–8.

18 David J. Karl, 'Proliferation Pessimism and Emerging Nuclear Powers', *International Security*, 21, 3 (Winter 1996/97), 87–119; Jordan Seng, 'Command and Control Advantages of Minor Nuclear States', *Security Studies*, 6, 4 (Summer 1997), 50–93.

19 Feaver, 'Optimists, Pessimists, and Theories of Proliferation', 770–2.

20 In this regard, I regret some of the wording I used previously which may have

implied that the debate was not policy relevant. See Feaver, 'Optimists, Pessimists, and Theories of Proliferation', 770.

21 Joel Larus, *Nuclear Weapons Safety and the Common Defense* (Columbus, OH: The Ohio State University Press, 1967); W. B. Wentz, *Nuclear Proliferation* (Washington, DC: Public Affairs Press, 1968); Lewis A. Dunn and Hermann Kahn, *Trends in Nuclear Proliferation, 1975–1995: Projections, Problems and Policy Options* (Croton-on-Hudson, NY: Hudson Institute, 1976); Richard K. Betts, 'Paranoids, Pygmies, Pariahs and Nonproliferation', *Foreign Policy*, 26 (1977), 157–83; John J. Weltman, 'Managing Nuclear Multipolarity', *International Security*, 6, 3 (1980); Dagobert L. Brito, Michael D. Intriligator and Adele E. Wick (eds), *Strategies for Managing Nuclear Proliferation* (Lexington, MA: Lexington Books, 1983); Shai Feldman, 'Managing Nuclear Proliferation', in Jed C. Snyder and Samuel F. Wells (eds), *Limiting Nuclear Proliferation* (Cambridge, MA: Ballinger, 1985); Daniel Caldwell, 'Permissive Action Links: A Description and Proposal', *Survival*, 29, 3 (May/June 1987), 224–38; Lewis A. Dunn, *Containing Nuclear Proliferation*, Adelphi Paper 263 (London: IISS, 1991); Lewis A. Dunn and Gregory F. Giles, *Nuclear Proliferation Contingency Planning: Defining the Issues* (McLean, VA: Center for National Security Negotiations, 1991); Mark D. Mandeles, 'Between a Rock and a Hard Place: Implications for the U.S. of Third World Nuclear Weapon and Ballistic Missile Proliferation', *Security Studies*, 1, 2 (Winter 1991), 235–69; Gregory Giles, 'Safeguarding Undeclared Nuclear Arsenals', *Washington Quarterly*, 16, 2 (Spring 1993), 173–86; Stephen Cimbala, 'Nuclear Weapons in the New World Order', *Journal of Strategic Studies*, 16, 2 (June 1993), 173–99; Robert D. Blackwill and Albert Carnesale (eds), *Coping with New Nuclear Nations* (New York: Council on Foreign Relations, 1993); and Peter D. Feaver and Emerson Niou, 'Managing Nuclear Proliferation: Condemn, Strike, or Assist?', *International Studies Quarterly*, 40 (1996), 209–34.

22 *De facto* US policy, of course, has always drawn distinctions, at the very least between friends and foes. Compare US policy to France and, for example, North Korea.

23 Feaver, 'Neo-optimists and the Enduring Problem of Nuclear Proliferation', 124.

24 Philip E. Tetlock and Aaron Belkin (eds), *Counterfactual Thought Experiments in World Politics: Logical, Methodological, and Psychological Perspectives* (Princeton, NJ: Princeton University Press, 1996).

25 Gary King, Robert O. Keohane and Sidney Verba, *Designing Social Inquiry: Scientific Inference in Qualitative Research* (Princeton, NJ: Princeton University Press, 1994), 87–9.

26 See the debate between John Lewis Gaddis, John Mueller and Robert Jervis. John Lewis Gaddis, 'The Long Peace: Elements of Stability in the Postwar International System', *International Security*, 10, 4 (Spring 1986), 99–142; John Mueller, 'The Essential Irrelevance of Nuclear Weapons: Stability in the Postwar World', *International Security*, 13, 2 (Fall 1988), 55–79; and Robert Jervis, 'The Political Effects of Nuclear Weapons: A Comment', *International Security*, 13, 2 (Fall 1988), 80–90.

27 The classic example of this in the proliferation field is how consideration of the policy aspects of Waltz's 'more nuclear proliferation is better' argument points to an implicit and dubious assumption in his theory: he adopts a system perspective that treats a paralyzed United States as equally desirable to a paralyzed Iran. See Feaver, 'Optimists, Pessimists, and Theories of Nuclear Proliferation Management', 770–2.

Notes on Contributors

Michael Barletta is Senior Research Associate at the Monterey Institute of International Studies, and Lecturer in National Security Affairs at the Naval Postgraduate School in Monterey, California. His current research focuses on the proliferation of weapons of mass destruction in the Middle East and Africa, and on foreign and security affairs in Latin America. This article is based on field research funded by the Program on Peace and International Security of the Social Science Research Council and the MacArthur Foundation, and the Institute for the Study of World Politics.

Ashton B. Carter is the Ford Foundation Professor of Science and International Affairs at Harvard's John F. Kennedy School of Government and Co-Director, with William J. Perry, of the Harvard-Stanford Preventive Defense Project.

Peter D. Feaver is an Assistant Professor of Political Science at Duke University. He has written extensively on nuclear proliferation and command and control issues. In 1993–94, he served on the National Security Council Staff as director for defense policy and arms control where his responsibilities included counterproliferation policy, regional arms control and other defense policy issues.

Victor Gilinsky is a consultant to energy firms and regulatory, financial and national security organizations. He served on the US Nuclear Regulatory Commission from 1975–84.

Timothy D. Hoyt is Visiting Assistant Professor in the National Security Studies Program at Georgetown University. He would like to thank Michael Barletta, Kory Sylvester, Henry Sokolski and Amanda O'Neal for their comments and assistance.

L. Celeste Johnson is an Associate in the Government Practice of DFI International, and a graduate of Stanford University and the John F. Kennedy School of Government at Harvard University.

Thomas G. Mahnken is Associate Professor of Strategy at the US Naval

War College. The views expressed in his essay are those of the author and do not reflect the official policy or position of the Department of Defense and the US Government.

Daniel Pipes is editor of the *Middle East Quarterly* and senior lecturer at the University of Pennsylvania. He has served in the Departments of State and Defense.

David C. Rapoport is Professor Emeritus of Political Science at the University of California, Los Angeles, and Editor of the *Journal of Terrorism and Political Violence*. Professor Rapoport is also Founding Director of the Center for the Study of Religion at UCLA.

Henry S. Rowen is Professor of Public Policy and Management at the Graduate School of Business, Stanford University, and senior fellow at the Hoover Institution. He has been president of the RAND Corporation, chairman of the National Intelligence Council, and Assistant Secretary of Defense for International Security Affairs.

Henry D. Sokolski is Executive Director of the Nonproliferation Policy Education Center. He served as the Deputy for Nonproliferation Policy in the Pentagon during the Bush administration and is the author of *Best of Intentions: America's Campaign Against Strategic Weapons Proliferation*, a critical history of US nonproliferation policy.

Frank von Hippel is on the senior research staff at the Center for Energy and Environmental Studies at Princeton University. During 1993–94, he served as Assistant Director for National Security in the White House Office of Science and Technology Policy. His areas of policy research include nuclear arms control and nonproliferation, energy, and checks and balances in policy making for technology.

Index

ABM (Anti-Ballistic Missile) Treaty, 56, 57, 62, 67
accidents, x, 23, 31n37, n38
Acheson–Lillienthal plan, 84
Adamov (Russian Minister of Atomic Energy), 89
ADB (Asian Development Bank), 113–14, 128
Advanced Concept Technology Demonstration, 77
advanced conventional weapons, xvi, xvii, 33–51
Afghanistan, 10, 27n12, 106, 108, 143
Africa, 100, 102, 104, 113, 115, 116; north, xviii, 105–6, 124; sub-Saharan, 103, 105, 106, 108, 122; see also names of countries
Agni I intermediate range ballistic missile, 38
Agni II intermediate range ballistic missile, 38
Agreed Framework, 55, 56, 68
Agreement of Cooperation, 93
Alaska, 67 .
Alfonsín, President, 151, 152, 153, 154, 155, 161n19, 167n63; administration, 150, 153, 154, 157
Algeria, 108, 137, 143, 144, 146
Alnasrawi, Abbas, 139
Amayreh, Khalid M., 140
American Political Science Review, 169
Amin, Galal A., 136, 139
Amirahmadi, Hooshang, 136
anthrax, 22, 25, 26, 76
Anti-Ballistic Missile (ABM) Treaty, 56, 57, 62, 67
antibiotics, 15, 25
anti-ship missiles, 35, 40; see also missiles; names of missiles
anti-terrorism, viii, xi, 15–16
apocalypse, 15, 26
Arabia, 143
Arab–Israeli conflict, 137, 143, 145
Arabs, 100, 119, 135, 143, 145; see also Arab–Israeli conflict
Arafat, Yasir, 137, 138
Aramar plant, 151, 155
area denial/sea denial capabilities, xv, 39–42, 45
Argentina, ix, xviii, 60, 61, 102, 105, 110, 113, 148–67
Arkansas, 21
Asia, ix, 58, 102, 113–14, 124, 125, 126; central, xviii, 105, 106, 116, 122; east, 3, 64, 102, 103, 104, 105, 109, 110, 111, 115, 116, 118, 119, 143; northeast, 104; south, 3–13, 37, 95, 103, 105, 114, 115, 116, 122, 175; southeast, 110, 115, 122; see also names of countries
Asian Development Bank (ADB), 113–14, 128
AsiaSat II satellite, 43
Aspin, Les, 72, 73
Atatürk, Kemal, 143
Atoms for Peace program, 8, 34
'Atoms for Peace' speech (Eisenhower, 1953), 86
Atrash, Sultan al-, 143
At-Takfir w'al-Hijra, 139
attrition, wars of, 17, 18
Aum Shinrikyo, x, 14, 17, 21–4, 31n36
Australasia, 122
Australia Group, 34
Avengers/Jewish partisans, 20–1, 30n31

Baghdad, viii
Balkans, 100, 122, 124
ballistic missiles, xvi, 20, 35, 36–8, 39, 43, 45, 55, 58, 68, 70, 72, 77, 81, 127, 135; see also missiles; names of missiles
Baltic states, 105
Bangladesh, 114, 115, 119, 128, 129, 138
Barletta, Michael, ix, xviii, 182
Barro, Robert J., 128, 129
Baruch Plan, 34
BDL (Bharat Dynamics Limited), 38
Beijing, viii, 42
Belarus, 68, 117, 130n11
Belgium, 102
Benvenisti, Meron, 137
'Berkeley Mafia', 110
beta burns, x
Bharat Dynamics Limited (BDL), 38
biological weapons, x, xi, xii, xv, xvi, 14–32, 64, 65, 66, 67–8, 70, 72, 73, 75, 76–7, 79; see also NBC (nuclear, biological, chemical) weapons; weapons of mass destruction
Biological Weapons Convention (BWC), 56, 68
Blight, James G., 173–4
Bloom, David E., 115
Boghammer speed boats, 40
Bohr, Neils, 4
Bombing to Win (Pape), 170
Bosnia, 143
Brazil, ix, xviii, 60, 61, 86, 102, 105, 110, 113, 115, 117, 119, 128, 129, 148–67

Customer:
Saghir Iqbal

L TUE PM

Twenty-First Century Weapons Proliferation: Are We Ready?

002-305-B1
UE-584-930

No CD

Used - Very Good

9780714681375

43124987